Whose
Rose Garden
Is It Anyway?

Art Buchwald

Whose Rose Garden Is It Anyway?

Illustrated by

Steve Mendelson

A Perigee Book

Perigee Books
are published by
The Putnam Publishing Group
200 Madison Avenue
New York, NY 10016

First Perigee Edition 1990

Library of Congress Cataloging-in-Publication Data

Buchwald, Art.
Whose rose garden is it anyway? / Art Buchwald ; illustrated by
Steve Mendelson.

p. cm.
1. United States—Politics and government—1981–1989—Humor.
2. United States—Civilization—1970—Humor. I. Title.
[PS3503.U1828W49 1990]   90-35322 CIP
814'.54—dc20
ISBN 0-399-51651-4

Designed by Beth Tondreau Design/Gabrielle Hamberg

Printed in the United States of America
1 2 3 4 5 6 7 8 9 10

This book is printed on acid-free paper.
∞

If you run three miles every morning,
you will add five years to your life—
but you will always be in pain.

—Sitting Bull

Contents

Contents

Contents

Contents

Contents

11

List of Illustrations

Introduction

Although it may look like it, this is not the complete history of the planet Earth. Admittedly, there are gaps in this definitive work because those who knew something wouldn't talk, and those who talked knew nothing.

I regret that CIA Director Bill Casey is no longer with us as he was the only one who could have shed light on the conversation between President Reagan and the Ayatollah Khomeini when they played golf at the Augusta National Golf Club.

I have tried to give Oliver North the benefit of the doubt after hearing his testimony that he knew right from wrong, but that he didn't know lying to Congress was illegal. North has provided me with almost as many columns as Richard Nixon. Was he a hero? I believe so—at least to every political cartoonist and humorist in the United States.

In this book I reveal, for the first time, Bill Casey's last words to me. They were, "Keep Reagan and Bush's name out of Iran-gate, and keep Bob Woodward the hell out of my hospital room."

If anyone fares better or worse in these chapters, it is the Gipper who, to this day, wears his Teflon on his sleeve as well as all over his body.

For eight years Reagan had the ability to drive through a car wash in a convertible with the top down—and the only one who got wet was Jimmy Carter.

I had no personal dealings with Ronald Reagan, other than

to review his trillion-dollar budget upstairs in his White House bedroom every night because the figures didn't balance. The President told me that a big-spending welfare mother in Chicago was to blame.

Ronald Reagan lost many sleepless days worrying about his country, and I credit him for providing me with half of the material in this work.

As you read on you will encounter many interesting characters.

I write with affection about ex-Attorney General Ed Meese, who appeared to have eaten the Constitution rather than read it. In his long years of public service, Ed could have either become a Supreme Court justice or been indicted—or both.

I always admired Nancy Reagan—and never more so than when Donald Regan revealed that she and President Reagan had consulted an astrologer. The American people heaved a sigh of relief because at last they knew where President Reagan was getting his advice from.

A footnote to history is Michael Dukakis, who said that he had never been treated by a psychiatrist. He announced this at the very moment in his campaign when everyone wanted to know *why* he hadn't been treated by a psychiatrist.

Then there was Gary Hart who, like the Duke of Windsor, chose love over his country. When Mr. Hart was caught in Bimini with a friend and there was an uproar, he announced that the people should decide whether or not he was fit to be President of the United States—and they did.

Now we come to President George Bush, who managed to win an overwhelming victory in the election despite the fact that he declared September 7 as the day the Japanese had bombed Pearl Harbor. This remark convinced me that I needed Bush as my president for the next four years.

I am not claiming that one couldn't find a better vice president than Dan Quayle, but I have no idea where. When Quayle served in the National Guard in Indiana during the Vietnam War everyone agreed that he was the right man in the right place at the right time. These days Washington sleeps easier just knowing that Dan Quayle is in the wings should anything happen to George Bush.

In these pages, I have disclosed that during the campaign George Bush seriously considered adopting Quayle as his son, because that would explain to the voters why he chose him as his vice president.

This is not the typical kiss-and-tell book. It deals with such subjects as men facing the firing squad and not being able to have a last cigarette because the Surgeon General has declared that smoking is bad for their health. . . . Parents and the dilemma of grown-up children who won't leave home. . . . Mothers who write term papers for their offspring. . . . Captain Lorenzo at the controls of an Eastern Airlines jet. . . . How to shoot Bambi with a semiautomatic weapon, and many more chapters on the life and times of America in the late eighties.

A New Limo

The President has a new car. He rode in it just after his swearing-in on Inauguration Day. News commentators gushed over its capabilities. As I understand it, the custom-built limousine is bulletproof, dustproof, has tilted seats, a smoke producer, a loudspeaker, a bar, a large-screen television, a kitchen (capable of cooking a meal for forty), a Jacuzzi, a steam room and a squash court.

What frightens me the most about this car is something Dan Rather said. He mentioned that the limo, and I am not making this up, was constructed in such a way that the President could conduct a nuclear war from it.

If true, this is very worrying.

I can just imagine the scene where the car salesman briefs the President on the features of his new automobile.

"Now, Mr. President, this button here controls the temperature, this one opens up the roof, this is the light dimmer and this one launches every ICBM in our stockpile."

"I see. Let me get it straight—this button opens the roof."

"No, sir, that's the temperature gauge. The one that operates the roof is next to it."

"I see. Then this button dims the lights."

"No, that one launches the nuclear missiles. The light dimmer is over here."

"Why can't the nuclear button be separated from the others so I don't get them mixed up?"

© 1989 St. Mendlen

"That would have added to the cost of the car, and the budget planners felt that since you would be using the nuclear button so seldom, it wasn't worth the money."

"What's this button for?"

"With that you can either start a conventional war or roll down your windows."

"Do you think that's the best place for it since my grand-children may be riding in the car?"

"If we put it higher, it could be confused with the stereo buttons. There was some talk of installing it in the glove compartment, but then it would be hard to reach from the back-seat."

"I am pleased to have such deterrent capability in my car, but what kind of signal are we sending the Soviet Union when half the controls in the back can start a war?"

"It was the CIA's idea. They told us that Gorbachev's limo has been equipped with four SS20s on the exhaust pipe, and that they are aimed directly at the United States."

"Well, all right. How do I receive the signal to launch my nuclear weapons?"

"It will come over this country music station. We're assuming that you will be listening to country music whenever you are driven to and from the White House. As soon as you hear the announcer say 'a kinder, gentler mushroom cloud,' you'll push the button."

"This one?"

"No, sir. That button is to defrost the rear window."

"I'll get it right. What happens if I push this one over here?"

"That turns on the car's flamethrower in case you're caught in a traffic gridlock."

"You people have thought of everything. I imagine that this button must be important."

"It could be the most important one in the car. It activates

19

the radar detector and warns you about every speed trap the
police have set up on any highway in the United States."

No Biz Like
the White House

The thing that bothered me most about the presidential campaign was that each of the candidates was in the hands of
highly skilled image-makers straight out of show business.
Every word and gesture seemed to be programmed by these
so-called media specialists whose only interest in politics was
to get a sound bite of their man on the evening news.

What frightens me is the possibility that these advisors have
followed the winner into the White House and continue to run
his life from there.

"Mr. President, the deficit has just hit the two-trillion-dollar
mark."

"Oh, my God, what do I do?"

"Well, first, you get up from behind your desk, very slowly,
and pretend that this happens every day. Then you walk over
to the window and look out at the Rose Garden for a couple

of beats, and finally you turn around, look straight into the camera and say, 'Oh, nuts.' "

"Two trillion dollars. Isn't there any action I can take?"

"You should put on some makeup. The polls indicate that forty-five percent of the public thinks your nose is too shiny. We have a saying on Madison Avenue. 'When you're President of the United States, never let the Russians see you sweat.' "

"Mr. President, Mr. President, Noriega has just closed the Panama Canal and wants twenty-five thousand tons of marijuana before he'll open it again."

"That sounds like a serious public relations problem, and could hurt my credibility in the South."

"That's true, Mr. President, and we'll get the writers on it immediately. In the meantime, do you have another tie?"

"What's wrong with this one?"

"It doesn't send the right message to Noriega. We want something flashy like the one Ronald Reagan wore the day we bombed Libya."

"Mr. President, this came in from the Treasury Department. In order to avoid going bankrupt, we'll have to raise income taxes."

"What shall I say to the American people? I made a promise not to raise them."

"We'll damage-control it, sir. We want you to stand over here next to the presidential seal and say, 'When I promised not to raise your taxes, I was drunk.' "

"I can't say that."

"That was a joke. We'll have you make the announcement in a cornfield in Iowa, and we will slip it in while you're driving a harvester across the amber waves of grain."

"I can do it."

"Mr. President, are you going to meet Gorbachev this afternoon?"

21

"I think so. Why do you ask?"

"We want you to upstage him by kissing him before he kisses you. The last time you were together he got all the best camera angles."

"Now, after Gorbachev you have the meeting with the Eagle Scout who will present you with a flag."

"I'm looking forward to that. Is it a debate?"

"Not exactly. But we aren't taking any chances. We have a kid from the White House mailroom who will play the role of the Eagle Scout during rehearsals. He'll throw every question in the book at you, and you'll pretend it's the real thing."

"I'm not afraid. I am a great debater. That's how I won the election. The trick is to be yourself so that everyone knows you are a real person. Does anybody have any good ad libs I can use when I exchange bons mots with the kid?"

The Reaganing of America

It was just eight years ago when the head of Warner Brothers studios called me in and said, "We're going to shoot a movie about a president of the United States in Washington."

"Great," I replied. "Who will play the title role?"

"I wanted Mickey Rooney but he's not available. What do you think of Ronald Reagan?"

"You've got to be kidding. He only plays nice guys."

"That's what everyone says. But suppose we had a president of the United States who really was a nice guy—even nicer than his best friend Jimmy Stewart. I want to cast Nancy Davis as Ron's wife and create a helluva wardrobe for her. This picture is going to have glitz."

"The audiences are dying for glitz," I told him.

He stood up from behind his desk and started pacing. "At the opening of the film I see Ronnie riding his horse right up to the front door of the White House, and the horse knocking on it with his hoof. All the servants are lined up and the head butler smiles and says, 'Welcome home, Mr. President. Your room is this way.' "

"That's all well and good," I said. "But what's the story?"

The studio head slapped himself on the thigh with a riding crop.

23

"Ron has come to Washington to root out waste and corruption in government, something the people there don't understand. But his strong leadership prevails and before he is finished, half of his own staff have either been fired or indicted."

"That is a good start."

"In the meantime, I'm going to have Nancy turning up at all of Ronnie's meetings, in different outfits, yelling at everyone she meets, 'Just say no.' "

"But where does that lead?" I asked.

"As the story unfolds, the plot poses the question, 'Can a nice guy spend eight years in the White House without becoming disenchanted with the government?' "

"Does Ron have a crisis of confidence?"

"Yes, he does. When underlings led by a Marine lieutenant colonel try to end-run the Oval Office and set up their own clandestine operation with the Iranians, Ronnie deals with it as a president should."

"How's that?"

"He says he doesn't know anything about it."

"Is that the major plot of the film?"

"No. The real story is that Ron makes up with the Russians."

"Nobody is going to believe that. Reagan hates the commies."

"That's the beauty of the plot. Ronnie, a man who detests Communists, finds good in all of them. We have a big scene on top of the Kremlin wall when Ron and Nancy embrace Mikhail Gorbachev and his wife Raisa as the Soviet troops march by in the May Day parade."

"I thought Brezhnev was in charge of the USSR."

"In the picture we're changing his name to Gorbachev and making the Russian leader much younger for dramatic effect."

"It's a good script, but there doesn't appear to be any conflict in it. When does Ron stand up and fight?"

"He doesn't—but Nancy does. This movie portrays the struggle between two strong-willed women trying to protect their men. I want to have a hair-pulling fight between Nancy and Raisa in front of Lenin's tomb."

"It sounds fine to me. How much will this production cost?"

He replied. "Would you believe a trillion dollars?"

Tora, Tora, Tora!

I came out of the house on my way to work one day, when I saw my neighbor, Clinton Fogle, planting a large American flag on his lawn.

"What's the occasion?" I shouted.

"It's Pearl Harbor Day, and I never forget it."

"Pearl Harbor Day isn't on the seventh of September," I said. "It always takes place during the third week of November."

"That's Thanksgiving," he reminded me.

"Of course it is, and that's why it has gone down in history as a day of infamy."

Fogle asked, "Do you remember what you were doing on September seventh, 1941?"

"I certainly do. I was celebrating the Labor Day weekend."

"Weren't you shocked when you heard that the Japanese had pulled a sneak attack on Hawaii?" he wanted to know.

"I didn't hear about it until December seventh. Our radio was on the fritz."

Fogle continued, "Well, I know where I was on September seventh. I was at a football game singing 'The Star-Spangled Banner.' "

"You have always sung 'The Star-Spangled Banner' at football games," I told him. "I would venture a guess that you are the most patriotic person in this Washington neighborhood, except maybe for George Bush."

He blushed. "I don't know why you would say I am a great patriot just because I recite the Pledge of Allegiance five times a day."

"That's not the only reason. You also seem to be able to smell out those who are good Americans and those who are not."

"I can't take credit for that. God gave me the gift."

"How do you tell the good from the bad?" I inquired.

"I guess everything begins and ends with school prayer. If a person is against our children using the name of the Lord in the classroom, he ought to go back to Massachusetts where he belongs."

"Would you test people for their patriotism?"

"You mean by urinalysis?"

"No, by oral and written tests."

"That's not a bad idea. I think one way to discover an unpatriotic American is to ask him if he believes we should have the right to bear arms. If his answer is no, it's a sure sign he is a latent Sandinista."

"Does the conservative wing have a monopoly on patriotism?" I asked.

"I should hope so. This country is divided as it has never been before."

"Between those who think that September seventh is Pearl

Harbor Day and those who have always thought it was December twenty-fifth?"

"No, it is divided between card-carrying members of the American Civil Liberties Union, and those who drink Coors beer."

"Fogle, I've never brought this up before. But do you think I'm a good American?"

"Do you have a picture of Ollie North hanging in your living room?"

"Not yet, but I'm looking for one."

"Frankly, I've never trusted you."

"Why not?"

"You don't put your flag out to commemorate the day Grenada attacked the United States."

"That's because I'm never sure whether it took place on Columbus Day or Lincoln's Birthday."

Snow in Miotango

"General Del Rio, I am Assistant Secretary of State for Acapulco Gold. I've flown down to discuss with you the misunderstanding between the United States and Miotango."

"You call it a misunderstanding? It's a monstrous catastrophe. Your grand jury has indicted me for the manufacture and smuggling of cocaine, heroin, marijuana, crack and adulterated decaffeinated coffee. How can you treat a friend like this?"

"It wasn't our doing. There was an overzealous assistant attorney general who put crime before our 'good neighbor' policy. Believe me, the Department is sick about it."

"Do I look like a man who would deal in dope?"

"Of course you don't."

"Do I look like a man who would kill Marxists?"

"Of course you do."

"Do I look like a man who would kill Communists while dealing in dope?"

"Apparently that's what the U.S. attorney in Florida keeps saying."

"Well, then, what's the problem?"

"General, we want you to terminate all the Marxists you can get your hands on, but we'd like you to cool it on the cocaine and heroin. It makes a mockery of Nancy Reagan's 'Just Say No' program."

"Don't you gringos understand? There is no money in killing Marxists. The bucks are all in snow."

28

"You've been on the CIA payroll for ten years, General. Surely they pay enough for your needs."

"The CIA pays chicken feed to Central American heads of state. I can't raise a family executing Communists without supplementary income from the Colombian Cocaine Manufacturers Association."

"Why not?"

"I'm sending my kid to an American college."

"General, I might be able to have the drug charges dropped if you promise to step down as the leader of Miotango."

"How can you ask me to step down at the very moment I have a 747 planeload of poppies flying in from Turkey?"

"It's not me, General. It's Congress. Some people are making charges that you have smuggled more dope into the United States than any freedom fighter in the Western Hemisphere. The CIA is embarrassed by all the hoopla, particularly because they're getting the heat. You have to mend your ways."

"So what am I supposed to do?"

"Our suggestion is to buy a home on the Riviera with your ill-gotten gains and we'll deny that you were ever in an illegal business of any kind."

"I would love to do it, but since being indicted I have become a folk hero in Miotango. As a matter of fact if the United States hadn't indicted me when it did, I would probably be buried in sand up to my head right now. Thanks to your government my people want to reelect me for life."

"That's the other thing I came to see you about. If you get reelected will you still work for us?"

"Of course, you've always treated me well. But I'm going to need money. It costs a lot more to put away a Marxist now than it did last year."

"I'll take it up with Washington. In exchange can we have your word if the Colombian cartel asks you to help smuggle in cocaine you'll just say no?"

"You have my word, not only as an officer and gentleman, but as a double agent for the Cubans as well."

Savings and Loans

While no one was looking, the savings and loan institutions have gotten themselves in debt to the tune of fifty billion dollars. To keep the entire industry from going under, there will probably have to be a taxpayer bailout in the very near future.

I saw the writing on the wall when Goodbar came to the door and said, "Each member of your family owes my savings and loan twenty-five thousand dollars."

"How can that be when we have never had a loan?"

"That's not the point. The savings and loans are in trouble and you have to bail us out. We expect every man, woman and child in this nation to ante up," he said.

"I don't get it. You people bankrupted yourselves and now you want the whole country to save you. I know life is unfair, but it's not that unfair. How did you get into such a mess?"

"It wasn't difficult. We lent money to people we thought were safe risks. Many were unable to pay back the money they borrowed, so we had to list them as bad risks. If you keep doing this for a while, it can cause you to lose a lot of money."

"Have you fired those who made the bad loans?"

"It's too late to punish anyone. When a savings and loan goes bankrupt we don't believe in taking it out on management. Now, are you going to make a voluntary contribution to get us out of the woods, or are we going to have to foreclose on your house?"

"If I help you on this, how do I know that the savings and loan down the street won't ask me to do the same for them?"

"When they ask, just tell them that you have already rescued us, and as far as you're concerned, that's good enough."

"Let's switch this around. If I owed you money and couldn't pay, would you bail me out?"

"As Dan Quayle might say, that's a hypothetical question and not worth answering. All we are doing is trying to save you if the savings and loans go belly-up. The American people owe us for the mess we now find ourselves in. How would you like it if our savings and loan went kaflooey right in front of your eyes?"

"I wouldn't like it, but I don't think I'd put it in the same class as the *Andrea Doria* going down. Why hasn't George Bush taken a stand on the savings and loan rescue mission?"

"Because he doesn't want to be the bearer of bad news. If the people find out what the bailout is going to cost each of them, there will be a taxpayers' revolt. To avoid this, the busted savings and loans are making house calls."

"Are other citizens donating money for this cause?"

"Yes, but they don't know it yet. We're trying to organize the bailout as quietly as possible."

"Why can't you go to Washington and get help from the government?"

"Because the government is handling so many failed savings and loans it is unable to take on any more. They told us to save ourselves by appealing directly to you for assistance. It's the only decent thing to do."

31

"It's hard to believe that one of the most important industries in the United States would have so much trouble keeping its head above water."

"When it comes to savings institutions, Americans must share the good times with the bad."

"I don't have twenty-five thousand dollars to donate to your bailout."

"We'll loan you the money at a very reasonable rate of interest. That's why savings and loans are in business."

Legal Theater

I met a lawyer at a party who looked familiar.

"Don't I know you?" I asked him.

"Maybe you saw me on Channel Four when I defended Alfredo Portman for inside trading on Wall Street. I had a four-point-three TV rating the day the verdict came in."

"No, I missed that one."

"I arbitrated a Holy War between three fundamentalist preachers from South Carolina, Jerry Falwell and the Ayatollah Khomeini."

"Maybe I saw you then. But didn't you plead Delta Domino guilty for stuffing U.S. Air Force missiles with Rice Krispies?"

"That was me."

"What kind of law work do you do?"

"I practice legal theater."

"I didn't know there was such a thing."

"You see it all the time," he told me. "You just don't recognize it. Legal theater is what lawyers do when they stand on the steps of the courthouse and try their case for the six o'clock news."

"Does it help the client?"

"No, but when people see me on the steps it attracts new business to the firm. It's amazing how much demand there is for a lawyer who has been on television."

"When you stand on the court steps with your client do you allow him to speak?"

"That would be a big mistake. After all, the client isn't too bright to start with or he wouldn't be in court."

"What exactly do you say to the media?"

"If it's a criminal case I declare the prosecutor is driven by political ambition and is vindictive beyond any normal bounds of justice. If I am handling a civil suit I charge that the other side has no case and should be fined for wasting the taxpayer's money. In legal theater it is not what you say, but how much TV time you can get that really counts."

He continued, "Sometimes I don't have to do anything to get on the air. I just walk with my client to the parking lot and let the reporters throw questions at me as I am slowly moving along. A lot of the news shows prefer that long walk to any dialogue you can exchange with their correspondents."

"There seems to be a lot more to practicing law than hitting the books," I said in admiration. "How did you decide to go into legal theater?"

"I had the choice of either becoming a lawyer or playing Hamlet. Legal theater gave me a chance to do both. My dream is to sit next to a witness at the Iran-contra congressional hearings and be on camera all day long."

"That must be every lawyer's dream."

"Actually, my real dream is to make each senator and congressman apologize for the way my client was treated."

"I guess that fantasy will never come true if you don't have anyone to represent in the scandal," I said.

"Rumor has it that Fawn Hall is looking for a younger lawyer," he whispered.

"You certainly would get on TV if you represented her."

"Not just any TV," he said. "I'd get on the Ted Koppel show."

"No one would ever forget you if you appeared on Ted Koppel's show with Fawn," I told him.

"The trick of legal theater is to always ask yourself before taking a case, 'Can this client cut the mustard on the Phil Donahue show?'"

"What was the most touching line you ever delivered?"

He replied, "This is an outrage. We are enormously disappointed by the verdict and intend to appeal."

"Did you write that yourself?"

"No, I saw it on 'People's Court.'"

Some Bush Questions

There have been many telephone calls asking what the presidential election outcome means to those of us who live in Washington.

Nothing much will change. Construction has now begun on an underground bunker at the Burning Tree Country Club for Vice President Dan Quayle. Bush handlers told me that this was being done to emphasize the important role the administration foresees for Quayle.

"Unlike the treatment of past vice presidents," one staffer said, "we intend to make full use of all of Dan Quayle's qualifications, which means we are finally going to get this country out of a lot of sand traps."

As far as we know, neither Mrs. Bush nor President Bush has an astrologer. The Reagans offered to turn over their own stargazer, but Bush's people felt that the President should appoint the astrologer of his choice to show the country that he is his own man.

There is no major decoration work to be done in the White House. The only question is, will Nancy Reagan leave behind the china she bought during her first term, or will she say, "I paid for these dishes and they are mine"?

Since George Bush claims to hail from both Texas *and* Connecticut, there is some question about what style of food they will be serving in the White House. The word around Washington is that it will most likely be barbecued quiche.

35

Domestic help could be a problem. During the last weeks of the campaign, Bush kept yelling at his cooks, "If you can't stand the heat, get out of the kitchen"—and they all left.

There will obviously be many differences between President Reagan and George Bush. Reagan always kept asking the American people to win one for the Gipper. Bush has no Gipper and will probably urge everyone to win one for Dan Quayle, who needs the country's prayers a lot more than the Gipper did.

George Bush has a larger family than Ronald Reagan, and he sees them frequently. This means lots of photo opportunities as each grandchild will insist on sitting on Bush's lap. Therefore we can expect to see more *People* magazine covers featuring Bush children than Princess Diana's and Fergie's babies combined.

Social life will remain about the same as it was under the Reagans. Rich people will still be welcome at the White House and treated just like you and me.

In the sports department, Bush is an ardent tennis player and Quayle is a devoted golfer. The good news is that if Mr. Bush travels abroad, Mr. Quayle, who is also an excellent tennis player, can fill in a foursome for him so that presidential business will not be interrupted.

The *in* university under Bush will be Yale; the *out* school will be the hated "H" word, which stands for Harvard. Anything coming out of Boston for the next four years will be viewed with the same seriousness as press communiqués from the Sandinistas.

It's hard for George Bush to follow Ronald Reagan's performance, because only President Reagan could get away with it. For example, for eight years the President cupped his ear to pretend he was hard of hearing each time he got on or off a helicopter or plane. No matter what the reporters asked, Mr.

Reagan just shrugged his shoulders indicating he had no idea what they were saying. Every once in a while he would shout back, "Yes," "No," and "So's your uncle."

But Bush can't do this, because if he pretends to be hard of hearing, Dan Quayle will offer to take over the presidency.

Not all people are happy about President Bush winning the election. I met one Democrat who said, "Everybody is concerned that something might happen to George Bush and then Dan Quayle will become president. But no one is worried about the effect of something happening to Dan Quayle and George Bush becoming president."

Smoke Gets in Your Eyes

The smokers and the nonsmokers had their greatest battle on a shuttle from Washington to New York not long ago. The smokers claimed the nonsmokers started it when a puffer lit up a Virginia Slim and an antismoking activist threw a pail of water at her.

The antismoker said she threw the water only because she thought the passenger was on fire. To show support for one of their own, all the smokers lit up and started blowing black tar at the nonsmokers, many of whom were senior citizens flying at half price.

Several nonsmokers put airsick bags over their faces and attacked the smoking section, assaulting the smokers with weighted briefcases and duty-free shopping bags.

The smokers rose as a group and set the airsick bags on fire with their cigarette lighters. The stewardesses put the fires out and to restore order, gave an extra demonstration on how to evacuate the airplane using the life jackets located under each seat.

To stop any further rioting the captain put on the "no smoking" sign. This angered a man who was not only a smoker but an executive of a large tobacco company.

"I know my Constitution. I have as much right to smoke as these tawdry people have not to," he said to a stewardess who was selling coffee tea or milk from a cart in the aisle.

"Smoking is bad for my health," the stewardess said.

"Medical tests show it doesn't hurt anyone's health," the executive told her.

"But they stink up my clothes."

"Sit down," a nonsmoking man said to the executive. "You're blocking my view of Philadelphia."

A lady in the smoking section started to hyperventilate. "I can't breathe," she cried. "I have to have a cigarette."

A smoker who looked like a Marlboro Man strolled down the aisle, lit up, leaned over and encouraged her to puff.

"It says no smoking on the sign," a passenger yelled angrily.

"This is an emergency," the Marlboro Man said. "Without a cigarette this lady could die."

"Stewardess, I want to speak to the captain," the nonsmoker shouted.

The captain came out of his cabin carrying an Uzi submachine gun.

"What are you doing with that gun?" the nonsmoking passenger gasped.

"We carry them now to break up arguments between smokers and nonsmokers. We used to have rubber bullets and water cannon, but they didn't have enough force to pacify people on the flights. Now what's the problem?"

"That man is permitting this lady to smoke and she's blowing it into the nonsmoking section. Throw them the hell off the plane."

"I can't do that. We have rules we must abide by." The pilot went over to the woman, who was lying on the floor. "Are you all right?"

"A couple of more puffs will do it," she said.

"Why don't you go outside on the wing of the plane?" the pilot suggested.

"Is that permitted?"

"Everything is permitted since deregulation."

Fit to Be President

The big question at the vice presidential debate was, "Is Senator Dan Quayle qualified to be President of the United States?" After listening carefully, I came to the conclusion that he is. I think what persuaded me was the answer he gave when asked what he would do if he were president.

He stated that first of all he would say a prayer, then he would meet with Bush's people, whom he had gotten to know on a first-name basis, and then he'd use his congressional experience to be President of the United States. This, of course, is a paraphrase of Quayle's answer to the question which he was asked three times.

I bought it all, even when Quayle compared himself to John Kennedy.

I even fantasized the scene. Bush and Quayle have won the election. As vice president with nothing to do, Dan Quayle has been persuaded by his father to take a course in remedial law. Dan is preparing for a true or false test, when a Bush aide rushes in and says, "President Bush has come down with a case of Mongolian flu and cannot function. According to the Twenty-fifth Amendment, you're going to have to take over as president."

Quayle says, "This is awful, but fortunately George Bush picked the most qualified person for the job. Harry Truman was the same age I am when he became president."

"You're no Harry Truman."

"That was uncalled for. Well, I better get ready. First, I will say a prayer for myself and the American people."

"That's a good idea, Mr. President. The American people need one."

"Then I'm going to meet with the President's Cabinet. I know all of them firsthand. What's the name of the little guy with the red hair?"

"His name is Red, sir."

"Okay, let's go and talk to the Cabinet. Hi, Doc. Hi, Sneezy. Hi, Dopey. Hi, Sleepy. Hi, Grumpy. Hi, Bashful. Hi, Happy. . . . You didn't think I'd know all your first names, did you? Now I've called you together because the President has Mongolian flu and I'm in charge. I'm qualified to be President of the United States because I passed the most important job-training bill in our history, and I know Margaret Thatcher personally. Are there any questions?"

"We have an explosive situation in the Middle East, Mr. President. The Iraqis and Iranians want to resume fighting. And if that isn't bad enough, Poland is boiling over, Africa is being devastated by locusts, and Pinochet in Chile is rounding up the usual suspects again. What should we do, sir?"

"Calvin Coolidge wasn't any older than I am when he faced a similar situation."

"With all due respect, sir, you're not Calvin Coolidge."

"That was really uncalled for."

"What action do you want us to take?"

"I'm going to relate a story that has prepared me for a moment such as this. I tell it at job-training centers and high schools and to the Veterans of Foreign Wars. My grandmother once said to me, 'You can do anything you want to if you just set your mind to it and go to work.'

"Now the Iranians and Iraqis may sneer at this common-sense advice, and the Poles may snicker, and Pinochet may laugh behind my back, but I'll choose my grandmother over them anytime."

"I guess that should take care of the problems we face today, sir."

"I am no younger than Checkers was when he moved into the White House."

"You're not Checkers."

"Will you cut that out!"

American Diplomacy

One of the things that made the Irangate hearings interesting was the discovery that so many private citizens were involved in conducting American diplomacy for all of us.

Albert Hakim, business partner of General Secord, and almost a father to Ollie North, testified that they went to Iran not only on arms business, but also to negotiate free-lance diplomatic deals. The trio promised that the U.S. would fight the Russians if they invaded Iran, get rid of the Iraqi president and arrange for the release of Moslem terrorists held by Kuwait.

There isn't a man or woman in this country who doesn't have a fantasy of being put in charge of our foreign policy.

This is my dream: I fly to Libya with my business partner, Albert Aagh Keem, and White House buddy Rolly West. We are escorted to Gadhafi's tent, where we present him with a chocolate cake and a Bible signed by Ronald Reagan.

"Your Royal Terrorist," I tell him in my dream, "we come to sign a peace treaty between your country and ours."

Gadhafi, ripping into the cake, says, "Do you have any Sara Lee flavors besides chocolate?"

"We have strawberry cheesecake, but we must have something in return. We want you to stop exporting terrorism in the Middle East."

"Everyone asks me that. What do I get in exchange?"

"We will sell you one thousand TOW missiles at our usual outrageously inflated prices."

43

"That doesn't seem very generous," Gadhafi says.

I take a deep breath. "We will set up a life insurance policy for you, and if we die first you can have all our money."

"You could do that for me?"

"Do you see this man?" I say, pointing at West. "This Marine colonel works for the President of the United States. He would not be here if he didn't have the right to give away the store."

"And who is this other joker?"

"This is Albert Aagh Keem. He's a poor, honest arms salesman who also translates for us on the side. Your Majesty, this is one opportunity in a million. If you sign a deal today we will assassinate all your enemies in Chad."

"I would like that very much."

"As private citizens of the U.S. our job is to make you happy, which the State Department cannot officially do."

Rolly West whispers in my ear. Then I say, "Mr. Gadhafi, I have something to suggest that as a head of state will blow your mind. If you sign this deal with us we will give you a midnight tour of the White House."

"I don't believe you have the authority to do that."

"Trust us. We'll show you the situation room, the Oval Office and Nancy Reagan's closet."

"I would love a tour of the White House. What do I do to get it?"

"Just sign the Bible and we'll give you all the spare parts you need."

"Are you certain your president supports this mission?"

"Do you think I would offer to show you the White House unless I had Mr. Reagan's permission?"

Rolly whispers in my ear again.

"If you would like to see where the dog sleeps at Camp David, that can be arranged too."

"And what is the price of the tours?"

"All we ask in exchange is that you give us ten million dollars to support moderate terrorism in Nicaragua."

Little Miss Shredder

When Fawn Hall testified to the congressional Irangate committee, there were sighs of envy in offices all over America. The sighs had nothing to do with Miss Hall's looks but rather with how she performed as Ollie North's secretary.

No one had ever seen a secretary who behaved like Hall, and after these hearings they may never see one again. Faithful, skilled and discreet beyond imagination, Fawn is the yardstick by which all future secretaries will be measured.

As might be expected, the National Security Council is having a difficult time finding a replacement for her.

"Miss Peters, if I asked you to shred my top secret documents would you do it?"

"I would if I had time, but I still haven't finished the As on the Rolodex."

"Forget the Rolodex. I would like you to alter several pages of the most confidential material I have in my safe."

"I'd like to but it would be wrong because I have a date with my boyfriend at five o'clock. Can't the altering wait until after the weekend?"

"This is hush-hush stuff, Miss Peters. If anyone finds out

45

what we're doing, we could get twenty years or congressional immunity, whichever comes first."

"That isn't worth perjuring myself for."

"How loyal are you, Miss Peters?"

"I'm loyal to a point, but this job is nothing to write home about."

"Suppose I asked you to smuggle out some very important documents under your dress. Would you do it for me?"

"Sure, if you're looking for a sexual harassment suit."

"Please, Miss Peters, I picked you for this job because you had the makings of a first-class shredder and paragraph-alterer. We may have to move against the FBI at any time. Are you willing to go that far?"

"Yes, because I respect you and everything you stand for—except for one thing. You might take the Fifth and leave me holding the bag."

"This country's security is at stake, so start deleting."

"What do you want me to delete?"

"Everything in pile A. Then I want you to shred everything in pile B. After that mix them in pile C, put them in your boots and trot out of the building."

"Why should I do that?"

"Because that's what Fawn would do if she were here right now."

"Boy, all you hear around here is what Fawn would do."

"I'm sorry I blew my stack, Miss Peters. Here is sixty dollars' worth of traveler's checks. Shred them and sprinkle them over Bloomingdale's."

"Okay. Is there anything else you want me to do before I start hitting the word processor?"

"Be careful, Miss Peters. The things you type on that processor could start World War Three."

"Why didn't you say so? What keys shouldn't I use?"

"It is not your job to ask. Fawn never questioned what went into her computer and what came out. Do you know why?"

"No, I don't."

"Because she was a team player. And do you know what made Fawn a team player?"

"Nope."

"She had the promise of limited immunity."

A Degree in Sleaze

"Washington School of Applied Ethics and Morality. Can we help you?"

"My son is coming to Washington this summer and I would like to know if you are giving any courses in hypocrisy, betrayal and sleaze?"

"Yes, we have an excellent curriculum that will lead either to a bachelor's degree in stonewalling or a master's degree in perjury."

"Can you give me some idea of what you're offering?"

"We have a popular class in lying. We hold moot congressional hearings in which the student is challenged to wriggle out of answering any compromising questions."

"How does he do that?"

"By using the Elliott Abrams defense. When asked a question the student is taught to reply something like, 'It probably happened but I don't remember it,' or, 'I don't remember it but if you say it took place I'll accept your word.' "

"Is Abrams the instructor?"

"No, he has nothing to do with the school. But the students look upon him as a role model."

"It doesn't surprise me. He's everybody's role model."

"If your son is working in Washington this summer I would advise that he take a seminar on special prosecutors."

"I didn't know you could take a *whole* seminar on them."

"It's essential if you're going to work for the administration. Let's say, for example, that while your son is in Washington, he gets involved in a defense factory bribery case. As a reward he receives stock and cash. As soon as it becomes public what he is up to, he is entitled to his own special prosecutor. We demonstrate how he can face up to a prosecutor while keeping damage to himself at a minimum."

"How is it done?"

"The student asks for immunity and then agrees to rat on all the other people involved with his scheme."

"But isn't that dirty pool?"

"No, dirty pool is another course where government officials learn how to help polluters get around the EPA."

"Since we're talking about morality, do you have any studies in adultery?"

"Your son can take adultery but he won't get any credit for it."

"What about greed?"

"Greed is required, and you can't graduate without it. We teach that there is nothing wrong with being greedy if it's in your country's best interests."

"My son hopes to work with one of the federal agencies. Is there a lot of sleaze involved in this?"

"It depends on how much work he does for the vested interests. We offer all the standard white-collar crimes. What our students do with them is their business."

"My son wants to know if you teach students how to shred incriminating documents."

"Each student is required to own a paper shredder and burn bag. The burn bag can also be used to carry his lunch."

"You have a fun school."

"We try to make our students good citizens, even if they have to lie to do it. As Ollie North said, 'There is more to government than rewarding your friends and punishing your enemies.' "

"How much more?"

"Come to think of it, not much."

The Friendly Skies

You might not know it, but the United States and the Soviet Union are still involved in arms negotiations.

Senko, the attaché at the Russian Embassy, told me they have hit a new snag.

"Gorbachev is demanding a Cessna-free Europe," he said.

"That's unfair," I told him. "There is no way we can promise that. We can control missiles, but Cessnas fly anywhere they want to. It wasn't our fault a light plane took off from Helsinki and landed in Red Square."

"Comrade Gorbachev thinks the U.S. did it to embarrass him and cause trouble between himself and Raisa Gorbachev."

"How could we do that?"

"The pilot flew so close to the Kremlin he could see Raisa taking a sauna. Raisa wants Gorbachev to keep small planes out of her bathroom."

"If it makes him so unhappy why didn't Gorbachev shoot down the Cessna?"

"He would have if he could," Senko answered. "We Russians are experts against a Stealth bomber, but our air defense is like Swiss cheese when attempting to bring down private planes."

"Then Gorbachev has a problem," I said.

"No, it's America that has a problem. We had the whole arms package tied up. Both sides agreed to give up middle-range missiles in Europe. We put testing on the table. We were ready to meet Reagan more than halfway. Then this decadent German youth blew up the whole deal. Now we don't know what type of weapons to ban in arms talks. Can you imagine what a chill this has sent through our crack Soviet Air Command?"

I asked, "How much damage can a tiny plane cause to a superpower?"

"The damage is in how we are viewed by the world. Not one Soviet fighter rose to shoot the Cessna down. No antiaircraft battery fired its guns. As far as Moscow's defenders were concerned the Cessna could have been flying the friendly skies of United."

"So what steps will you take to rectify the situation?"

"Gorbachev just made his air defense commander an inspector in a Chicken Kiev factory in Smolensk. All the men charged with defending Moscow have been stationed at 7-Eleven stores in Chernobyl. Several Soviet marshals have now been assigned to waiting on U.S. Marines in the GUM department store."

"Gorbachev has taken all the necessary steps. What more does he want?"

"The General Secretary will not make an arms deal with the U.S. until you promise to keep Cessnas from using Red Square as a landing strip."

"Tell Gorbachev that we have no control over what our NATO friends do with their light planes," I said.

"He doesn't believe you. The comrade leader says the German Cessna could never have made it unless it had sophisticated American guidance equipment. Gorbachev believes you intend to violate the arms treaty with Piper Cubs."

"If he thinks such a thing, where does that leave the talks?"

"Up in the air. The Soviet position has always been that

we're willing to give up everything, except we will not permit small aircraft to land on Lenin's tomb. Without guarantees we will break up the talks."

"But why?"

"If you don't promise us a Cessna-free Europe how can we be sure you won't build Star Wars?"

"Would you believe it if I told you that the landing of the Cessna worried Americans no end?"

"I wouldn't believe it," Senko said.

"It was just a shot in the dark."

Fabulous Garbage

I used to spend a lot of time worrying about the garbage barge that sat off Long Island, New York—after it journeyed to the Gulf of Mexico and back. Newspaper reports indicated that absolutely *no one* wanted the 3,000 tons of refuse and that is why the barge returned.

I found out that this information was wrong. When I approached the barge in the Central Islip inlet, a man with a shotgun shouted, "Stand back or I'll shoot you. What are you doing here?"

"I just came to see the garbage."

"That's what everyone says, but we're not fooled. You want this trash for yourself."

"That's not true. We have all the garbage we need in Washington and we don't want any of this stuff."

"You may have garbage," he said, "but it's not the high-grade New York variety."

"What's so special about New York garbage?"

"It contains everything from pickles to forged traffic tickets. We have nuclear waste and McDonald's coffee cups. People in New York have a very high standard of living and therefore they dispose of only the best refuse. You couldn't find a better variety of trash than we have on this barge, and we're not giving it up to anyone no matter how much you beg for it."

"I'm not going to beg. New York is entitled to its own rubbish. What kind of landfill will your garbage make?"

The man laughed. "Only the finest in America. Did you know Atlantic City would fall into the sea if it weren't for Manhattan trash?"

"What I don't understand is if you have such great slop why no one would take any of it when your barge sailed south."

"That was a goodwill trip in which we wanted to call on southern ports and Mexico to bring regards from Mayor Koch," the man said. "And it was very successful. When we showed up with the waste in Mexican waters they met us with gunboats, planes and helicopters. Old-timers said they had never seen a garbage scow given that kind of greeting by the Mexican Navy before."

"That's a real honor."

"The U.S. Navy is talking about bringing us to the Strait of Hormuz to show the people in the area that the United States means business."

"Why would they want you to do that?"

53

"We could show the American flag, and if the Iranians hit us, how much damage could they do?"

"This barge has really paid for itself. At the rate you're going there is no sense dumping any of the refuse into the sea. You could make more money selling it to tourists."

"We're considering that. There are a lot of people from Greenwich who would give anything for our bilge."

"Did you ever dream when you loaded the scow that its cargo would become this sentimental to so many people?"

"New Yorkers are funny that way. When they are loaded down with trash they keep screaming for someone to take it away, and when it's gone they cry for someone to bring it back. Hey, what are you doing?" he yelled.

"I just picked up a crushed Coca-Cola can and a Kool-Aid wrapper."

He raised his gun. "Put it down or I'll shoot. That is the property of the people of Central Islip and the EPA."

"I'm sorry. Every time I see a scow filled with New York garbage I lose my head."

"Justice For All"

"May I speak to the Attorney General of the United States?"

"I'm sorry, he is in conference with several lawyers."

"Justice Department lawyers?"

"No, his own lawyers. They're discussing the Wedtech case. They want to get that straightened out so the Attorney General can devote all his time to defending himself in the Iraqi oil pipeline scandal."

"He's much more active than most attorney generals," I said.

"That's not the half of it. The AG may have to face a special prosecutor for his role in the Iran-contra affair."

"I guess an attorney general's work is never done."

"You'd be busy too if every special prosecutor in the country was cheek to jowl with you."

"Look, I don't want much of his time. I just wish to ask him how he is doing in his fight against organized crime."

"The Attorney General has not been able to get around to fighting organized crime because he is too involved in giving depositions regarding his blind trust."

"That shouldn't take him all day."

"You'd be surprised how blind the AG has been concerning his blind trusts."

"Well, you tell him for me it doesn't look nice for the highest law-enforcement officer in the land to be seen sneaking around so many grand jury rooms."

"That's an attorney general's job."

"But he keeps going in for himself and not on behalf of the government."

"The AG is a very fine lawyer and he's a whiz at testifying under oath. He'd be willing to handle government business if they would just leave him alone on his personal affairs."

"They can't as long as there is a smoking gun."

"Are you finished?"

"No, I'm not. I would also like to speak to the AG about the recent resignations in the Justice Department."

"The Attorney General has instructed me to tell anyone who calls that nothing should be read into the fact that a few disloyal turncoats jumped ship before the skipper lowered the flag."

"The rumor on the street is they resigned because the AG kept tiptoeing in the sleaze."

"That's ridiculous. The AG has never been convicted of any crime. He will go down in history as having had more friends invest for him than any other Reagan Cabinet officer. That's why the President considers him a great attorney general."

"But what about the government? What did he do for the government?"

"How could he do anything for the government when he was being badgered all the time by political enemies looking into his finances?"

"They were out to get him because he had bad judgment, weren't they?"

"You said it, I didn't."

"If I could only talk to the AG for one moment I would wish him a nice day."

"After he finishes meeting with his lawyers he is going to have to huddle with his accountants, so everyone can get the papers together for the Senate Judiciary Committee."

"Do you think with all the pressure the AG might resign?"

"What for? He loves the job. When he came over from the White House he took an oath of office that he would clear himself and his friends of any wrongdoing, even if it tied him up for the entire four years."

Help Wanted

Most commencement speakers lied to the graduating classes of 1987. They said that America wants them to become outstanding doctors, lawyers, nurses, dentists, scientists and college professors.

No one wants any such thing. What we really wish they could do is become dishwashers, busboys, waitresses, taxi drivers, chambermaids and gardeners.

Ebell Bowl, who gave the commencement speech at Luna Lake Tech, was one of the thousands of speakers who admitted he made a mistake. We discussed it at a sidewalk café on Cape Cod, waiting for coffee that never came.

"I should have told the class of 1987 that their generation owes it to our generation to provide the basic services we all need, and I don't mean genetic engineering."

"It doesn't count for a kid to climb the ladder of success if no one can get a cup of coffee," I said.

Ebell continued. "My message to the graduating class should

have been that none of us can enjoy the American dream if young people will not carry away our dirty dishes."

"I remember when I finished college how much I looked forward to being a bellhop at a resort hotel. I couldn't have cared less about upward mobility."

Ebell became agitated. "I know what I should have said in my speech. This country will be great only when there are enough students to pump its gas."

"You could have made the point that since there are no illegal aliens available, everyone with an engineering diploma should pick grapes."

Ebell said, "Higher education means bupkes if there is no one to clean our hotel rooms. I don't want astronomers to tell me the world started with a bang. I want someone to explain why my air conditioner won't work. We don't need investment bankers, and marketing geniuses—not as long as the country is crying for lifeguards and people to make Dunkin' Donuts."

"Why is there such a shortage of help?" I asked Ebell.

"Nobody will work," he replied. "The trouble is that kids don't think six dollars per hour is a fair wage for jerking sodas, particularly since they can get twice as much from their parents if they promise not to drive sixty-five miles an hour."

Ebell added, "Attitudes have changed in recent years. At one time the greatest thrill in the world for a young person was to wait on his friends in a restaurant. Now the biggest kick for a college student is to be waited on. What's happened is that both the haves and have-nots want somebody else to do their menial work. The haves want it all; the have-nots want it now. But nobody wants to work for tips."

"If everyone is sitting down, who will mix our malted milkshakes?"

"I made a lot of mistakes at the graduation. I shouldn't have told the students their job is to stop a nuclear holocaust. I should have assured them that the most they can do for peace is clean fish so people won't go hungry in Southampton."

"Even if you had said it, they wouldn't have listened."

Ebell continued. "Not one of those youngsters has a right to demand a piece of the American pie if he or she hasn't paid his dues to Wendy's. This country can't survive if its graduates insist on bypassing the summer jobs that go begging."

"Had you mentioned that in your talk, you would have received a standing ovation—from the parents."

"Not only that," said Ebell. "We might also have been served our coffee."

Living Well

Donald Trump and his lovely wife, Ivana, were eating breakfast in the window of Tiffany's, which they had recently purchased. Donald sipped his orange juice and made a face. "It tastes funny," he said.

"What's wrong with it?" Ivana asked.

"I don't know, but if I bought Florida I could make better juice than this."

"What part of Florida?" Ivana wanted to know.

"The whole state. There's no sense in just owning a piece

here and a piece there. How does Trump Disney World sound to you?"

"It's all right with me but I thought you were going to buy Mexico and corner the refried beans business."

"There is no reason why I can't have them both. How does Trump Refried Beans grab you?"

"It has a nice ring to it. Are we going out on the boat today?"

"The boat's in dry dock. I'm adding anti-mine-sweeping gear to it."

"Don't tell me you've bought the Strait of Hormuz."

"No, but I have an option on it as soon as Iraq and Iran work out the details of a cease-fire. It'll be renamed the Strait of Trump."

"Donald, you never cease to amaze me. You would buy Saint Patrick's Cathedral if you had a chance."

"Maybe not the cathedral, but I'd certainly consider acquiring the air rights over it. What do you think of Trump Saint Patrick's?"

"I like it," Ivana said. "What are you doing after breakfast?"

"I'm going to fly out to Jackson Hole, Wyoming."

"The government won't let you own Jackson Hole."

"I didn't say I was going to buy it. All I want is a ninety-nine-year lease so that I can build a casino there. Trump Jackson Hole fits in nicely with the other stuff I have."

"It will attract a lot of people who were afraid to go to the wilderness before."

"What are your plans for today, Ivana?"

"I'm having my hair done."

"That's a good idea. I'll buy you the Elizabeth Arden company. Trump Elizabeth Arden sounds great to me."

"I don't want to own Elizabeth Arden. I just need somebody to do my hair."

"But Ivana, you wouldn't have to tip anyone if it was your company."

"Donald, you are a compulsive shopper. You don't have to buy everything just because it's there."

"That's easy for you to say. But if I don't acquire something every day, I get sick to my stomach. I have a good mind to make a bid for Venice, Italy. Then I could merge it with Verona. I'd like to call it the Trump Romeo and Juliet Estates. If someone purchases a condo, they get free swimming rights in the Venice canals."

"Donald, I never know when you're joking."

"I never joke about real estate, dear. If I can make a go of Venice, then maybe they will let me build a shopping center on Saint Peter's Square."

"What name will you put on it, Donald?"

"I'll have to give that a lot of thought."

She Does Nothing

The worst thing you can ask a woman these days is, "What do you do?"

I made this mistake the other night when I turned to the lady seated next to me at a dinner party and posed the question.

"I don't do anything," she said. "I make breakfast for the family and then I clean the kitchen. After that I call the telephone company to find out if they plan on sending anyone to fix the phone, and then I go to the supermarket with a long list of things that we're out of."

"But you're doing something," I disagreed.

"I'm really not worth much," she sighed. "After the supermarket, I pick up my youngest child from kindergarten, and leave him at the baby-sitter while I go off in search of fertilizer for the lawn. I don't wear nice suits, and I never carry a briefcase."

"Look, if you don't want to talk about it, it's okay with me."

"I feel so worthless," she continued. "Sometimes when I want to have fun I go to the shoemaker and get new heels put on my shoes. But then I have to make up for it by taking the car to the garage because the brakes squeal, and the electrical system keeps dying on me. I've risen as high as I can in life."

"You do more than most women who work outside the home," I assured her.

"It's not true. Those women are suing people and figuring

63

out celebrities' income taxes; they're removing gallstones and merging peanut companies with coal mine monopolies. All I'm doing with my time is carting overdue books back to the library, driving my mother to the dentist, and trying to find a sump pump for my basement. I'm almost ashamed to be in this room with so many women of accomplishment."

"You're being too hard on yourself. Let's change the subject. What do you think of this lamb?"

"I never eat lamb. Nobody in my family likes it. But they do enjoy beef stew and it only takes me three hours to cook the whole thing. I love to be in the kitchen. No one has ever taken me out to lunch just because they wanted to sell me a new pension plan."

I must have touched a nerve somewhere because she wouldn't stop.

"Did I tell you I also compact garbage?"

"No, you didn't."

"What I do is take the garbage, put it into the machine and push a button, and then it gets compacted into a bag. But that's not all. When I've crushed enough garbage, I have to take it out of the compactor and insert a new bag. Now do you know what I do?"

"I'm very impressed," I answered.

"It's not as hard as it sounds, especially for those of us who went to Radcliffe. What else would you like to know about me?"

"Do you have any dreams?"

"I dream of a big strong man coming to my house and saying, 'I am from the University of Virginia Tau Omega fraternity and part of my hazing assignment is to wash all your windows and bathe your dog.' I know it's too much to hope for, but I need something to keep me going."

"Have you seen the Gauguin exhibit at the National Gallery?" I asked.

"I've been meaning to go but I have to wallpaper the kids' rooms, wait for the piano tuner to turn up, hem my daughter's dress, and buy a wedding gift for my niece, as well as make popcorn for my husband and his friends when they come over to watch the baseball playoff game."

"I don't understand why you keep putting yourself down. You do quite a bit for somebody who officially does nothing," I said.

"It's so little compared to that woman over there who is giving my husband her business card."

A Meeting in Philly

I went up to Philadelphia to join in the celebration of the 200th birthday of the United States Constitution. It's an event that not many people in the country paid attention to, particularly since Jimmy and Tammy Bakker were celebrating their wedding anniversary and garnering all the headlines.

It's amazing how little we know about the Constitution.

For example, I found out that Independence Hall was originally constructed by the William Penn Insurance Company, and the Liberty Bell was rung every time a horse and carriage went over a cliff. The insurance company agreed to lend their property to the sovereign states on the condition that it would get to write Medicaid policies if a nation was ever born.

This is not known: The first Constitution was written as a TV sitcom for Bill Cosby. After all three networks turned it down, the writers decided to sell it to the United States as a possible blueprint for the law of the land.

This is not known: The second version of the Constitution was shredded by a young secretary who worked for a Colonel North on George Washington's National Security staff. When asked why she did it, the secretary said, "Ollie told me that sometimes there are things higher than the written law."

This was the smoking gun that Congress had been looking for and they demanded North testify.

It is not generally known, but Ollie said, "You can't call me as a witness because there is no Constitution which says you have the right to."

The convention delegates immediately passed a Constitution which they proudly showed to North. He read it and said, "I'll take this one here."

"What are you taking?" Alexander Hamilton wanted to know.

"The Fifth Amendment. The founding fathers wouldn't want me to incriminate myself, would they?"

Rufus King, the delegate from Massachusetts, was furious. "Who's the wise guy who inserted the Fifth?" he demanded.

"I did," said Robert Morris of Pennsylvania. "But there is a loophole. We can always make North testify by giving him limited immunity."

"Aw," said Charles Pinckney of South Carolina, "this Constitution is full of loopholes. I'll vote for capital punishment and we'll hang North on the square. It's the kind of thing they would do in Philadelphia."

"The Constitution says you can't do that," said James McHenry of Maryland. "By the way, where *is* the Constitution?"

"It's gone," someone yelled.

"I know nothing about it," said George Washington. "But if someone on my staff took it I'm sure he had a very good reason."

It is not widely known, but Roger Sherman of Connecticut came stomping in and cried, "I have just found out where the Constitution is. It's in a numbered bank account in Switzerland."

"What's it doing there?"

"It was deposited by General Secord, who has been selling guns to the Indians."

"Let's ransack Secord's house and find the number."

"We can't. That's unlawful search and seizure."

"Why did we put unlawful search and seizure into the Constitution?"

"Because we needed some boilerplate for the first page."

Ask the
Air Travel Lady

The Air Travel Answer Lady is here to help. Just send your queries to "Dear Airy," and she will favor you with a reply.

Dear Airy: I am taking a flight from Washington to Atlanta. We've been sitting on the runway for four hours. How do I know if I will have enough air to breathe until we take off?—PATTY FAYE DIMETRES

Dear Patty: Four hours is not too long a time to wait on a runway these days. What I do for my own safety is carry a canary in my pocket. When the canary keels over dead I know it's time to slide down the emergency chute.

Dear Airy: I was told I could fly to San Francisco for ninety-nine dollars. But when I arrived at the airport I was informed that that particular fare was only good on Columbus Day. I asked them if they had any other bargains and they told me they had a red-eye special to El Paso with intermediate stops in Charlotte, North Carolina, and Billings, Montana, for $355. Is someone giving me the business?—JANE COHEN

Dear Jane: Your airline is only charging you what the market will bear. Thanks to deregulation its fares must compete with other carriers on the same route. This is how the fare war works: Various airlines announce bargain tickets for the same destination, which are sold out just as you get to the counter.

You then have the choice of paying the regular fare or canceling the flight, which carries a penalty of five years in prison.

Dear Airy: Are there any regulations spelling out the width of seats and leg room on American carriers?—PHILIP AND MYRNA AIELLO

Dear Philip and Myrna: There are strict rules concerning the transport of pets and domestic animals in flight, but they do not apply to humans. For example, pets are not required to eat airline food, but human passengers are. The reason for this is the FAA knows every pet is dear to someone. But the government still considers human beings to be excess baggage.

Dear Airy: When the flight I'm on has a near miss in the air, do the people on my plane wave to the passengers on the other plane, or should they wave to us?—KAY ROBERTS

Dear Kay: In a near-miss situation either side may wave first, but only the pilots are permitted to make rude gestures.

Dear Airy: Why do you see so many little kids flying on planes these days?—KATHY BYE

Dear Kathy: More children are flying now than ever before because it's cheaper for a mother to travel with her kids than to put them in a day-care center.

Most of the mothers you see on planes have no particular destination in mind and are just killing time until their husbands can take them to Burger Chef for dinner.

Dear Airy: Do airborne pilots receive extra pay for telling you what cities you are flying over?—JOHN R. PROFFITT

Dear John: No, they are all volunteers who delight in giving a tour of the earth at 40,000 feet. These pilots believe a passenger will lose his sense of awe if he doesn't know he has just flown over Topeka, Kansas.

Pay Raise

There has to be a solution to the congressional pay deadlock. Congressmen and senators need more money and the taxpayer is adamant about not giving it to them.

There are some people who are against the raise because they think it's too much. Then there are others who are against it because this is the first time in their lives that they have been in a position to turn down *anyone* for a pay increase. Consequently, they want to make the most of the opportunity.

My taxi driver is one of them. "I say no raise," he declared, as we started out for the office. "They get too much money anyway, and they don't do a thing for it."

"That's a harsh judgment, Rico. Many legislators work day and night, and then have to travel long distances on weekends in order to give the American people the best laws that money can buy. Would you prefer they be paid the same wages as the workers at McDonald's?"

"They tried to sneak the raise in behind our backs because they were too chicken to vote it up or down. If Congress had come to me and said, 'Rico, we need this to educate our children and feed our families,' I might have given them the increase."

"That's very good for you, Rico. How many raises have you handed out in your life?"

"That doesn't matter. I'm a good judge of character, and I know when someone should have a pay increase and when they shouldn't. I read the papers like everybody else. Besides, I never thought an across-the-board raise was a good idea. I'd like to see the lawmakers paid on a piecework basis. Members of Congress would be rewarded according to their level of production. If a legislator shows up every day on the Hill, he is given a standard fee. If he introduces a bill in Congress, he gets an extra amount for it, and if the bill is passed, he receives a bonus."

"Would you give them anything for attending a PAC breakfast to raise money for their election campaigns?"

"No. They would be on their own for all fund-raisers. At the same time I might offer them a fee for going to a prayer breakfast."

"How much should they get for waging a filibuster?"

"In that situation we would be very generous because it puts a lot of wear and tear on the body. I'd also pay piecemeal for those who give speeches on the floor of the Senate, but I would like to see a system whereby the person making the shortest speech gets the most money."

"Would I be correct if I presumed that each time a representative voted, he would get a stipend?"

"Yes. I'd have the sergeant at arms sit at a table and pay everyone in cash as they came down the aisle."

"Rico, I think you're onto something. No one has ever thought of compensating lawmakers for what they actually do—not even Trotsky."

"It's the only way Congress is going to get a raise from me."

"You're a good man and a fair man, but suppose they don't accept your plan?"

"They have no choice. I don't think anyone has been fairer than I have to the people on Capitol Hill. But I can't justify throwing money away on large pay raises when there are so many potholes in this country still waiting to be filled."

Drop Dead

The Reverend Oral Roberts' statement that he has raised people from the dead brought snickers from some nonbelievers, but apparently he is not the only one who has been doing it.

Reverend Felix Doberman of the "TV Temple in the Shady Glen" claims to have been raising souls from the dead long before Oral vowed to go to heaven if church members didn't send in their dues.

I asked Doberman how he raises people from the dead.

He replied, "First I lay my hands on them, and then say, 'Everybody up!' "

"That's all it takes?"

"That and a hefty donation to the TV Temple in the Shady Glen. I can't bring anyone back to life if he's not willing to support our electronic congregation."

"How many dead have you raised?"

"At least one thousand in the live audience. I've also raised a lot of them who were watching me on television, so all I can do is take their word for it—plus whatever donation they want to make. I've known of so many miracles you wouldn't believe it. I've heard of men and women stretched out in their coffins who rose and danced as soon as my son made his initial pitch for money."

"Where did you get the idea of bringing back the dead as a fund-raiser?"

"I'm always consulting God on how to obtain fresh resources. He told me there is nothing that excites people more than coming back to life."

"Do you think Oral Roberts really brought many parishioners back?"

"Oral is a good ol' Oklahoma boy, and the way he's been acting lately I believe anything he says. What worries me is that there are too many ministers claiming they can raise the dead. When they see there is money in it, all the TV evangelists are going to be claiming they are able to do it, and professionals like myself and Oral will be competing with frauds."

"Perhaps they should issue licenses to trained faith healers."

"That would mix church and state and restrict donations from secular humanists. Frankly I think Oral should have kept his mouth shut. He was raising a lot of dead and no one knew about it. Now it's a big story and you can't tell the ones who have the touch from those who don't."

"Are Jimmy and Tammy Bakker into dead-raising?" I asked.

"Not that anyone remembers. Jimmy raised a lot of other things though, and there is some question about where the money went. As for Tammy, she said if Jimmy did it she'll forgive him."

"Certainly the Reverend Jerry Falwell hasn't raised anyone from the dead."

"No, he hasn't, though he tried to do it with the PTL Club."

"Why couldn't he?"

"Because the PTL really *is* dead, and there is no way of bringing it back."

"Has Jimmy Swaggart ever raised anyone from the dead?"

"No, but he's sent an awful lot of people to hell. Jimmy tells his audience to either give money or drop dead."

Polling the Readers

Every news outfit is taking polls concerning current events. In a matter of hours you can now find out where America stands on any subject. I've decided to go into the same business. Here are the results of my latest nationwide poll:

1. When Bud McFarlane and Oliver North went to Iran they brought with them a Bible and a chocolate cake. In exchange the Iranians mined the Strait of Hormuz. Who got the best deal?

The U.S.—48 percent.

The Ayatollah's Bible class—42 percent.

The CIA baker who made the cake to launch the first Iranian-American Friendship Cookbook—10 percent.

2. Does President Reagan know any more now than he did before he had lunch with Admiral Poindexter?

Knows more—10 percent.

Knows less—15 percent.

Can't remember who Admiral Poindexter is—75 percent.

3. After hearing the President talk about his role in the contra supply network in Central America, do you believe the President has:

A longer nose—35 percent.

A shorter nose—50 percent.

About the same—15 percent.

4. Do you agree that Ollie North should have permitted someone else to install a security system around his house?

Agree—14 percent.

Disagree—14 percent.

Should have bought a pit bulldog instead—72 percent.

5. If anyone from the White House is indicted for crimes concerning Irangate he should be given:

An immediate pardon—33 percent.

An immediate pardon and a lecture tour—45 percent.

An immediate pardon, a lecture tour, a million-dollar book contract, a Bible and a chocolate layer cake—22 percent.

6. If you had your choice of picking a fall guy for the contra hearings, who would you choose?

Elliott Abrams—21 percent.

Bill Casey—20 percent.

Judge Robert Bork—59 percent.

7. Who should be in charge of Kuwaiti-American tankers in the Persian Gulf?

Sly Stallone—76 percent.

James Bond—14 percent.

Arnold Schwarzenegger, if all else fails—10 percent.

8. Who would you most like to see stand by the President in a crisis?

Fawn Hall—15 percent.

Donna Rice—20 percent.

Joan Collins—65 percent.

9. What would you do with the Iranian-contra money that has been stashed away in Swiss bank accounts?

Give it to Attorney General Ed Meese to help Wedtech get back on its feet—25 percent.

Give it to Mike Deaver so he can get the Justice Department off his back—25 percent.

Give it to Tammy Bakker so she can save her face—50 percent.

He's in Charge

When President Reagan told the country that the buck stops in his office, he wasn't kidding.

"Mr. President, five countries in Central America have just signed a peace plan to make the Nicaraguans and the contras stop fighting."

"Did I know anything about it?"

"No sir, you didn't."

"Well, that's where you are wrong. Everything that happens winds up here on this desk."

"Yes sir. I almost forgot."

"Can we still supply the contras under the plan?"

"No sir, and the Soviets and Cubans aren't permitted to supply the Sandinistas. The five countries want everybody out of Central America."

"What kind of peace treaty is that?"

"It's a terrible one. That's why I brought it to you—because the buck on this one stops with you."

"Of course it does. This is a presidential decision that only the elected leader of all the people can deal with."

"You're right as rain, sir. What do you want to do now?"

"Think it through. When the buck stops on my desk I don't just throw it back without thinking about it. I want to know how we can abide by the terms of the treaty and also supply the contras with weapons and nonmilitary support."

"We can always sell snowmobiles to Iran."

"We did that once and it didn't work. Do you know why? Because the buck stopped with Admiral Poindexter instead of with me. Had I been in charge of the buck I would have never let Colonel North do so many good, bad and ugly things. I didn't know what was going on, but I should have because that's what presidents are for."

"Yessir, Mr. President. Do you want to send our people to Central America to find out what is going on there?"

"I do if it's clearly understood that it is my decision to do so. If there is anything I hate it's people thinking I don't know what is going on. What's this buck doing on my desk?"

"It's the trillion-dollar budget you're offering the country."

"That isn't my budget. I won't take the blame for it."

"You're going to have to, sir. You've insisted that this is as far as the buck goes, and that includes accountability for the finances of the country."

"The free-spending Democrats are responsible for this budget. How many times have I said fiscal matters don't stop with me?"

"If you insist, sir, you can say that, but it looks bad after announcing that you make all the decisions in the White House."

"Couldn't we arrange to have the budget presented as a covert operation through a bank in Switzerland with a presidential finding?"

"I don't think so, sir. There are too many people who know about it."

"How much of the buck will have to stop with me?"

"The whole thing, Mr. President."

"That's an awful lot to get stuck with. Doesn't the CIA have a solution to this problem?"

"The only answer they came up with, sir, is to put the budget in your wife's name."

"Guess Who?"

The fun of watching the seven Democratic presidential candidates on TV is guessing their identities. The other day it was my turn to have the gang over, and this is how it went.

"Who is the fellow from Arizona?"

"He's the one wearing the dark suit."

"Six of the seven have dark suits on."

"Well, he's not the guy with the bow tie."

"How do you know that?"

"Because there is only one guy in the presidential race with a bow tie and he's from somewhere in the Midwest."

"I recognize a candidate."

"Which one?"

"The fellow with the mustache. That's Jesse Jackson."

"How can you be sure it's Jesse Jackson?"

"He is the only one in the campaign who has a mustache, just like the other guy is the only one who has a bow tie. This makes each of them very different from the others."

"I think that's Joe Biden of Delaware at the end."

"Are you positive?"

"Yes, because he's attacking the size of the Republican deficit."

"They all have attacked the size of the Republican deficit. The person you say is Biden could be any of the seven."

"It could even be Dukakis. People confuse him with Biden when they're debating."

78

"It's hard to tell Dukakis from the others because he doesn't look like anybody."

"Any idea who the fellow in the light suit is?"

"That's probably the candidate from Iowa. I don't know his name, but he's always getting into an argument with the senator from Tennessee whose name I think is Gephardt."

"No, dummy, the senator from Tennessee is named Babbitt."

"I thought Babbitt was from Illinois. It isn't easy to keep them straight."

"They all look like excellent prospects to me."

"And they each have their own personality, which causes them to stand out in a crowd—and makes it easy to identify with them."

"Who is the one for taxes and against war?"

"I think Jackson. No, it could be Simon."

"You haven't been listening. All seven are for taxes and against war."

"Have any of them come out against lying in government?"

"As far as I can tell most of them have taken a position against lying in government."

"Well, at least they agree on something."

"I think they agree on everything."

"How can you have seven candidates who agree on everything?"

"Because they don't want to make anybody mad at them."

"What's most peculiar is that Jesse Jackson is the one making all the jokes. When did Jackson start telling jokes?"

"When Gary Hart got caught in Bimini."

Phi Beta Money

Word from the old alma mater is that the cost of private education is going up faster than the national debt. A recent College Board survey revealed that the price of a diploma at one of the more expensive schools is now $75,000, which does not include gas, oil or ski trips during the school break.

Can parents afford to send a kid to college for $75,000 and still find happiness? The answer is, most people can't afford to send them for half of that. And yet for some reason the older generation continues to do it. Thanks to their own sacrifice, parents are making their nut and their children are growing up in the rich academic environment everyone has told them they are entitled to.

In order to get a better picture of what exactly is going on I talked to some of those involved in the tuition struggle to see how they feel about it.

One student at Georgetown University took the news calmly. "Nobody wants to force our parents to come up with seventy-five thousand big ones, but if that's what we young Americans have to pay for a good education, I say it's money well spent. Dad had it easy when he went to college so he never knew the cost of a diploma. Now he's learning the hard way, and he'll be better for it."

The drama concerning heavy tuition is being played out everywhere. I saw a father at Johns Hopkins say farewell to his son at the gate. As he bade him goodbye, the father gave the young man his cuff links, tie clasp and gold watch. "This is it," the father told the boy. "When they are gone you're on your own."

"Where will I find you?" the boy wanted to know.

"Your mother and I will be in the basement of a federal housing project in Baltimore. Don't worry, the move has nothing to do with your tuition. We always planned to do it that way."

A president of one of the Ivy League schools defended the high-priced costs and said that $75,000 barely pays for books and a half-baked history teacher.

"It's wrong," he explained, "to use the figure seventy-five thousand dollars as the cost of a four-year education, because now everybody will expect one for that. We have a different plan at our school. We insist that parents throw everything they have into our rotunda and allow the school to take what it needs."

"That sounds like a fair way of doing it," I agreed.

"Parents think we make money on tuition costing seventy-five thousand dollars. There is no way we can get in the black by filling our classrooms," the president said. "We don't even make a profit on Shakespeare."

"What do you make money on?" I asked.

"Towing students' cars away. If it weren't for our police towaway program we would never have been able to construct a new science building."

The final person I spoke to was a football player attending a great Texas university.

"How do you feel about a seventy-five-thousand-dollar college education?"

He replied, "I don't think that's a lot of money to pay a linebacker. After all, we have given up a great deal to play football for our school."

"I believe you misunderstood me. The *student* is expected to pay the school, not the other way around."

"Why would a college football player want to pay the school anything?" he asked.

"Perhaps to get a better education."

"I'd rather see the seventy-five thousand go into new shoulder pads, where it belongs."

Courage

The Dan Rather "black hole," as it has become known in news circles, is one of the most unusual events to have happened in television.

This is what took place. Dan was down in Miami to cover the Pope's visit and to anchor the "CBS Evening News." To Dan's chagrin CBS Sports was broadcasting a whale of a tennis match between lady stars Lori McNeil and Steffi Graf. Dan was informed that the "Evening News" might have to be cut to make time for the tennis. Rather was furious and said if CBS Sports cut into his show then CBS Sports could do all the news that evening.

It was a standoff until six-thirty P.M. rolled around and Rather was told he had to hold off on the Pope until the tennis game was over. Dan, in fury, took off his mike and walked out of the studio to call his boss in New York.

This is where it gets interesting. While Rather was in the hall the tennis match ended. But there was nobody in the studio to present the evening news. So CBS went to black—pitch black—while CBS network executives from New York to Key Biscayne were screaming at each other, "My TV set is on the fritz!" After six minutes of blackness Dan came back on the air with an upbeat report on the Pope. But it was too late.

Ever since that night, known as "Black Friday at Black Rock," the CBS brass have been scratching their heads trying to figure out what happened and what can be done about it. Chairman of the Board Larry Tisch said, "This will never happen again." Howard Stringer, the CBS News president, said it even more strongly. "This will never happen again!" Three thousand CBS executives opened their windows and shouted, "This will never happen again!"

It is one thing to say it, but another to actually do something constructive.

A source at CBS told me that one of the ideas the executives came up with is to station a pit bulldog by Rather's desk. Every time Dan makes a move toward the door the bull will start chewing his leg.

Another idea, in case the pit bull doesn't work out, is to put Rather in chains in the control booth with Mike Wallace holding the key.

A news producer wants to let Dan sit in the umpire's chair at the tennis open and adjudicate the match on center court. Hopefully, by calling the matches, Rather will develop as much interest in tennis as he has in Afghanistan. It will also give him an opportunity to go straight from McEnroe to Judge Bork without a break.

A TV expert on black holes has come up with voice-over audiotapes that would automatically start playing if CBS screens all over America darkened. The voice would say, "Don't turn the dial. You are now watching George Bush visiting a West Virginia coal mine," or, "The blackness you now see on your screen is a picture of the U.S. Supreme Court from the neck down."

Whether CBS will resort to any of these strategies is not known at this time. Rather feels terrible about the blackout and as penance has offered to wear tennis sweaters every night on his show.

To make matters a lot worse, Nielsen took a survey and discovered that 25 percent of the viewers would want to watch women's tennis, 20 percent said they'd rather tune in to the "Evening News," and 55 percent said if they had a choice they would prefer to stare at a black screen.

Peace in Our Time

It appears we have an agreement with the Russians to remove medium-range nuclear missiles from Europe. The negotiations were tough and both sides worked hard to put a deal together.

How did it happen?

One of the Americans on the delegation, thought to be a CIA man, went to a Soviet delegate and told him, "You might as well make a deal. We know for a fact your medium-sized missiles don't work."

The Soviet delegate, certain to be a KGB man, cried, "You've been spying on us! That violates the Geneva Convention."

"Don't get so excited," the CIA man told him. "Ours don't work either."

"You're sure?"

"We couldn't even light a Christmas tree with one. For years we knew your missiles were no good—but it was only recently we found out ours are bummers."

"How can I believe you?" the KGB man wanted to know.

"Don't take my word for it. Inspect our contractors' spare parts. If that doesn't convince you the missiles won't work, nothing will."

The KGB man was suspicious. "Why are you telling me all this?"

"Because we want an arms treaty, and the only way to get one is to convince you that what we are both removing from Europe doesn't matter since they won't fly anyway," the CIA man said. "If we were to take ours out unilaterally the political fallout would be awful. If you take yours out alone you get the same flak. We have to remove them together so there will be peace in our time."

"Wait a minute," the KGB man said. "What about the Pershing missiles in West Germany? If both of us give up our missiles, and the Germans keep theirs, Bonn could become the biggest threat to Europe."

"Don't worry, comrade. The German missiles don't work either."

"How can we be certain that all your medium-sized nuclear weapons don't work?" the KGB man asked.

"As part of the treaty we will test-fire every missile as it is removed from its hole."

"At what target?"

"Iran. It's always good for a soft landing. If for some reason the missile isn't a dud, then it's 'Bye-bye Tehran.' "

"So what are you saying?"

"We sign a treaty and remove all medium-sized weapons from Europe. Then we go out and buy white tie and tails to wear when we get the Nobel Prize."

"Let's drink to glasnost and Gorbachev."

"To Beverly Hills and Ronald Reagan."

"I can see the day," the KGB man mused, "when every missile will be turned into a plowshare."

"And every plowshare will be sold to the Russians to help the farmers get on their feet."

"We must make peace by eliminating all weapons that don't work."

"Except for one," the CIA man said.

"What weapon do you refuse to give up for the cause of peace?"

"Minesweepers."

I Love Paris

PARIS, FRANCE—They are celebrating the 100th anniversary of the *International Herald Tribune* in Paris and I'm here for the party. I'm proud to say that I have been continuously associated with the Trib for thirty-eight years. Fourteen of them were spent in Paris and were the happiest years of my life, except for the first three, when I lived there as a bachelor.

I went to Paris as a student in late 1948 and lucked out by getting a job on the *Tribune* in early 1949. The position was restaurant and nightclub critic and the pay was twenty-five dollars a week. I had impeccable credentials for reviewing French restaurants. Prior to living in Paris I had dined for three years in U.S. Marine Corps mess halls. Then for three more I ate in the school cafeteria at the University of Southern California, and finally, in Paris I took my meals in Montparnasse at a Polish cooperative called the Hôtel des États-Unis.

Writing about food in Paris was no problem. But wines were a little trickier. So I did what almost every American in France was doing at the time—I faked it. I was told by friends that if the wine bottle had a neck it was a burgundy, and if it had shoulders it was a bordeaux. When distinguishing reds from whites, it was every man for himself.

To make the gourmet job less boring I took along an Irish-American lady from Warren, Pennsylvania, who offered to tell me which dishes were hot and which ones were cold.

The key to the good life in Paris was writing about restaurants. If someone wanted to eat well he had to come to me.

One time the late Aga Khan called and asked if I could recommend a good restaurant. I said I would go one better and take him there. We had a great lunch and when the check came there was no move on the Aga's part to pick it up, so I took it. When I handed in my expenses the feisty managing editor, Eric Hawkins, said, "How dare you take the Aga Khan to lunch?" "I had to," I protested. "I still have relatives in Pakistan."

The Trib didn't keep me on the food beat forever. I started covering other stories of interest, such as the wedding of Grace Kelly and Prince Rainier, the coronation of Queen Elizabeth, the feud between Aristotle Onassis and Stavros Niarchos, the state visit to Paris of Roy Cohn and David Schine, the opening of the Istanbul Hilton, the discovery of the Dead Sea Scrolls in Israel, the breaking of the "Six-Minute Louvre" record, and Elizabeth Taylor's futile attempt to walk through the Rome Olympics without getting pinched.

I also covered the International Set, which had only the most beautiful women as members. (It was French law.) Unfortunately there was this Irish-American lady from Warren, Pennsylvania, who kept following me around, so I never could sit down with them and get their real stories.

It was a time of turmoil on the continent. I almost had a duel with movie producer Walter Wanger over *Joan of Arc*. James Hagerty, Eisenhower's press secretary, took me to task for writing a spoof of his press briefings, and I got caught crashing a fancy costume party in Venice dressed as Louis XIV.

I mention these things not to brag, though anyone who has ever worked on the Paris *Herald Tribune* tends to do a lot of that sort of thing, but rather to show you why I'm so happy to be part of the 100th anniversary celebration.

You cannot return to Paris after having lived there for fourteen years without getting teary-eyed. To celebrate the anniversary of the Trib I want to go back to all the fleshpots and lowlife I knew when I was a boy columnist. The trouble is there's this Irish-American lady from Warren, Pennsylvania, who keeps insisting that since she was the only one who would eat with me in Paris thirty-eight years ago, she has a right to tag along.

One Sad Fan

I came in the house one recent Sunday and my wife whispered, "George is in the living room waiting for the football game to start."

"Didn't you tell him there is no game this week?" I asked.

"He refuses to believe me."

I walked into the room and found George sitting on the couch. He put a fistful of potato chips in his mouth and pointed at the screen. "Oouhouhouh," he mumbled.

"There is nothing wrong with the TV, George. The teams are on strike."

George looked at me as if I had lost all my marbles and grunted, "Umumumumum."

"It's nobody's fault, George. It's a question of power and who gets to keep it. Would you like to see a movie?"

George shook his head, crawled to the TV set and started feeling the glass with his hands.

"You have to believe me, George. There is nothing you can do to bring on a football game."

He rubbed his head against the screen.

"George, you're getting hair oil all over the TV set," my wife said.

I made a sign for her to hush up.

Then George began hitting the glass with his head. I pulled him away and gently put him down in his chair. My wife gave him a handful of pretzels.

"Dubidubidou," he babbled, spitting out half the pretzels.

"What does he want now?" my wife asked.

"He wants to know why there is no football."

"You told him that."

"The reality of the strike hasn't sunk in on everyone." I took a wad of dollars out of my pocket and waved it in the air. "This is why they're striking. The players want more of these and owners want to give them less. Surely you can understand that, George."

He jumped up, rushed to the screen and slammed it with his two fists.

"Don't get mad at the set," I begged. "The TV has nothing to do with the strike. You can hit it all day and you still won't see an NFL kickoff."

Apparently George didn't believe me because he started sniffing around the back of the cabinet.

My wife came over and whispered, "Get him out of here."

"It's not his fault there isn't a game. The man has never done anything on Sundays but watch football. You can't take something like that away from a person and expect him to act normal."

"Get him out of the house," my wife repeated.

I looked at George, who was examining the electrical outlet in the wall to make sure it was working.

"Why don't you take him outside and throw him a stick?" my wife suggested.

"George," I said, "you better go home. Someday the owners and players will make up their differences, and then you can come back and we'll sit and cheer for the team of our choice. We'll call you when the strike is over."

George looked hurt and shoved some popcorn in his mouth. Then he went, "Ouuurnnnournn."

"What is he muttering about now?" my wife asked.

"He says NFL football sucks."

"He said that?" she gasped.

"Yes, but that's not what is scary. He said he's speaking for millions and millions of American people."

Write On

My friend Senator Bearman decided not to run for president.

"Did it have anything to do with your submitting one of Judge Oliver Wendell Holmes' opinions to the *Reader's Digest* as your own?" I asked him.

"Holmes is dead. Do you think it matters to him who gets credit for something he wrote?"

"Right, Senator. But your opponents say you've done things like this since law school."

"I have always written my own stuff, including George Washington's farewell address, which some have called the finest speech this country has ever heard."

"You will be remembered for it."

"I have never used the words of anyone else without attribution," he maintained. "I am going out to speak to my supporters, who are devastated by this. Come with me if you want to see the real Bearman."

I followed him to his headquarters where 500 men and women waited patiently.

Bearman began, "Friends, Romans, countrymen. I come to bury Caesar, not to praise him. The evil that men do lives after them. The good is oft interred with their bones."

"That's good," I said to Bearman's campaign manager. "Did you write it?"

"No, the senator pens his own resignation speeches."

Then Bearman said, "I am not frightened of the future. The only thing we have to fear is fear itself."

I was so taken with this statement I started to write it down. The aide said, "I wouldn't do that if I were you. The senator has it copyrighted."

"But doesn't he want all his thoughts to be distributed throughout the country?"

"He doesn't care." Then, like rolling thunder I heard Bearman's voice. "I have nothing to offer but blood, sweat and tears."

"Are my ears deceiving me?"

"What can I tell you? The man is a natural communicator," his manager told me.

The senator stretched out his arms. "I must go down to the seas again, to the lonely sea and the sky. And all I ask is a tall ship and a star to steer her by."

"I never heard a politician put it that way before," I admitted.

"The senator likes to recite sea poems. It makes him feel close to the people."

"When does he get time to write all this stuff?" I asked.

"Anyone can find it if they are running for President of the United States."

"Then there is no truth to the talk about the senator plagiarizing other people's work."

"Have you heard one thing that didn't sound as if it just came fresh out of the oven?"

"Can't say that I have," I replied. "He's on a roll."

"You won't believe what is coming next," the campaign manager said.

The senator looked out at his supporters and spoke, "Oh, London is a man's town, there's power in the air; and Paris is a woman's town, with flowers in her hair. So if you can't stand the heat get out of the kitchen."

I went up to Bearman to congratulate him. "Let me guess, Senator. When talking about the heat you were quoting Harry Truman."

"You're wrong. They were my words and I scribbled them on an envelope while driving over here."

The Soft Dollar

Paris—The last time I saw Paris the tourists still controlled the main boulevards and sidewalk cafés. Americans were smiling and the French were glum. Unfortunately all this has changed. Now the French are smiling and the Americans are glum.

"What happened?" I asked the doorman at my hotel.

"Your dollar went soft and our franc went hard," he said. "Nobody pays attention to anyone who has soft currency dribbling out of his pocket."

"It's temporary," I protested. "We are working on a new chemical process to harden the dollar. Soon it will be as tough as the yen."

"If you say so. Did you want to take a bus or the metro?"

"I can afford a taxi," I said. "Americans may be poor but we're a proud people."

"Even if I found you a taxi you couldn't go anywhere."

"Why not?"

"All the traffic in Paris is standing still. Nothing is moving. You see those cars out there in the street? They have been there since last Thursday."

"What's wrong?"

"It's the hard franc. Everybody now has money to spend so all the French are trying to get to a store or a restaurant at the same time. They might be able to make it except the workers are on strike."

"Are they blocking the streets?"

"No, the police are blocking the streets to prevent the workers from jamming them."

"Why are they protesting?"

"They want more hard francs so they can be part of the traffic tieup."

I said to the doorman, "I recall the days when the dollar was strong and every store had a sign, 'English Spoken Here.' "

"I remember that also," he answered. "We even gave you discounts for your traveler's checks."

"And you sent our packages to the airplane as a courtesy."

The doorman scoffed, "You Americans thought it would last forever."

"It would have if someone hadn't stomped all over the dollar. Tell me the truth, do the French respect us anymore?"

"They don't disrespect you. They ignore you. To them you are no better or worse than a Swedish tourist. Remember, there is nothing you can do for the French. They have everything."

I finally said, "There is more to life than hard currency, good living and gridlock."

"Why didn't you tell us that when the franc was soft?"

"I need a taxi."

"Where are you going?"

95

"To a fine French restaurant."

"What are you going to use for money?"

"I have a credit card that permits me to charge up to two thousand dollars."

"That should do it if you don't order a fancy wine."

"Don't worry about me," I said. "I know how to order a French meal. When I was here the last time I had the greatest dinner in the world at a bistro called Chez Bébé for twenty-five dollars a person."

"Bébé is no longer there."

"Where is he?" I asked.

"He's out in the traffic, trying to take his mistress to Maxim's."

Forbidden Jaws

Cape Cod—How bad is the ocean pollution along the East Coast these days? I'll tell you how bad it is. The sharks no longer consider it safe to go into the water.

Perhaps that's an exaggeration. The truth is that the sharks are swimming around, but nowhere near the shore. A submarine picked up on sonar the conversation of a school of sharks about 200 miles off Cape Cod. The sonar operator identified the sharks as Jaws I, Jaws II, Jaws III and Jaws IV.

What follows is a transcript of that discussion.

Jaws I: Don't go near Long Island. All the beaches have been turned into cesspools.

Jaws II: Ditto for New Jersey. Every bit of medical garbage known to man has been dumped into the water there, including blood contaminated with AIDS.

Jaws III: How can anyone live like that? Even squid don't poison their own water.

Jaws IV: I don't mind eating garbage but I'm not going to swim through the other stuff they're pumping into the sea.

Jaws I: I hear that it is so bad off Far Rockaway that you can get violently sick just by nuzzling your head against a swimmer's leg.

Jaws II: The people are not only releasing raw sewage from the land, but they are pumping it out of their boats as well. There is no way we can go near the beach without getting herpes.

Jaws IV: Maybe we shouldn't stay here. The ocean currents could bring the stuff out to where we are now.

Jaws I: I would like to bite the arm off the person responsible for dumping all the medical swill into the sea.

Jaws II: I would too, but only if I could hear him scream a lot.

Jaws III: And thrash around in helpless agony. . . .

Jaws IV: That's all well and good, but what do we do about food? All the marine life in the area is now contaminated. Even the people on the beach are unsafe to eat.

Jaws I: That's outrageous. No one should be permitted to contaminate human beings. They're our meal ticket.

Jaws II: I can't believe that people who would dump all their waste into the sea would make sharks the heavies in the movies. For old times' sake, why don't we take one fast swim into shore and scare them to death.

Jaws III: We can't scare them if they are not allowed to go into the water.

Jaws IV: I hate to swim in red algae.

Jaws I: Just when we thought it was safe to go into the water we got sucked in by chemical waste. I guess we have to scratch Long Island as a good place for lunch.

Jaws II: It's not just Long Island. The whole ocean tastes funny. I say that all sea creatures should pronounce the entire East Coast off limits until people get their antipollution act together.

Jaws III: I hear it's not safe around Martha's Vineyard or Nantucket either.

Jaws IV: Could we be declared an endangered species?

Jaws I: But we are not an endangered species. These people are throwing all their bilge into the sea just to save money.

Jaws II: And to think people call us sharks.

New Book Rules

There is good news from the Frankfurt Book Fair in Germany. The scorekeeping for book reading has been revised. The International Book Readers Association has decided that you no longer have to read a book from beginning to end to get credit for it.

Grant Fingerlift, who heads the scoring division of the IBRA, told me that book customers can now be given credit for reading as little as half a book. He explained, "We discovered that while more books are being sold, people are reading less. The book buyers were demanding points for books they didn't finish, so we had to bow to the pressure. In the future, anyone who reads two hundred pages, fiction or nonfiction, may announce that he has read the book."

"Everyone in America stands to gain by the rule," I said.

"There are a few regulations. For example, the half book must remain at your bedside for at least a month, and a marker must be placed in it where you left off reading. You win a five-point bonus if it gathers dust."

"I have a half-read book by my bedside now called *Presumed Innocent*. Suppose at some future time I finish it. Can I receive any more points?"

"Yes, but it's rare for someone to complete a book after they have read only half of it. A novel that has been only half-read eventually takes on an odor."

"Does that present a problem for you?" I asked Fingerlift.

He said, *"Presumed Innocent* is one of the most talked-about books of recent years. People all over the country claim to have read it. But we don't know who has and who hasn't. We're beefing up our investigative staff so we can get at the truth."

"If someone can tell you the ending will you accept that as proof they have read the entire book?"

"No, because many readers are starting to read books from the back, as a way of pretending they've read the whole book. We feel this is very bad sport, and we intend to expose anyone who does it."

"Bob Woodward wrote a book about Bill Casey. I never made it to the halfway mark. Do I get a score for that?"

"We'll give you nine and a half points for reading two hundred pages, and another five points if you believe them."

"Why did the IBRA go to so much trouble to change its scoring?"

"Our only object is to encourage book buying. One of the things our research has shown us is that people hesitate buying books because they are afraid they will have to read them. Now we've ruled that just because you've purchased a book doesn't mean you have to open it. We feel this will make the book business much more appealing."

"I wish you'd had these rules when Pat Robertson's book came out. It's still sitting on my TV set and God knows when I'll get to it."

"There are some books that do better sitting on a TV set."

"One more thing," I said. "Is the scoring retroactive?"

"Not necessarily. Our new scoring system is for those who are trying to keep up with other people's reading habits and don't have time to read every book. As long as they have good faith, we'll give them any score they want."

Waltzing with Bush

Vice President George Bush has been getting a lot of publicity lately and much of it is well deserved. I saw him at the coming-out party of a cornhusker's debutante daughter in Iowa and he was telling us why the people in Iowa didn't vote for him in a straw poll.

"The farmers were all playing polo," he said. "And those who weren't playing polo were big-game hunting in Africa. Nobody stayed home to vote for me."

It sounded plausible. "Do you know the girl who is making her debut here in Iowa?"

"No," the Vice President told me, "but I met a Polish mechanic on my trip to Eastern Europe and he told me his niece was coming-out here, so naturally I said I would go. That mechanic would put any Detroit worker to shame. We ought to bring over thousands of them to get our auto industry on its feet again."

"Have you ever been to a coming-out party in Iowa, Mr. Vice President?"

"No, but I've seen a lot of them in West Virginia. A coming-out party is as American as apple pie. We probably wouldn't have white ties if it weren't for the balls. I'm curious to find out if Iowa does it the way we do back home."

102

"I heard that after the girl dances with her father she throws herself on a fiery haystack to prove she's ready to be dated."

"That's different from the way we do it," the veep said. "The girls back home don't have to do anything more than curtsy to announce they are coming-out in society. Are there any other questions?"

"Mr. Vice President, you said on the 'Larry King Show' the other night that the Cystic Fibrosis Foundation was fighting Judge Bork's nomination. Did you misspeak?"

"Yes, and when I found out I did I issued a retraction saying I was pleased to hear that the group did not oppose Judge Bork. I feel that straightened out the matter quite well."

"They thought your apology was as bad as your original statement. You made it look as if they were supporting Judge Bork."

"Are you calling me a wimp?"

"No, sir."

"Because if you are, here is my war record. I am not a wimp. If I were I wouldn't be attending a cornhusker's daughter's coming-out party when I could be fox hunting in Virginia."

"Mr. Vice President, you are not doing so well in the polls. Rumor has it you're trying to get President Reagan off your back."

"That's a damn lie. The thing I believe in the most is loyalty. President Reagan has made mistakes—we all do—but they are his mistakes and nobody else's. I would like to get the record clear right now that I was out of town when the errors were made, and by the time I got back it was too late for me to do anything about them. I'm not one of those vice presidents who says those are the President's mistakes and these are mine—because I didn't make any. But that doesn't mean I'll turn my back on the President even if he refuses to back me for the nomination after all I have done for him in the last seven years."

"Why is the Reverend Robertson doing so much better in the polls than you?"

"Because he is using prayer as a political issue."

"What are you using as a political issue?"

"Stand-tall leadership."

"That won't even get you the white-tie vote in Poland."

Give Me Some Margin

There are many young people who work in the stock market investing billions of dollars of other people's money. These young investment advisors have known only success, so Black Monday hit them very hard.

One I know personally is Baby Duckett, a blue-chip specialist who was handling the money of almost everyone in our neighborhood. On paper we were all millionaires and worshiped his investing know-how. Like most Wall Street advisors, Baby is thirteen years old.

When the "Slide for Life" happened I rushed down to Baby's house to find out what was going on. His mother was standing on the lawn with other investors.

"He won't come out. He's crying," she said. "He has never lost money in the stock market before, and he says it's unfair."

"It's *our* money he lost," I yelled. "How does he explain that?"

"He thinks that more people sold stock on Monday than bought it. When this happens the Dow Jones usually goes down."

"It could be a reasonable explanation," I agreed with Baby's mother. "Why didn't he sell with the others?"

"Baby doesn't know how to sell. He only knows how to buy. For goodness sakes you can't blame him for what the market did. He's only a child."

"Two weeks ago I was a nouveau-riche—now I'm a nouveau-pauvre. Baby has to answer for that."

The mother said, "Baby is taking this very hard. He told me he doesn't want to grow up in a world where there is a chance of losing money in the stock market."

"He can say that now, but he's the one who took us down the river with General Motors and IBM. Why did he pick those two dogs?"

"Baby never picked them," Mrs. Duckett said. "What he did was lay out the *Wall Street Journal* stock pages on the floor and let the cat walk over them."

"That's how he played the market?"

"That's how most people played it. For two years the cat couldn't do anything wrong."

"If I had known that I would have paid the cat our fee," I said. "I think Baby should come out."

She yelled up to the bedroom window, "Baby, there are some people out front who want to see you."

Baby finally came out. His eyes were red and he was sniffling.

"Tell the nice people you're sorry you lost their life savings, Baby," his mother said.

"I don't want to."

"Be a good boy. They can't do anything to you because

you're a minor, and any investment counselor under twenty-one is not responsible for losing somebody's farm."

Baby said, "I'm sorry I lost your money—but now is the time to buy because there are a lot of bargains around and this is only a correction, and Reagan is bullish and the German mark will never destroy the dollar, as long as J. P. Morgan is alive." He took a piece of chalk and started writing orders on the sidewalk.

His mother beamed, "The nice thing about investment advisors is they don't stay sad very long."

Mr. President

The President held a press conference recently. It was his first one in eight months. Now Mr. Reagan can return to his usual way of communicating with the media—yelling.

This is how the Commander in Chief deals with the fourth estate:

The President steps out of his helicopter onto the White House lawn.

A reporter, trying to shout over the din of the copter, says, "MR. PRESIDENT, ARE WE AT WAR WITH IRAN?"

The President cups his hand over his ear and shakes his head.

When the question is repeated he yells back, "NO, I'M NOT SORRY I NOMINATED JUDGE BORK."

"MR. PRESIDENT, DO YOU THINK THERE IS GOING TO BE A STOCK MARKET CRASH SIMILAR TO THAT OF 1929?"

The President furrows his forehead and then points his finger at the questioner. "IF IT WILL HELP OUR CONTRAS IN CENTRAL AMERICA THEN I SAY A CRASH PROGRAM IS SOMETHING I WOULD SUPPORT."

Now the dog is getting away from Nancy, so the President grabs the leash. It's hard to control the dog and listen to a question at the same time, but the President manages to do it.

"MR. PRESIDENT," comes a voice that can barely be heard above the sound of the copter, "WHAT ABOUT NEW TAXES?"

"WE'RE GOING TO BRING THAT UP WHEN GORBACHEV COMES TO THE UNITED STATES. IF HE WANTS A MISSILE TREATY WITH US HE BETTER STOP FIXING UP OUR MARINES WITH RUSSIAN GIRLS IN THE MOSCOW EMBASSY."

The President has made it halfway to the White House. Questions continue to be thrown at him from the press pen. He pauses to listen to one from a network correspondent.

"MR. PRESIDENT, IS CONGRESS RESPONSIBLE FOR ALL THE TROUBLE IN THE COUNTRY?"

"YES, AND TO SHOW GOOD FAITH THEY HAVE TO GET OUT OF AFGHANISTAN."

"I MEAN CONGRESS, NOT THE SOVIETS."

"I KNOW WHAT YOU MEAN. IT'S NOT MY FAULT THAT CONGRESS HAS ITS FEET IN CEMENT AND WON'T PUT UP THE MONEY FOR STAR WARS."

All the newspaper people are writing furiously because these freewheeling questions and answers could mean a new turn in White House policy.

Thanks to the dog dragging him, the President is almost to the White House door and Mr. Reagan's aides, who have been biting their nails, sigh with relief.

"MR. PRESIDENT," comes a chilling voice from the back of the press pen, "DO YOU THINK THE DOLLAR SHOULD GO UP OR DOWN?"

"I CANNOT SAY WHAT I INTEND TO DO ABOUT IT, BUT I WILL BE MEETING WITH MY SECRETARY OF DEFENSE TO MAKE SURE WE HAVE ALL THE WEAPONS THAT ARE NECESSARY."

As the dog pulls Mr. Reagan through the door, Helen Thomas yells, "THANK YOU, MR. PRESIDENT."

By this time the White House staff are congratulating the President on the press conference.

"You really socked it to them, Mr. President," his press secretary tells him.

"They haven't laid a finger on me since we put those extra propellers in," the President mutters.

"Give the dog some credit too," Nancy says.

Mr. Reagan smiles. "This job is all about communication. If I can communicate by yelling, and my voice remains strong, I will never have to worry about holding a prepared press conference again."

Give as Much as You Can

In an election year, everyone from the presidential candidate to the lowly senator is begging for dollars, and it is not fun.

I walked into Senator Moondecker's office. He was on the phone, yelling, "Look, Trilby, we sent you two envelopes and nothing came back. The next time you want me to get a bill passed for you making it possible to transfer liquid gas through kindergarten playgrounds, forget you know me."

"Some people just don't have any gratitude," I said.

"I don't know what's going on," he complained. "Last time I had eight hundred thousand dollars—this election I have three thousand dollars. All the lobbyists claim their home offices have frozen them out."

"Maybe it's the stock market," I suggested. "A lot of guys who help politicians are now in quicksand."

Moondecker replied, "They should give, especially when there is a stock market crisis, because only the Senate can get them out of their misery. What I resent is that nobody is buying tickets to my breakfast."

"How much is your breakfast?"

"Ten thousand dollars a plate, but you get hot coffee and Danish. I've only sold forty tickets."

"Maybe you ought to get Jim and Tammy Bakker as your speakers. They sell tickets better than anyone."

"Last time I made one hundred and forty thousand dollars on my bingo game. This year I can't give the cards away. You'd think people would donate to make sure their candidates get in."

"There must be a lot of voters that your computer hasn't heard from."

The phone rang and Moondecker picked it up. "Yes, I know who you are," he said. "You're Ogilvy of Beeswax Honey and you want me to introduce a bill barring all Japanese honey from the United States. How do you expect me to do this without a war chest? Do you think honey bills grow on trees? Ogilvy, how would you like to be an admiral in the S.S. *Moondecker Navy*? It will cost you twenty-five thousand dollars and you get to sit on the deck of all Senate trade meetings. Thanks, Ogilvy, your bees are safe with me."

Moondecker said, "This is not my idea of fun, but if I don't do it somebody else will and heaven knows what kind of senator he'll turn out to be. At least I can be trusted."

"Do all senators do their own fund-raising?" I asked.

"All the ones I know do. Of course those who sit on the Armed Services Committee can raise a lot more than those stuck with investigating Judge Ginsburg. Some of the big fellows even have their own PACs and they channel money to other senators—then you really owe them for being nice to you."

"It seems there are many ways of raising money in the government. What is the weirdest thing you've done?"

"I offered to confirm a guy for an ambassadorship for fifteen thousand dollars."

"That sounds dangerous," I said.

"I'll say. He turned it down."

For the Minds of Men

The nomination of Douglas Ginsburg to the Supreme Court, or "l'Affaire Ginsburg," as we call it, left deep wounds in the nation's capital. It turned liberals against conservatives and conservatives against liberals and pragmatists against true believers.

In the past the liberals had a fairly loose attitude about smoking marijuana joints, and the conservatives always linked pot-puffers with agents of the devil.

But when Judge Ginsburg revealed that he had used grass at Harvard, everyone lost his ideological compass.

I happened to be at a bipartisan party the day after Ginsburg confessed to using a foreign substance while teaching law at Harvard.

Dabney, a fighting liberal, was horrified. "I'm shocked beyond words," he said. "How could we have a Supreme Court justice who is turning on?"

Template, whom we all think of as the conservative's conservative, was defensive. "The man had a few reefers when he was a student. Surely we are a forgiving nation."

Dabney was finding it difficult to control his temper. "That's easy for you to say because conservatives have no regard for law and order. But nobody knows how a man or woman will

111

rule on the Supreme Court once he's had a taste of the weed. I could not, in good conscience, support a pothead. We liberals owe that much to Nancy Reagan."

Template threw his hands in the air. "We can't judge people by what they smoked in the sixties. Even the President says it is not Ginsburg's deed but his confession that counts. Besides, if grass wasn't good for your health, why would cows eat it?"

I intervened. "I don't understand it. The liberals are dead set against the use of marijuana and the conservatives are all for it. Is it possible this has more to do with politics than with smoking?"

Said Dabney, "Liberals are for strong law-enforcement and tough judges. We have to protect the Constitution. The eight justices on the Court have never smoked a joint in their lives. We can't afford to have a forty-one-year-old justice tempting them."

Template, the conservative, protested. "If we are going to judge people by what they inhale we are never going to get the court the President wants. Let's not forget Ginsburg said he smoked his last marijuana cigarette in 1979. Surely this country has a statute of limitations on Harvard professors who make mistakes."

I responded, "I believe you miss the point. Although Ginsburg may have quit in 1979, many Americans would look at him differently than they would the other eight justices. They'd wonder if his eyes were glazing over from the case he is hearing or from what he has hidden in his robes."

Template asserted, "It's typical of the liberals to kill a Reagan appointment because he had some Acapulco Gold in his youth. I'll tell you something. I would rather have a Supreme Court justice who relaxes in his chamber with a cigarette than one who is against prayer in the schools."

Dabney, the liberal, was not having any of it. "Marijuana

is the most serious issue to face the Supreme Court since Bork's beard. I don't care what a man thinks," he said, "it's what he puts in his mouth that counts. For all I know Ginsburg could be a great justice, but I wouldn't want to have to check out the plants in his windowboxes every time he writes an opinion."

Ain't Going to Sin No More

The climate in Washington is such that in order to be a political candidate for any office you must confess to every sin you committed in your life.

Winkel, a presidential contender, couldn't understand it. He asked his campaign manager, "Why do you want me to expose my private life to the public?"

"Because if you don't they will think you are hiding something much worse. What is wrong with going on TV and telling everyone you were a shoplifter when you couldn't afford to buy your mother a gift for Christmas?"

"I never was a shoplifter and I could always afford to buy my mother a present."

"I didn't say you couldn't, sir, but we're in a tough battle. Blaisdorf has confessed to hiding out with a college cheerleader in a motel in South Bend, Indiana. Squiggly has told the world he used the Lord's name in vain when he sailed in the America's Cup. Rocabottom has fessed up to leading a panty raid on the USC Tri Delt sorority, and Duggan has admitted to reading *Penthouse* magazine since he was nine years old. We're the only ones who are not begging for forgiveness."

"It seems to me that the country would vote for the one candidate who has nothing to hide."

"Maybe. But we would be taking too big a chance. Think back, sir. Couldn't you have committed adultery in your youth?"

"It was so long ago. Who can remember?"

"Maybe it happened in Iowa when you were too tired to think?"

"I never committed adultery. I wouldn't have been able to handle the guilt."

"Okay then, have you ever been drunk and disorderly and arrested and tossed in the can?"

"Certainly not. I don't drink."

"We have to come up with something. You never smoked pot?"

"Never, not even from a potted plant."

"Sir, have you ever flirted with a woman other than your wife?"

"Why should I do that if I intended to be President of the United States?"

"The voter is going to find you awfully dull. What about wild beach parties?"

"I went to beach parties but only in my capacity as a life-guard. This is getting ridiculous. I know of nothing I have done that the public need forgive me for."

"There has to be something we've overlooked. Have you ever gone to Bimini in a boat with a volunteer from your campaign?"

"Yes, but she slept on a minesweeper when we got there."

"That's it! You have to say that you sailed out of Miami with another woman who was a model and also happened to be a good friend, and you're not going to sin anymore."

"But I hardly knew the girl."

"By the time we're finished denying it, the whole world will love her. Then finally the public will know you as a swinging human being who made one mistake but still belongs in the White House."

"Will adultery make me human?"

"A lot more human than supporting a balanced budget."

The Minority Minority Report

I think everyone should make up his own mind about what the Iran-contra affair means without coaching from people on Capitol Hill. I must admit I was not satisfied with the majority report or the minority report issued by members of Congress, so I have written my own based on hundreds of hours of watching the hearings on television.

Testimony by people who worked in the White House confirms that the object of the exercise was to exchange missiles for goodwill. They succeeded in this because relations between Iran and the United States have never been better. It's doubtful if the two countries would be peacefully sharing the Persian Gulf if some bright person hadn't come up with the idea of financing arms for the contras.

Attorney General Ed Meese's role in Irangate was questioned by the majority report. I take exception to this. Meese's handling of the case was just right. He was neither too hard nor too soft on the suspects. One of the reasons people criticize Ed Meese is that he plays a twofold role in the administration and this gets confusing at times. I personally am perplexed because every time I see Meese enter a grand jury room I never know if he is there to testify for the government or himself.

As far as we know, no crimes were committed during Irangate—except for perjury, misuse of government funds, obstruction of justice, embezzlement, tax fraud, destruction of vital evidence and profiteering on military equipment. But since all of these crimes were done to save the Western World from going Communist, the special prosecutor should pack up and get the hell out of Washington before he hurts somebody.

President Reagan did not know anything about Irangate. This is obvious to anyone who saw him on TV during the period it was occurring. Had Mr. Reagan been involved he would have been nervous and ill-at-ease. But during the time the arms were being shipped he was relaxed and at peace with himself. Evidence at the hearings indicated the President was not only unaware that Admiral Poindexter and Colonel North were involved in a covert operation—he didn't know either man was in Washington.

Ollie North is the most interesting person in Irangate. The only connection he seems to have had with the scandal was that Fawn Hall worked for him as a secretary. Fawn Hall, one of the more mysterious figures in the affair, made North shred reams of evidence linking her with the case. She prevailed on the Marine colonel to alter documents that might indicate Miss Hall was having her government salary deposited in a Swiss bank account. Why did North cooperate? He testified, "I believed in what Fawn was doing and there was no hanky-panky involved."

In almost every instance North was just following orders and therefore he should still be treated as a hero.

The one person who didn't lie on the stand was Bill Casey, the CIA Director. Had he been alive during the hearings it might have been a different story. In his last words to Bob Woodward before passing away, Casey said, "Irangate is nothing but a third-rate burglary and therefore I am not a crook." The key to the entire mystery is somewhere in that sentence if someone could just break the code.

Admiral Poindexter's role has still not been resolved. Because he was national security advisor his office was located in the White House right next to the President. Poindexter, as NSC advisor, had only one duty and that was to keep all information about national security away from Mr. Reagan. Whenever someone tried to carry a message to the President, Poindexter would trip him and say, "The buck stops here."

Unlike the majority and minority reports, mine is written far more objectively because I'm not worried about the political ramifications. I was the one who wanted Albert Hakim appointed to the Supreme Court.

In conclusion, I recommend that the President give everyone involved a full pardon. After all, nobody saw, heard or said anything to justify their being indicted. And even if they did it's silly to make a federal case of it.

Gorbachev's Visit

The White House burned the midnight oil trying to put together an itinerary for Mikhail Gorbachev's visit to Washington.

"Scratch Gorby's address to a joint session of Congress. They won't let him speak there."

"Now they tell us. Well, we have to allow him to speak *somewhere*. What about asking him to address a day school in Fairfax, Virginia?"

"Better still, the Daughters of the American Revolution. They're always looking for an inspiring message."

"I'm not sure the DAR would give him a standing ovation. We have to arrange a forum for Gorbachev befitting his position as chief of the USSR."

"Perhaps he could address a thousand-dollar-a-plate prayer breakfast for Jerry Falwell."

"Won't it disturb Jerry to share scrambled eggs with the number one commie in the world?"

"No. Even if he isn't Christian, Gorbachev sells a lot of tables."

"Well, let's look into it. Now we promised the Kremlin that Gorby would get TV exposure. What shows do we book him on?"

"What about 'Wheel of Fortune'? It would be great for Soviet-American relations if Gorby won a jeep on the show and Vanna White gave him the keys."

"I'd rather see him on the Phil Donahue show. It's more

serious. Phil could ask what it's like to be red rather than dead."

"Why would Gorby do it?"

"He just wrote a book on glasnost and he knows Donahue has the best show to promote it."

"I prefer to put him on Johnny Carson. Johnny could do an anti-Soviet monologue and have Gorby in stitches."

"Wouldn't it be better to book him on Ted Koppel?"

"We're trying to lighten up the summit. With Koppel you don't get laughs."

"I'd rather go with Geraldo Rivera. He could open a safe underwater in the Soviet Embassy and have Gorby describe the contents."

"Okay, that takes care of TV. Now what do we do for sightseeing?"

"How about Jimmy and Tammy Bakker's Heritage USA park? Gorby would not only get a chance to go on some very scary amusement rides, but he could see how we raise money for religion in the United States."

"I'd rather send him to Disneyland."

"Khrushchev went to Disneyland. It might bring back bad memories for Gorbachev. Best he attend a pro football game and let him see our fans in action. That should scare the hell out of the USSR."

"Are we still dragging him down to Wall Street?"

"No way. All he has to do is show his face on the floor of the exchange and we'll have another Black Monday."

"There would be no harm in letting him go to Las Vegas. Everyone in Russia says Gorbachev's a crapshooter."

"Hold it. Suppose he loses and demands on-site inspection of all the roulette wheels? What then?"

"We give him a ringside table to see Frank Sinatra and have Frank ask him to stand up in the middle of the show."

"Good idea. Well, the calendar is filling up. Here is the last item. We have to find a typical American family for Gorbachev to visit. Anybody have any ideas?"

"How about Ferdinand and Imelda Marcos?"

Late Flights, Faulty Luggage

The Department of Transportation has come up with a dandy solution to the disastrous air transportation problem. Because of so many complaints from the public it has ordered the airlines to list all their flight delays and report the losses of and damage to luggage. These figures will be made available to travelers so they can decide which is the best carrier to fly.

I was about to embrace the plan when I suddenly remembered that it was the Department of Transportation who messed up the airlines in the first place.

To clarify what was going on I went over to the DOT building to get additional information on the order. I was referred to the Deputy Secretary for Mollifying Irritable Air Travelers and Their Loved Ones.

"By knowing how many planes from each airline were tardy today, is there any benefit to me?"

"If you are informed which airline has a lousy flight record you can take a different one the next time you fly out of Albany."

"What do I do if the only airline from Albany is the one with the lousy record?"

"The knowledge of a late flight schedule can help you decide when to get to the airport. For example, if the plane takes off two hours late, you can use the time to do something exciting in Albany."

"That's great thinking. It's no wonder you were the people who devised a way to bust up the air controllers' union."

"We're serious administrators," he said. "DOT is going to fine every airline company one thousand dollars for failing to report that they were late."

"That fine should break most airlines," I agreed. "Can we talk about luggage? Suppose an airline confesses it has an excellent record on flight arrivals, but a dismal one handling luggage. How do I deal with that?"

"We advise people to take the flight but leave their luggage behind. On the other hand, if the carrier has a poor flying record, but good baggage handling, we advise the passengers to send their luggage on it and board a plane which leaves at another time."

"Can you really shame an airline into flying straight by forcing it to report its faults?"

"The Department of Transportation thinks so. We're going to slap the wrist of any carrier that kicks in a person's suitcase. No aviation executive will be able to face his stockholders again and inform them that Joan Collins' luggage was lost somewhere between Paris and Anchorage. We want the airlines to be humiliated into changing their ways."

"I hope it works, because the Democrats are pretty angry now and they are threatening to take the flying of planes into their own hands," I told him.

"The Department has a contingency plan," the man said.

"What's that?"

"Put all the Democrats on standby."

The Wimp Vote

"George Bush is making a mistake," Whiner told me.

"In what way?" I asked.

"By declaring he is not a wimp he's alienating the wimp vote in the country."

"So what?"

"He needs a lot of wimps to win the election."

"I didn't know there were many," I said.

"There are a lot more of us than there are of them," Whiner answered. "And don't forget wimps vote as a bloc."

"You'd think Bush's people would have researched it."

"By denying he is a wimp, Bush is sending out a message that there is something wrong with being one. That's what the wimps are crying about. The question we would like to put to the Vice President is what's wrong with being that way if it's how you feel?"

"I guess nothing if you don't flaunt it."

"There are some of us who think Bush is a secret wimp and is afraid to come out of the closet."

"I don't believe that," I protested. "I think he honestly hates wimps—perhaps it has something to do with his having grown up in Texas."

"There are a lot of wimps in Texas. We're all over the map, and when we get upset we can be a mighty force in deciding who our next president is going to be. If Bush thinks the macho voters are going to put him over the top without wimp support he's crazy."

"What makes a person a wimp?" I inquired.

"It's definitely genetic. It's passed down through the male side of the family. You can always spot a wimp because he whines and cries a lot and continually loses at arm wrestling."

"Women don't like wimps, do they?"

"They say they don't, but most of them marry one. Shere Hite, who did a sexual survey, says ninety-three percent of all American women have slept with a wimp. Women prefer them because wimps are afraid to yell at their mates."

"So by attacking wimps Bush could lose the spouse vote as well?"

"It seems that way. No woman wants a president who doesn't remind her of her husband."

"Are you predicting the wimp factor will decide the 1988 election?"

"I believe so. The wimps are sick and tired of being denigrated by politicians and football fans, and we intend to introduce Wimp Power into the White House. By insisting he is not a wimp, Bush is endorsing the prejudice we have had to live with for years. We may be snivelers but we have rights too."

"Suppose all the candidates ignore you. What will your people do?"

"Sit the election out. Wimps don't have to vote unless they want to."

"It appears that Bush has a lot of apologizing to do before he gets your support. What can he do to make it up to you?"

"I'd like him to go on television and say he respects wimps and admires their way of life. He must come out for equal job opportunities and fair treatment for all wimps. And finally, Bush has to promise to appoint a wimp to the Supreme Court as soon as possible."

Pillow Talk

Ronald Reagan got into bed and sighed. "Mikhail is really a nice guy."

Nancy punched her pillow with her fist.

"He's feisty but he has a sense of humor," the President went on.

Nancy punched her pillow again.

"Why are you doing that?" Ronald asked.

"I can't believe it. I was publicly upstaged by a Communist," Nancy said, hitting her pillow once more.

"You're just imagining things," Ronald said. "Raisa wouldn't upstage you."

125

"Where do you get this Raisa stuff from?" Nancy demanded.

"Well, he calls me Ronnie, and I call him Mikhail, so I don't see anything wrong with calling her Raisa, and the two of them calling you Nancy. That is what summits are all about."

"I don't care what you call her, she humiliated me and she did it on purpose."

"No one could humiliate you, Nancy."

"How would you know? You were locked up in meetings all day and you had no idea about what was going on outside."

"What did she do?"

"For one thing she wouldn't let me know if she was coming to tea or not. I had egg on my face when I couldn't tell the press what time she was arriving."

"You know how Russians are about their tea."

"That's the point. When she came she didn't want tea, she wanted coffee. I had to go out in the kitchen and make a fresh pot."

"It doesn't matter. We signed an intermediate-range-missile treaty. I never thought the Russians would do it."

Nancy sniffed. "I knew you'd take her side instead of mine."

"You're overreacting, Nancy."

"You don't know about the tour of the White House I gave her with the TV cameras covering us."

"How could Raisa upstage you in your own house?"

"She kept straightening my paintings," Nancy cried. "And every time I told her a historical fact about the White House she topped me with two I didn't know. I'm sure the KGB briefed her on every piece of furniture on the ground floor."

Ronnie acted shocked. "I didn't know this or I would have demanded a fifty-percent reduction in Soviet conventional forces."

"You're just saying that because you want to go to sleep," Nancy said, pounding her pillow again.

126

"Look, when we go to Moscow you can get back at her. You can be late for tea and we'll get the CIA to help you bone up on the Kremlin so you know more than Raisa does."

"Suppose she doesn't invite me to visit the Kremlin? Are you still going to sign a long-range-missile treaty?"

"Probably not," Ronald said.

"You just want me to shut up."

"You're taking this too hard, Nancy. Men understand peace, but it's more difficult for women to realize what is at stake. If you and Raisa don't hit it off, it isn't the end of the world. But if Mikhail and I don't—it is."

"Every time Raisa Gorbachev saw reporters she broke away from me and talked to them. She never stopped pushing me aside to look into the TV cameras. I don't call that glasnost."

"So what do you want me to do?"

"You're the President of the United States. My question to you is, are you going to let the Russians pull the wool over your eyes?"

Ronald replied, "Of course not, my little babushka."

Hart and the Press

I hope he doesn't mind my saying so, but I think Gary Hart is campaigning the wrong way. By insisting on discussing the issues and not his private life, he is losing votes and alienating the majority of the country.

If he is serious about coming back, this is what he should be saying when he holds an impromptu press conference on a cold and windy street corner in New Hampshire.

"Senator Hart, can you give us some idea about how you would solve the problem of the worst budget deficit in history?"

"I will not discuss such issues publicly. The country's deficit happens to be a private matter between myself and my wife. Why don't you ask me serious questions about Donna Rice?"

"Gary, don't you think it's your duty as a candidate to reveal what you intend to do about the Star Wars program which will cost the nation billions of dollars?"

"It's nobody's business what I plan do about SDI. I will answer your questions about Bimini and Miami, but don't try to get me to tell you about my defense strategies. It has nothing to do with why I am in New Hampshire."

"Mr. Hart, don't you believe the public has a right to know where you stand on Social Security?"

"No. I am prepared to answer any questions you have on my philandering, but my thoughts as to how I feel about Social Security will remain in my bedroom."

"Senator Hart, since you got back in the race everyone has

128

been talking about your position vis-à-vis farm subsidies. Are we to assume that you will back farm subsidies if you become president?"

"I never said I would back farm subsidies. This is something the media made up. My family is furious with the innuendos you people have printed that I favor more acreage for soybeans than I do for alfalfa. Everyone makes mistakes and I have admitted mine. Now I'll be happy to take questions concerning where Donna Rice slept when she came to Washington."

"Senator, I think you're trying to change the subject. We, as responsible newspaper people, want to know if you will ask for a new tariff on pig iron and steel to stop the flooding of foreign metal to these shores."

"I do not have to answer that question. Why don't you ask if there were any other women in my life besides you-know-who?"

"With all due respect, Senator, that is not news. It's our job to inquire about your attitude toward improving relations between the United States and Norway."

"There you go again. How would you like it if someone asked you if you had had relations with Norway? I've got to get my campaign on the track again, and you people refuse to let me do it. If you really want to be fair, why don't you print pictures of me on the *Monkey Business?* I'll tell you why— because it would ruin the one story you all have on your minds, which is politics."

"How can we find out where you stand on the issues if you insist they are private matters?"

"Follow me around. If anybody wants to put a tail on me go ahead, but they will be very bored."

"Does that include day-care centers, Mr. Hart?"

"I don't have to answer that question. But I will respond to anything you want to know about my trip to Las Vegas."

"Could we talk about where you see America going?"

"When you ask me that I only become angry and defiant. Why are you all so obsessed with political trivia? The only thing the voters are interested in is what a man does in his personal life."

If you follow this script, Gary, they can't lay a finger on you.

Swords and Plowshares

Ronald the Lionhearted and Mikhail the Magnificent met on the top of the mountain in a heavily guarded white tent.

"I am here," said Mikhail, "to turn my medium-sized swords into medium-sized plowshares."

Ronald the Lionhearted said, "We are willing to turn our medium-sized swords into plowshares also. But how do we know you won't cheat?"

"Cheating is foreign to us," Mikhail assured Ronald.

"I cannot take your word for it, because every time we agree to turn our swords into plowshares you turn your plowshares into long-range offensive weapons."

Mikhail the Magnificent retorted, "And what about your multiheaded spears that can be hurled over the walls of our forts?"

"The spears are defensive weapons and once we perfect them we will share them with you," Ronald replied.

"I am not a fool," Mikhail declared. "You can have peace or spears, but you can't have both."

Ronald said, "Which brings me to another subject. If we turn our medium swords into plowshares we insist that you reduce your conventional cavalry by half."

Mikhail responded, "Everything can be put on the table, but we will not give up the cavalry until we are certain your plowshares are not aimed at us."

Ronald the Lionhearted gritted his teeth. "I will open my plowshare sites to verification only if you do the same."

Mikhail the Magnificent was skeptical. "How can we be assured you don't want to sneak in on a Trojan horse?"

Ronald laughed. "We have no intention of attacking you, Mikhail. Our only desire is to force you to stop stockpiling swords."

"What do you have to fear? We both have enough long-range swords to cut up every man, woman and child in the countryside," reminded Mikhail. "The only reason we have swords is to deter aggression."

Ronald the Lionhearted then spoke. "I would like to discuss what we could do with all the plowshares that are going to be made from the swords we destroy."

"Can't we sell them to the client states we support?" Mikhail suggested.

"No, because if we sell plowshares to them they will only be turned back into swords," Ronald said.

"You could take all the plowshares and dump them into the sea."

Ronald agreed. "We will only do this if your soldiers get out of Macedonia."

Mikhail said angrily, "We will never withdraw from Macedonia until your fighters leave the desert of Zin."

Ronald countered, "If we turn our swords into plowshares will you free the captured slaves you are holding in your dungeons back home?"

Mikhail replied, "They're my captured slaves and I can do anything I want with them. What right do you have to tell me who I can chain up in my stockades? If you must know, the only people I have enslaved are those with the skills to make swords into plowshares."

Ronald lowered his voice. "Don't get mad, I'm just making suggestions. Let's get back to disarmament. If you agree to eliminate your medium-sized swords, sign this paper."

Mikhail said suspiciously, "Why are you so anxious to conclude a treaty?"

Ronald replied, "I knew Errol Flynn and I know what medium-sized swords can do to human beings."

Thanks for What?

The worst thing about sending a Christmas gift is not knowing if the person received it.

This scene is being repeated in homes all over America.

"It's funny," said Ethel Americus, "the Blauvelts never thanked us for the ant farm we sent them."

"Maybe they didn't like it," Tom Americus suggested.

"Even if they didn't they should at least have had the manners to acknowledge it. Ant farms are not easy to find," Ethel sniffed.

"Perhaps they never received it," Tom suggested. "Mail service is lousy, particularly around Christmastime."

"Then we better put a tracer on it, and find out if it was delivered."

"That's a good idea. But what if the postal inspector interviews the Blauvelts? They'll suspect we were checking up on them," Tom said.

"We *are* checking up on them," Ethel declared. "If they got the package and didn't acknowledge it they deserve to be embarrassed. We went to a lot of trouble to get them a gift. Expecting a little thank-you from them is not out of line."

"They have no right to ruin our Christmas," Tom said.

"I could call Loretta's sister and ask her if she knows whether they received it or not," Ethel mused.

"Ah, the heck with it. If they're going to behave like ingrates I say we write off the ant farm as a bad investment," Tom told her.

133

"I still think they didn't get it. Loretta would be the first to sit down and send a thank-you note," Ethel said.

"Then how come we never heard from her when we gave the daughter a shower curtain for her wedding?" Tom asked.

"We never heard from Loretta's daughter. The bride is supposed to thank us for the gift, not the bride's mother."

"Everything is 'gimme' with the Blauvelts. The rotten thing is he makes more money than I do."

"I have an idea," Ethel declared. "Why don't we drop in on them and while you keep them occupied I'll scout around and see if the ant farm is anywhere? Then at least we'll know if they got it or not."

"I wouldn't do that. The fact the farm isn't there doesn't mean the Blauvelts didn't get it. They could have given it to their daughter."

Ethel asked, "Should I call her up and ask her point-blank if she got the ant farm?"

"That's a good idea. When it comes to gift giving at Christmas I always believe in confrontation."

Ethel dialed the phone. "Loretta, is that you? . . . Did you have a divine holiday? . . . Wonderful, so did we. What did you get? . . . Uh, huh, a new rug, a fur coat, a TV, and a bottle of Opium perfume. Did you receive anything from your friends? . . . An umbrella stand, ashtrays and door chimes that play 'Old Macdonald Had a Farm.' Anything else? . . . You haven't opened up all your gifts yet. . . . Well, if you're not going to open the others, at least find the one with the wrapping that has reindeers jumping over Santa Claus on it. . . . I'll wait. . . . You mean it's from us? As I live and breathe, I had forgotten we sent you anything. . . . You don't have to say you like it if you don't. It's a silly little present but I thought you would be amused every time you saw the ants digging out of the sand. . . . You don't have to gush. Tom and I never expect anyone to acknowledge our Christmas presents. We give for joy, not for thanks."

Flynt vs. Falwell

Our eight Supreme Court justices have been hard at work boning up on one of the most complicated First Amendment cases in history.

The issue concerns Larry Flynt of *Hustler* magazine (boooo) who lost a lower-court decision to Jerry Falwell (yaayyyy) for causing the good reverend emotional distress by parodying him in a fake advertisement.

A lower court ruled that the ad, which said Falwell had sexual relations with his mother in an outhouse, did not libel him, but hurt Mr. Falwell's feelings to the tune of $200,000.

Let the Supreme Court record show I am not a reader of *Hustler* magazine, nor do I stand at the magazine racks sneaking looks at it when no one is around. The only thing I have in common with the publication is we're both protected by the First Amendment.

As Justice Oliver Wendell Holmes wrote in one of his famous opinions many years ago, "I never saw a purple cow, I never hope to see one. But I can tell you anyhow, I'd rather see than be one."

It has to be granted that ludicrous exaggeration is a tricky business and if done properly can inflict great pain and suffering on the intended victim.

That is why Supreme Court Justice Brandeis once said in a footnote, "Parody can sometimes be truer than truth and righter than rain."

If Falwell gets his $200,000, how many others will file suit claiming they have been made sick to the stomach by some creator of burlesque?

It isn't the money we worry about (most cartoonists and funnymen make between eight and nine hundred thousand dollars a year) but the chilling effect that a decision in Falwell's favor will produce amongst publishers and editors, who have never been too sure whether they wanted satire in their papers in the first place.

Without a Doonesbury, our publications would take on the ugly gray dull look of a *Pravda*. John Marshall, our fourth Supreme Court Chief Justice, had this in mind when he told the graduating class of the Harvard Law School, "The Founding Fathers warned us that if you can't make fun of Jerry Falwell, then how can anyone send up Tammy Bakker?"

What do I want the present Supreme Court to do? I want them to compromise.

There are solutions that would satisfy everyone. It means fooling around with the Constitution a little bit, but no court ever minded that. I suggest the following:

The Supreme Court should order people dealing in parody, satire and humor to be licensed by the federal government and placed under court supervision.

Let us say Ed Meese objects to a Herblock cartoon because Herb has made Ed look like a barnyard animal. Meese, if he gets emotionally sick, can demand the immediate withdrawal of Herb's license for a period of ten days, or the rest of his term as attorney general—whichever comes first.

Under these conditions Block would think twice about putting jowls on Ed Meese's cheeks.

It isn't easy being on the same side of an issue as Larry Flynt. But a lot is at stake here. As Justice Hugo Black tried to tell the Court years ago, "You have to defend cheap, sleazy magazines to protect the constitutional rights of the expensive sleazy ones."

I believe it is the role of the parodist to make fun of every well-known figure in this country, regardless of position, sex, pay scale or standing in the community—with one exception. They would have to first beat me with a rubber hose before I made light of the eight freedom-loving justices who smile down on all of us from the highest court in this land.

Buy-Out

Scrooge & Marley, the Wall Street investment bankers, have just announced that they plan to make a serious attempt to take over the Christmas Holiday for 100 billion dollars.

"This could be the largest, unfriendly buy-out in history," Scrooge cackled at a press conference. "We are offering ten dollars a share to every man, woman and child who has an interest in Christmas, provided they sell by December twenty-fifth. Since we have almost total control of the stock right now, it makes no sense for anyone to hold out and refuse our offer."

Scrooge said that he had been secretly buying up Christmas stock for over a year because he felt it was grossly undervalued.

"Its parts are worth far more than the whole. What we intend to do is spin off the unprofitable enterprises such as the eggnog division and the reindeer transportation company, and hold on to the big money-makers, which are Christmas cards and fake snowflakes."

"How about Christmas mail-order catalogues?"

"We're going to keep them, but we may dump the Christmas tree business because it has such a low profit potential. If we make this deal, we're going to be up to our ears in debt, so every dollar counts."

"But without trees you won't have a market for Christmas decorations," a reporter pointed out.

"That's probably true, but we were planning to get rid of the decoration business anyway because we need the cash to buy Del Monte Catsup from Nabisco."

"Where are you going to get the money to pay for Christmas?" someone else asked.

"Bob Cratchit, my accountant, has advised me to issue junk bonds. We'll offer the bonds to the public at twenty percent interest, which is junkier than Drexel Burnham. If we can't dispose of enough of those we will sell off the world rights to Santa Claus."

"Santa Claus is sacred. You can't unload the rights to him and still call yourself a Christmas company."

Scrooge said, "Bah, people can do anything they want in an unfriendly takeover. Cratchit has discovered that the old Christmas management tolerated unbelievable waste in their operations. They even gave free shopping mall space to high school choirs who wanted to sing 'Jingle Bells.' Believe me, if Scrooge and Marley succeed in this buy-out, we're going to run a lean and tough holiday ship."

"But," said a reporter, "Christmas excess is essential to a happy holiday season."

"If it's so essential, then we ought to make people pay for it. Spreading Christmas cheer doesn't come cheap."

"Sir, why did you decide on an unfriendly takeover rather than a friendly one?"

"Because the Scrooge and Marley company never gets involved in friendly bids. When we made noises about our plans, the present Christmas board of directors told us to butt out. So we decided to go for it on our own. At the beginning we never thought Christmas was much of an investment. But then we realized that everyone on Wall Street would treat us with new respect when they saw how much debt we were in."

"Do you believe the present Christmas stockholders will go for your bid?"

"Of course. Christmas has been a losing proposition for most people, and Scrooge and Marley are offering them a way to bail out."

"Suppose present management says that Christmas is not for sale."

"My answer to them is, 'Humbug.' Somebody is going to acquire the holiday sooner or later, and better Scrooge and Marley than the people who bombed Pearl Harbor."

Pray for Money

Things are really bad in the TV fundamentalist business. I didn't know how bad until the Reverend Juniper Tube, the "King of Video Prayers," knocked at my front door and asked for a donation.

"Reverend, I didn't expect to see you working door-to-door for contributions."

"I'm in Chapter Eleven and I need four million dollars by Friday or they are going to take my chapel with the Rolls-Royce on top away from me. If you donate fifty dollars a month for life I'll give you this picture postcard of the Holy Mercy Mud Baths in Palm Springs."

"I don't believe I want a postcard of a golf course. Why are you in such dire financial straits?"

"It all started when the Reverend Jimmy Bakker committed adultery and got kicked out of his PTL empire. Jerry Falwell took charge from Jimmy and Tammy to prevent Jimmy Swaggart from making a hostile takeover. Then everyone without sin started throwing stones and all our donations dried up."

"But Reverend, you did nothing to have your viewers turn against you."

"It doesn't matter. One fundamentalist preacher looks like another on TV. We got tarred with the same expense account. In the old days all I had to do was promise parishioners that if they sent in ten dollars I would wipe out the killer bees in their gardens and the checks rolled in. I once offered a keychain of our dog Babel riding the merry-go-round in the Noah's Ark amusement park and I raised five million dollars in an hour. But you don't see money like that anymore. I would love to get Tammy and Jimmy by their throats and smite them with a sword."

"That's no way for a TV man of the cloth to talk," I said. "Remember, when television donations fall off, a man of God must turn the other cheek."

"Where did you hear that?"

"It was either on channel four, five, seven, nine or Johnny Carson. I remember it because I was so impressed I sent in one hundred dollars.'"

"How about giving *me* a hundred dollars?" the Reverend said.

"I can't believe you have stooped to asking for a paltry hundred dollars when you are known as the Good Shepherd of VISA cards."

"Tammy didn't do me any good either," the Reverend Juniper moaned. "Once they showed the price of her clothes and the size of her closets, people started calling her a greedy Imelda Marcos. I'm desperate. If you don't give me a large contribution right now God is going to call me home."

"That's an old Oral Roberts trick," I told him. "If you want to play with the big boys in the evangelical game you have to come up with something more original."

"What if I said I need cash so I can run for President of the United States?"

"Pat Robertson beat you to that one. He's got the hell and damnation electorate all tied up."

"Suppose I told you I need the money because Jimmy Swaggart is putting out stories about my one-night-stand in Patachello?"

"You didn't have a one-night-stand in Patachello, did you?"

"Of course I didn't. But after all the stuff that's been in the papers people believe every TV minister had a one-night-stand in Patachello."

"Good point," I said. "Well, I guess there is nothing wrong with giving you a few bucks since you can't get it from TV. What do you intend to do with it?"

"I'm going to give it to God as hush money."

No Man Is an Island

This is what hurts: when you discover a summer haven you really love, and someone else finds it after you.

Irving's Falls is my resort. I believed it was all mine, and I reveled in the fact that I was the first human being ever to walk along its shores, if you didn't count the Big Brothers Camp down the road, the Club Med at the South End and the Holiday Inn and marina on the North Shore.

Then Stern showed up one day and destroyed it all for me.

"What are you doing here?" I asked him.

"Who says I'm not supposed to be here?" he wanted to know.

"I discovered this place," I protested.

"Good for you. Now I discovered it. And *Town and Country* discovered it before we did, and the English in the 1600s discovered it before *Town and Country.*"

"That's not the point. By coming here, you have ruined my summer. How can I enjoy myself knowing that you have found Irving's Falls," I cried. "Just the thought that you, a Washington resident, are enjoying the island, makes it a real downer for me. I have a good mind to leave and go to Martha's Vineyard, which nobody knows about yet."

Stern said, "Pretend I never arrived. I'll try and stay out of your sight."

"It doesn't help. The place can't take any more summer people. We don't have enough septic tanks for new immigrants."

"That's baloney. Every resort has one more septic tank for those of us who come after the last guy."

"You're a vacation spoiler. You just found out that I was here and you landed because you don't have an original idea of your own. How dare you want to bathe on a beach with those of us who have been doing it for twenty years."

"Has it ever occurred to you that every resort needs fresh blood? Don't you remember when you came here and you were the new boy on the tennis courts? Well, that's the way I feel now. Maybe later on I'll resent those who follow me, but at the moment I just want to get a foothold on some property before the real estate values go any higher."

"There are no houses for sale," I told him.

"There are if you have a million dollars, which doesn't include beach privileges. If I become a homeowner, will you still object to me being here?"

"Of course I'll object. Folks like you are responsible for residents like me having one less parking spot in town. When I first came to Irving's Falls, it was possible to park in front of the A and P all day long. Now you get ten minutes to buy your groceries and after that they tow away your car."

144

"What do you want from me? I deserve a vacation as much as you do," Stern whined.

"I'd like you to go somewhere else and leave us alone. Let us make scrimshaw for the day tourists, and not have to keep an eye on the freeway exit to see who is coming next."

Stern pleaded, "Give me a break. Let me be the last one in. I won't tell anyone. It will be just you, me and Walter Cronkite. Irving's Falls will be our dirty little secret, if you don't count *Women's Wear Daily.*"

Gorbachev's Mail

Mikhail Gorbachev said during his interview with Tom Brokaw that he received 80,000 letters from Americans in one year. Here are a few his staff would not let him read.

Dear Mr. Gorbachev,

When Mr. Yeltsin, the former Secretary of Moscow's Communist Party, is tried for adventurism, will you pardon him if President Reagan promises to pardon Colonel North?

Joan Bialek

Dear Comrade,

I am a Wall Street broker and I am happy to inform you that this could not be a better time to invest in the stock market. A few years down the road when glasnost has been revealed as an anti-Soviet CIA capitalist plot, and you have been given the boot by the Politburo, you will be grateful that you put your hard-earned savings into safe, reliable American securities.

Just think, Comrade, you can spend your September years on a golf course on the Black Sea while all your friends are huddled around a fire on Gorky Street trying to keep their fingers from falling off in the cold.

As soon as you reach Washington, visit one of our convenient downtown offices and let us show you how you can own a piece of America.

Sincerely,
Andy Krulwich

Dear Mikhail,

I heard what you said to Brokaw about human rights and I agree with your hardline policy. I want you to do something about my cousin Duba. I'm requesting this for your benefit, not his. Duba can be one swift pain in the neck to anyone who is trying to preserve the Soviet way of life. He's always yelling at KGB people in the streets and meeting with newspapermen in his one-room apartment and printing underground poems criticizing your wife's clothes. You would be doing yourself a great favor if you put him and his entire family on the next plane to the United States, so Duba would become Reagan's problem and not yours.

You don't owe me anything for this suggestion. I figure Duba has made your people suffer enough.

Lenny Domyan

Dear Mr. Gorbachev,

I understand the treaty you wrote with Ronald Reagan requires both countries to destroy all intermediate nuclear missiles. I have a question to ask. Where are you going to bury the warheads? If you haven't decided yet may I put in a good word for Cleveland?

Ziggy from the Carryout

Dear Mr. Gorbachev,

You said in your interview that you tell your wife everything. Does she tell you everything in return? For example, has she ever said, "Mikhail Sergeyevich, although you are the leader of the nonfree world I am one of the few people who knows you never throw your socks into the laundry hamper."

Peter the Great, Jr.

Dear Mr. General Secretary,

I wish to inform you that I was very hurt that you would talk to Tom Brokaw before you talked to me. After all, I'm the one you have to sign the treaty with. Mr. Brokaw may be the chief anchorman of NBC, but I would like to remind you that I am not a potted plant.

Sincerely,
Ron Reagan

Home Sweet Home

If this were an unusual situation I wouldn't write about it, but it's happening more and more in this great land.

Mrs. McDougal whispered to Mr. McDougal in their bedroom, "Is he still here?"

Mr. McDougal replied, "Seems to be. I saw him eating breakfast this morning and reading my paper. Tell me again exactly what the conversation was two weeks ago."

"He said he wanted to come home for Christmas, and I told him, 'Son, that's wonderful. Your old room is waiting for you.' "

"Did he say anything about coming back for good?" McDougal asked.

"Not that I recall. He told me he just wanted to be part of the family for the holiday season."

"Then why the hell is he still here?" McDougal demanded.

"Perhaps he doesn't know the holidays are over. He was always weak on keeping time."

McDougal said, "I believe we should confront him and ask him what his plans are for the year."

"I did that already," Mrs. McDougal explained. "He claims he has no idea, but he'll do something. He's waiting to hear about a roofing job from a guy in Minnesota."

"That's not good enough. This is my house and I want to know how long he's going to be staying here!" McDougal yelled.

148

"Hush, he'll hear you."

"Tough. He's thirty-one years old. He should be able to figure out when Christmas is over."

"Well, I have no intention of telling him to get out. You should see the fear on his face when I ask him to go down to the store and buy milk and bread. He looks like a drowning puppy."

"He has to go out and do something," Mr. McDougal said. "He's been in safe harbors too long."

"But he is so happy. I never saw anyone eat so much and sleep so late and watch TV so religiously. He told me the only thing that would make him happier is if he had his dog with him. It's the only thing he really loves," said Mrs. McDougal. "You can't separate a child from his dog."

"He's not a child and if he misses the dog that much let him go back to it."

"Maybe we should both talk to him. We could tell him Christmas is over and we are looking forward to having him come back for Easter or the Fourth of July, whichever comes first."

McDougal agreed. "That makes sense. We'll promise to forward any messages to him from the guy in Minnesota. He's got to understand that we're kicking him out for his own good."

Mrs. McDougal said, "He'll never believe that. He'll think we don't want him because he's one more mouth to feed."

"If he believes that, it's a better reason than I can come up with for booting him out in the cold," McDougal grumbled.

"Why don't we wait one more day, just in case he decides to leave on his own?"

"No way. He doesn't have a job and the chances of his friend calling him are no better than a thousand to one. We better pray the guy in Minnesota doesn't move in with him."

"It's funny," Mrs. McDougal reflected. "I thought of all our children he would leave the nest first and never want to come back."

"You don't know until they reach thirty-one how becoming a grown-up is going to hit them. Let's go downstairs and have it out."

"What are you going to say?"

McDougal replied, "How about, 'Por favor, hijo, but our casa is *not* your casa.' "

Snow Job

Every time it snows in Washington there is a dilemma: Who is important enough to report to work and who is unimportant enough to stay home? This year, during our big storm, the U.S. government announced that only "essential" employees need come in for work.

"That's me," said John Medlin, starting to put on his galoshes.

His wife Bobbie asked, "Where are you going? You're not essential."

"How do you know I'm not essential?"

"Because if you were essential they would have told you so in advance of the storm."

"Izzat so," John huffed. "Well, the last time they asked only essential people to show up I went in and not one person questioned my essentiality. Everyone was very, very glad to see me."

Bobbie retorted, "They're not going to throw you out when you show up in a snowstorm. Maybe they thought you were one of the homeless."

John was perspiring. "If I believe I'm essential to running the government—you, as my wife, should think so too."

Bobbie was not moved. "If you were essential it would show up in your paycheck. I don't see anything in your grade level to indicate you are needed when it snows in Washington."

"How do you know the work I do does not become secret

during a weather crisis? The last time it snowed like this everybody in the office piled restricted papers on my desk. They wouldn't do that if I wasn't necessary to the operation."

"Why wouldn't they dump papers on your desk? You were probably the only nonessential person who reported for work that day."

John snapped at Bobbie, "This is a ridiculous argument. How can you debate the issue when there are only a handful of top management people who know whether I am essential or not?"

Bobbie replied, "That's just great. But you have to be careful when it snows in Washington. Suppose you show up today with all the really essential people and they see you at your desk. They may think you're after their jobs and they could make your life miserable for you."

"Essential people aren't like that. I've shoveled snow with them and not one has a mean bone in his body. Your problem is you feel that since I'm not essential to you, there is no way I can be essential to Uncle Sam. I'm ready to go to work right now if it means being pulled on a dogsled. We must never let this country go down because of a minus-five wind-chill factor."

"You're really sticking to your story that the government can't run without you?"

"I have a good reason. All our neighbors heard the same news bulletins we did. They know I work for the government. How does it look to them if I am not considered essential at this grave dip in Washington's weather map?"

"Why don't you take your briefcase and ride around on the bus for a few hours?" Bobbie suggested.

"Enough already. I'm off to the department and I'm working today whether they pay me or not."

"If you don't take any pay that will definitely make you nonessential."

"I'm going in for one reason. I want to see who the higher-ups think are essential in the office. I'll bet there isn't one of them who didn't get there without apple-polishing the department manager's head."

"Stay home. Why aggravate yourself?" Bobbie said.

"Who is aggravated? If I go in and no one else does they will have to promote me to the head of Policy, Plans and Printouts."

"Is that good?"

"Good? I'd be in charge when an earthquake hits six on the Richter scale."

Hail to Somebody

The thing that disturbed me the most about the Republican race for president was how hostile the candidates were toward each other.

In order to convince voters that they were worthy of occupying the White House the candidates tried to distance themselves from Ronald Reagan and use his mistakes to show why new blood is needed in Washington.

This is the way it seemed to go every time I saw the six GOP contenders on television.

"What do you think of the deficit, and if you became president what would you do about it?"

"I'm appalled by the waste and pork and cannot understand how anyone in his right mind could get us into such a mess."

"Do you blame Ronald Reagan for the huge debt?"

"No, I don't. But I do blame the people around him who never told him anything about it. That's why I want to be elected—so no one will pull the wool over a mediocre president's eyes again."

"Do you believe a vice president should warn his president when the chief is practicing voodoo economics?"

"No, because there is nothing wrong with voodoo economics if done in moderation."

"I think the Vice President should come clean with what he advised the President to do on the deficit and when he advised him to do it."

"All I can say is I gave the President the best advice he ever had, but I would never tell the public what it was."

"Did you tell the President to exchange the Stealth bomber and one hundred MX missiles for hostages in Iran?"

"As vice president I have no intention of revealing what I said to the President. Sure, he's made a lot of mistakes—but who hasn't? I'm not going to criticize him just because he is a lame duck. And while I'm on the subject I would like to see the senator's tax returns for the last ten years so we know what kind of blind trust his wife has been in."

"I'm not releasing my tax returns until you release your notes on what you and the President said to Lyn Nofziger."

"Gentlemen, may I just say something? While you are arguing about Iran and blind trusts the dollar is falling. I know who is responsible for the fall. His initials are R.R."

"Let's get on to the INF treaty with the Soviets. It's a bad treaty, and speaking as a Republican and a friend who has always admired the President, I say Ronald Reagan should be impeached for signing it."

"As vice president I say there is nothing wrong with the treaty. Sure, it's flawed but so is Senator Dole's thinking on soybean reform. I've asked the senator to produce his financial records and all he can think of doing is impeaching the President."

"Spoken like a true wimp. You wouldn't know a good INF treaty if you saw one. That's the trouble with being vice president. You have had no experience on how to run a government."

"Get off my back, because I'm liable to shoot a silkworm missile over your bow."

"Why did you say that?"

"I always get applause when I use it in my speeches. I think we should talk about schools."

"I'm for good schools."

"So am I."

"I think when kids go to good schools they learn to read and write."

"The Republican Party must start anew. Do we want the old tired ways of Bush and Reagan? The answer is no. We must reach out to the grass roots and have them tell our leaders 'Washington does not understand America.' We have to get rid of those who work inside the Beltway and replace them with those of us who live at Trump Towers in Council Bluffs, Iowa."

Super Bowl Talk

Now that the Super Bowl is history I would like to have the last word on what it all means. Although some people (with inferior teams) have mixed feelings about the game, it does serve a purpose. It allows those who would otherwise be normal American men and women an opportunity to let off just enough steam so they won't kill each other. Football is the great leveler in all our lives—possibly the only thing that separates us from four-legged animals.

Let me give you an example of why I believe pro football, with all its faults, should not be abolished.

On the Monday after the game I arrived at National Airport and was placed by a dispatcher in a beat-up taxicab, driven by a giant of a man with deep black eyes, a beard and two gold front teeth. For those who haven't had the chance to take our taxis at National Airport, the majority of drivers are shipped to Washington by camel dealers from the Third World. The cabbies are not only unable to find an address in Washington, they can't find one in the Third World. Because they don't know where they're going, they turn around and stare at you while they drive at high speeds.

When I gave Attila my address he spat out the window, cursed in what I thought was a Khomeini accent, and headed into the highway traffic at seventy miles an hour.

I knew to save my life I had to do something fast. "How did you like Doug Williams' passing at the Super Bowl?" I asked him.

156

He spat out the window again. "We killed them. The Denver defense couldn't cover Sanders and Clark at the same time."

"You can say that again," I said, noticing him thaw in front of my eyes. He had even slowed down to sixty. "Dexter Manley earned his keep."

"You can say that again," the driver said. "But the real credit has to go to Joe Gibbs."

By the time we got to the special teams you would have thought we had shared the same locker at Forest Hills High School. My driver turned into a teddy bear and even stopped for a red light. Here we were, two strangers from different cultures, one from the first world and the other from the Third World, and the only thing that could have brought us together was the Super Bowl. It was a miracle.

Football not only brings taxi drivers and their fares together. It also stops strife in the family. There is a male cousin in our family with whom I find it hard to spend more than ten minutes. If it weren't for football I'm not sure what would happen at family gatherings.

"They stopped Elway!" Tyrone shouted at me before I got my coat off.

"They also stopped the Three Amigos," I told him.

"Darryl Green stopped the Amigos," he said. Tyrone was exaggerating his knowledge of the game, but when football is the subject, a man is entitled to his opinion, particularly if he's a blood relative.

"You're probably right," I agreed. From then on I lost my urge to kick him in the stomach.

Family, friends, cops—there isn't anyone who can't be tamed by asking his opinion of the NFL and the Super Bowl. Everyone is an expert at football and willing to prove it to you, and you don't have to be Jimmy the Greek to say how the players are bred.

If anyone has doubts that football is a civilizing influence on the American people, all he or she has to do is watch the fans in the stadium on television. When you see how they claw the camera you have to conclude that these people are dangerous, and should not be trusted with a nuclear bomb. But as long as you give them Super Bowls the chances of them committing homicide are no more than three to two.

The downside is, now that the football season is over there is nothing to talk about. That's why I have a deathly fear that Attila will kill me next time he takes me home from National Airport.

A Case of A-Meesia

The Centers for Disease Control just announced a new health hazard. It is called "A-Meesia," known in medical circles as "Attorney General's Disease."

Dr. Covey Extra, who discovered it, said A-Meesia has reached epidemic proportions in the Justice Department, and has even infiltrated the Cabinet in the White House.

"What are the symptoms?" I asked Dr. Extra.

"Loss of mind is the main one. The person is unable to remember any details when testifying in regards to crimes involving himself or his friends."

158

"He goes blank?"

"Completely, particularly when it has something to do with the law. At these times he can't distinguish right from wrong."

"Are you sure this is a new disease?"

"I'm quite certain. I had an attorney general in the other day and I asked him to read a memo on the Iraqi pipeline. He couldn't do it. Then I handed him a paper concerning Wed-tech and he said, 'I never saw this before.' "

"What was wrong with that?" I asked.

"He had read it out loud in my waiting room an hour before. It was a textbook case of A-Meesia. The man had lost all recollection of who and what he had been involved with during the last seven years."

"It sounds like there is a pattern to the illness."

"If you lose your memory once, it is not serious. But when you continually lose it in public, then you are sick."

"Can you contract A-Meesia from other people?"

"That's the easiest way to get it. My patient confessed to me he was constantly having financial relations with his friends."

"Where have you witnessed the most cases of A-Meesia?"

"I saw a lot of it during the Irangate hearings. So many people were losing their memories we had to set up a MASH unit outside the Senate hearing room."

"Is there a cure?"

"Some people in the administration have been taking an aspirin every other day. But it hasn't stopped them from forgetting everything."

"Suppose," I said, "A-Meesia is psychosomatic and people are pretending they have lost their memories so they won't be indicted by a grand jury?"

"We thought of that but rejected it. A-Meesia is a real disease and has to be dealt with as such. That's why we're doing a lot of work with rats. If we can find out why white rats forget, then we may discover why government lawyers do the same thing."

"Do you have any leads?"

"We suspect it might be the asbestos in the Attorney General's ceiling. But then again he might have caught A-Meesia when he was working as counselor to the President. We don't have much to go on. But we have to find an answer. There is nothing so sad as seeing an attorney general on the witness stand who doesn't know what time it is."

"I'm sure you'll find a medical solution."

"Maybe, maybe not. I just received this specimen bottle back from the Justice Department lab."

"Whose is it?"

"Nobody over there can remember."

By George—By Dan

The George Bush–Dan Rather brawl, which historians now refer to as The Nine Minutes That Shook the World, left many Republicans embittered. Strangely enough, none of them were Bush supporters. While outwardly outraged at Dan Rather for beating up on their candidate, the Bush people privately rejoiced at their good fortune.

"Our boy is no longer a wimp," a Bush campaign chief told me. "He stared at the toughest anchorman in television and Rather blinked."

There seems to be no joy in the other Republican camps. Managers of Dole, Kemp, Robertson, Haig and DuPont met in a Pizza Hut in Ames, Iowa, to discuss the ominous turn of events.

"The Vice President was ambushed by CBS," the Haig man complained. "This means only one thing. CBS must sandbag our candidates too. We can't let Bush walk away with the antimedia vote just because an anchorman verbally assaulted him on the evening news."

The Dole manager was even more bitter. "Rather owes it to us to make our guys look lousy. If he doesn't rough us up, Bush walks into the White House. When it comes to TV dumping on candidates, there is such a thing as equal time."

Al Haig's aide said, "The thing that gets me mad is, not only did Bush go up in the polls because of CBS, but the money is pouring in. It's not George Bush money but anti-Rather money that is flooding his headquarters."

The DuPont man had a suggestion. "What if we go to CBS and apologize to Rather on behalf of the Vice President? Won't that make him look like a wimp again?"

Pat Robertson's representative spoke up. "I think we should pray the whole thing blows over. God tells me it's hopeless to believe Rather would get into a shouting match with all of us after he saw how much good it did George Bush."

"George never even answered Rather's question," Pierre DuPont's man grumbled.

Kemp's lieutenant replied, "He didn't have to answer the question. All he had to do was sit there and object to Dan's asking it. It was a setup from start to finish and we're the losers."

Haig's man said, "Rather should never have let Bush go on his television show. After all, how does an anchorman defend himself against a vice president of the United States who stonewalls him right through the commercials?"

"Dan should have known what he was getting into when he tangled with a Yale man," the Kemp representative added.

"Will George do any future interviews with Rather?"

"I'm sure of it," the Dole manager answered. "I heard Bush is so in love with CBS News that he has offered to fill in for Lesley Stahl when she goes on vacation."

The Haig man slammed his hand onto his pizza. "I say CBS owes us equal time. Dan Rather has to be as rude to us as he was to Bush or we sue."

The DuPont rep suggested, "Maybe in place of an interview Dan could moderate a debate and push our candidates when they don't answer his query."

The Kemp aide agreed. "Yes, and we'll invoke the unfairness doctrine. Whenever Rather asks our candidates a tough question we'll act wounded."

Dole's aide said, "Senator Dole will go along with it just to bring some sanity to this race."

Kemp's man raised his hand. "We're all assuming that Rather will play along with us. Suppose CBS won't let him. How do we win the antimedia vote then?"

Dole's man declared, "We'll get Sam Donaldson to yell at us from a meat-packing plant in Pocatello, Idaho."

Ivan the Terrible

The real meaning of the thaw in Soviet-American relations is that the Russians can no longer be cast in spy novels and movies as the bad guys. Arnold Schwarzenegger's film *Red Heat* is the first of many that portray the Evil Empire in a good light.

This has required Hollywood producers to revise their scripts.

"Hold it, Richard. We're doing a complete rewrite of *Ivan the Terrible.* First we have to come up with a different title."

"What do you suggest?"

"How about 'Ivan the Good Ol' Boy'?"

"Are you sure?"

"Richard, don't you understand? We can't make Soviet citizens the heavies anymore. People won't accept it. The Russkies are the salt of the earth, and it's our job to portray them that way. Now let's take it from the top of the script: Ivan

163

works for the KGB, which is the agency in charge of dams and reclamation projects in his country."

"In the original version the KGB was the notorious Soviet Secret Service."

"How wrong can you be? Why would Ivan, one of our two heroes, have anything to do with the Secret Service?"

"He's not a hero in the draft I have here. He is a villain with plans to blow up the Williamsburg Bridge in New York City."

"Change it. Make Ivan the one who is going to save the bridge."

"So who's trying to blow it up?"

"What about Noriega and his crazy crew of Panamanians?"

"You'd like to portray Noriega's people as the loonies?"

"Why not? What could be better than the Soviets and the Americans working together against the little twerp's empire? Let's do it like this. Sam, our American hero, and Ivan meet at a Soviet-American softball game on Red Square. They take an instant dislike to each other."

"Why?"

"Because Ivan is short and Sam is tall. But they team up anyway to try and find the psychopathic bridge bomber in Manhattan. Although they are miles apart ideologically, the two men know that their lives depend on each other. They also feel that if Raisa Gorbachev and Nancy Reagan can hit it off, they can at least give it a try. For starters, the men learn each other's tongues. Ivan, who comes from Leningrad, teaches Sam fluent Russian, and Sam, who lives in Miami, teaches Ivan fluent Spanish."

"Do we still keep Hilda the American civil engineer in the script?"

"Yes, but let's make her a milkmaid from Kiev instead."

"You want a milkmaid to discover that the Williamsburg Bridge is going to fall down?"

"Of course. That's what makes glasnost for real."

"It's your picture."

"You bet it's my picture. The time is ripe to show the Soviet people as decent, warm, loving human beings who want peace, and oil furnaces that work. When the milkmaid dies trying to save the bridge from falling into the river, there won't be a dry eye from Albuquerque to Kharkov. That is perestroika.

"The message I'd like to convey in this film is that it is possible for two men to work together in harmony in spite of the fact that one believes in God and the other doesn't."

"Which one believes in God?"

"I don't know. You're the writer."

Lonely New Hampshire

New Hampshire can be a lonely place once the primaries are over. I realized this when I saw a sign on the border that read, "Will the last reporter leaving Manchester please turn out the lights?"

I stopped for gas at a 7-Eleven in the town of Boot. The gas man, seeing my press credentials on the windshield, put his snow cap on and rushed over.

"If you want a wider shot you can set your TV cameras over there," he said.

"I'm not here to set up cameras," I told him. "I just need some gas."

"Don't you want to know my opinion of George Bush?"

"It's too late. Nobody in the United States cares what you think about Bush anymore."

"Dan Rather cared what I thought. He stuck his mike in my mouth for two minutes."

"Dan's only interest now is South Carolina."

"That isn't what he told me. He said what people in New Hampshire think about Bush could change the results of the election. I gave him some Twinkies because he let me say hello to my mother."

166

"I would like a cup of coffee."

"Jack Kemp always had a cup of coffee before he went out on the campaign trail. He sat right on that box over there next to Gary Hart."

"Get off it. Jack Kemp never sat next to Gary Hart."

"Kemp didn't know it was Gary Hart. He thought it was Warren Beatty."

"What was Gary Hart doing in a 7-Eleven?"

"He said he was looking for a voter to talk to—any voter."

"This seems to have been a busy store."

"We're the last 7-Eleven before you get to Concord, so everybody loads up here. Tom Brokaw bought a Spam sandwich from me last month and asked if I was going to vote for Dukakis. I told Tom I would if it assured me of getting on the evening news. We in New Hampshire can't make up our minds unless we know we're appearing on prime time.

"I was about to call it a night when Ted Koppel came by with his crew and asked me to go on split screen as a typical Boot, New Hampshire, resident. I told him I'd be delighted since I had already done it for Dan Rather, Bryant Gumbel, Oprah Winfrey and Phil Donahue.

"Ted said he was looking for someone who wasn't so overexposed, so I called up my cousin who had only been on '60 Minutes.' The trouble with you TV fellers is you think that you can just drive up and find a New Hampshire media virgin who has never been interviewed on television."

"You can relax now," I said. "New Hampshire has had its day in the sun."

"Don't sit near the cornflakes," the man cried. "Barbara Walters sat there when she talked to me about Mrs. Dole. She asked me lots of personal questions about her."

"Did you answer them?"

"It was hard to because Mrs. Dole only came in a couple of

times, bought frozen yogurt and ate it in the car. You can't get a real fix on a candidate's wife from that."

"But Barbara didn't care?"

"She couldn't have been nicer, especially when she found out my brother drives a plow for the Department of Transportation. You want any pictures of me holding up the photo that the Reverend Robertson left behind showing the Russian missiles in Cuba?"

"Why did he leave it behind?"

"He said the people of New Hampshire were the only born-again voters who knew he was telling the truth."

Post Office

I went down to the post office one day and it was locked tight.

"It's closed until the Fourth of July," a man who had been sleeping on the sidewalk said.

"Are you homeless?" I asked him.

"No," he said, "I'm just waiting to pick up a parcel post package of cookies my mother sent me for Christmas. It's easier to sack out here than go home every night."

"How can you be sure the post office won't open until the Fourth of July?" I wanted to know.

"It's all over town. They have a big deficit and this is the only way to make it up, unless they get a bank loan from Mexico."

"But my letter is very important," I said. "If I can't mail it in by midnight I may not win a free sweepstakes cruise to Puerto Rico."

The man looked at my envelope. "This letter will never fly. It only has a twenty-five-cent stamp on it."

"That's the new price they announced for a first-class stamp."

"Do you think the post office can handle this envelope for two bits? It costs a fortune to deliver a letter on its appointed rounds through dark of night."

"So what stamp should I use?"

"That's for each person to decide for himself—but be generous. Remember, workers in the post office aren't there for the money."

"How can they operate the system at a profit if they keep their stations closed?"

"Very slowly. You see, in order to bring the deficit down they have to reduce the services most people expect. The fewer services the post office provides, the less it has to charge for its stamps. Heaven knows what a twenty-five-cent stamp would cost if postal offices were open all day long."

I looked in the window.

"What do you see?" he asked me.

"A long line of people," I replied.

"Oh, that's the Express Mail line left over from 1987."

"I also see a mountain of junk mail."

"That's not junk mail. Those are windows of opportunity which make it possible for people to win millions of dollars, cabin cruisers or new homes in Arizona. There are also magazines full of lingerie ads, not to mention thousands of catalogs that keep the factories in Hong Kong humming."

169

"Why don't I sneak around the back and drop my letter in with the junk mail? Perhaps it will get out faster."

"I doubt it because this post office has been designated a 'Priority A' station, which means you can't mix first-class mail with junk mail."

"Why not?" I asked.

"You don't want to risk the first-class mail infecting the junk mail. A country that doesn't respect its fourth-class mail doesn't deserve to have an excellent postal system."

"Is there some station that is open on days other than July Fourth?"

"There is one in Maryland and one in Virginia, but nobody knows exactly where they're located, since they are mail drops for Ollie North."

I said, "Then I'm stuck with this post office."

He assured me, "You'll get to like it. To introduce the new twenty-five-cent stamp they have promised to serve free coffee to the first ten people in line."

Wrong Number

Ever since they broke up the phone company people seem to be showered with wrong numbers.

I believe these calls are not accidental but are placed by a syndicate of perverts stationed in boiler rooms around the country. The purpose of the wrong-number dialer is to ring up when a person least expects it and cause the victim to break his toe on an end table.

What is the payoff for someone making a wrong-number call? It gives the dialer a sense of power he or she never had before, and a way for many of the callers to get even with their mothers.

This is how the team assigned to my house works: The first dialer rings only at bathtime. I can't afford to ignore the phone because it might be Ed McMahon telling me I won ten million dollars in a sweepstakes, so I slosh across the floor and pick up the receiver. At which point the caller hangs up. Like all idiots who receive wrong numbers I keep screaming "hello!" into the phone until I realize it is futile. I return the receiver to the cradle and say to my wife, "How could he know I was in the bath?" My wife replies, "That's not the question. The question is, how did he know you'd get *out* of the bath?"

My second caller has a thick accent and it wouldn't surprise me if he was in the country illegally. Here's how this wrong call goes:

"Hello, Sam," he says.

"This is not Sam. There is no Sam in this house."

"Who you?"

"I'm the person who owns the phone. You have the wrong number."

"You tell Sam he better call me or I smash his face in."

"Okay, I'll tell him," I say. "But you still have the wrong number."

"You tell Sam I'm going to smash him in his face for giving me the wrong number."

One of my other dialers sounds like a kid. Those calls go like this: "Grandpa?"

"Yes, this is Grandpa. Is this Jason?"

"No, it's Nicholas. You're not my grandpa."

"You're right. You shouldn't use the phone when your parents aren't there."

"My daddy's right here."

"What are you bothering my kid for?" a man's voice says.

"If he's for real, which I doubt, he called my number by mistake."

"Then why did you answer the phone? He's only five years old."

While I get my share of wrong numbers during the waking hours, I have observed that most of the calls come very early in the morning. They are made by people who sound just like teenagers, and they get extremely angry at me when they find out they're not talking to Bubba.

If you tell the person on the phone you don't know where Bubba is, they accuse you of locking him in the furnace room, which you had no right to do.

There is only one thing worse than a Bubba caller and that's a heavy breather, who checks in at three o'clock in the morning. The first time he started breathing I handed the receiver to my wife and said, "It's for you."

"How do you know? It could be a woman."

"Do you think there are female heavy breathers?"

She rolled over and said, "Why don't you ask her?"

This is just a sample of my wrong-number callers. There are only two conclusions you can come to about why they are so numerous. One is, there are a lot more crazy people in the country than the census shows; and the other is, the telephone lines are even more fouled up than anyone imagines.

Hot Line

The United States has installed a new hot line to the Soviet Union to prevent accidental war. Instead of phones, the system uses desk computers. That's the rub. Anyone who has ever watched someone using a computer at an airline counter, a hotel registration desk or a department store has to be very nervous. Computers and the people who use them never seem to be in operation at the same time.

This is my nightmare:

"I want to speak to Mr. Gorbachev on the hot line."

"Just a minute, sir. I don't show any Mr. Gorbachev on my screen. Do you have a first name?"

"Mikhail Gorbachev. Hurry up, the survival of the whole human race depends on your networking Gorbachev in the Kremlin."

"Do you know his Social Security number?"

"No, but if you don't connect me in the next three minutes your body will turn into a glass of heavy water."

"Let me try bypassing the computer by way of Armenia. Hold it, I'm flashing a telephone number for Maxim Gorky. Will he do?"

"I want M. Gorbachev and no one but M. Gorbachev."

"Sir, the hot-line terminal on the other end says the Bolshoi Ballet is sold out, but it is willing to trade two house seats for a pair of tickets to *Phantom of the Opera.*"

"Tell your computer to try Gorbachev at his dacha."

"We have no access to his dacha, but I can get you an airline seat on Aeroflot to Raleigh, North Carolina."

"Your computer was supposed to be programmed to immediately put me in touch with the leader of the Communist world. How do you explain this foulup?"

"I don't know, sir. We talked to someone in the Soviet Union the other day."

"What did you say?"

"We confirmed he had a double room at the Holiday Inn in Atlantic City."

"The clock is running. Is there no way of jumping the program so I can get through directly to the Politburo?"

"I'll try this. I'll retrieve all the Gorbachevs in the Moscow telephone book and then sort them out in my memory bank."

"Did it work?"

"No, the only thing the computer says is a Mrs. Gorbachev owes Bloomingdale's $12.50."

"Where did you learn to run a computer, young man?"

"National Airport. The machines there are much easier to work than this one, sir. I could get a Russian on my Delta Airlines reservations screen anytime I wanted to."

"Hurry, man, someone has goofed and World War Three is upon us."

"Do you want me to feed that into the computer?"

"Why not?"

"Uh, oh—something has gone wrong because it says we transmitted a faulty entry on a rental car in Lincoln, Nebraska."

"Forget it, I'll call Gorbachev on the phone."

"You don't have to—he *is* on the phone."

"Why didn't you tell me?"

"I thought you wanted to speak to him on the computer."

"Mikhail, I'm glad to talk to you. I don't want you to get mad, but tomorrow morning you are going to be receiving one hundred million *Reader's Digests* in the mail. Just send them back to us and we'll pay the postage. . . . No, Mikhail, these aren't the same operators who will be running Star Wars. The Star Wars programmers are being trained by Eastern Airlines."

The Truth, the Whole Truth

The only thing you see when world leaders meet is their exit. All you hear are pallid declarations as the leaders face the microphones.

"We had a very fruitful exchange which will eventually lead to mutual understanding," the Premier says.

The U.S. Secretary of State then speaks. "The discussions were frank and open and we hope someday they will produce positive results for the entire region."

Diplomacy demands the two people make such statements. But you have to read between the lines to get the real meaning.

This is what the Premier really wished to say when he described the talks as fruitful. "When the Secretary of State tried to blackmail me by threatening to cut off ground-to-air missile deliveries, I had no choice but to throw the fruit bowl at him."

While the Secretary of State really wanted to say, "What can you expect from a man who has devoted his entire life to being short?"

And so it goes. Here is the dialogue—and what the leaders were really thinking:

The Premier speaks into the mikes, "We had sharp exchanges but now we can move forward." ("The Secretary wants peace and he wants the Russians at the table. How can he have both? The trouble with the American is he plays too much tennis and the sun gets to his head.")

"I want to say," the Secretary of State declares, "the areas of agreement are far greater than those of disagreement. I have gotten to know the Premier better and that was worth my entire trip." ("If I had seen how little I was going to get out of all this I would have brought De Tocqueville with me and stayed in the hotel.")

The Premier is next. "Two great nations can agree to disagree, but this should not stop them from supplying each other with helicopters." ("Not only is the American Secretary of State wrong on everything—he is also boring. Anyone who can put my entire cabinet to sleep with his final peace offer deserves a Nobel peace prize.")

The Secretary, not to be outdone, asserts, "I intend to come back and continue the discussions we have had today, because only by talking across the table will we be able to reach solutions to knotty problems that confront the Premier and myself." ("Even if he agreed to everything, I could not accept the terms because I did not understand a word he was saying.")

World leaders know their remarks will be shown on television and sent around the world. That's why they don't want to look like losers.

The Premier has a lot going on in his head when he is speaking into the mikes, but he realizes it is wise not to let on what it is—such as, "If we didn't need the new F-16s I would have spilled water all over his pants."

The Secretary of State always bites his tongue so he won't blurt, "The Premier is stubborn and obstinate and doesn't know up from down. All he wants is war, and if he keeps doing what he's doing he's going to get one. Not only do I disagree with him diplomatically, I don't even like him as a person."

The Premier looks at the microphones and declares, "We are now going to have a friendly lunch." But what he says to himself is, "Inviting him to lunch was a mistake. He'll continue to talk and it will just give me another headache."

Now Hear This

Larry Speakes was roundly criticized for putting words in President Reagan's mouth. As press secretary he made up quotes that he attributed to the President, causing untold damage to Mr. Reagan's reputation as the commander in chief of everything he utters.

People in the White House press corps were not so much amazed at Speakes' resorting to such subterfuge as they were puzzled about why the President allowed it.

The best explanation is that President Reagan never worried about what Speakes said at his briefings so long as it sounded good to the public.

There were some close calls for the Gipper, however. One time Speakes came into the Oval Office and said, "Sir, we have just secured Grenada. Is there any statement you'd like to make?"

"How about, 'Fourscore and seven years ago our forefathers brought forth on this earth a new nation and that is why we have nothing to fear but fear itself'?"

"It's a bit wordy," Larry said.

"Well, you have the idea, just kick it around and use anything you want to."

"I will say, 'This is one of the greatest victories against Communism in our lifetime and is a signal to our foes that we will never negotiate out of fear nor fear to negotiate.' "

"That's fine. Good night."

"But sir, it's four o'clock in the afternoon. You have to make a speech this evening at your state dinner for Margaret Thatcher."

"What are you going to tell the press I said?" the President asked.

"I might tell them you said Prime Minister Thatcher has brought us nothing but blood, sweat and tears."

"I hadn't planned on saying that. Why can't you report that when I made my toast I had no comment."

"The press won't like it. Don't worry. I'll think of something."

"You're very good, Larry."

"I see it this way, Mr. President. A press secretary's job is to make the President look better than he really is. If I can have you expounding brilliant things we both win."

"How do we both win?"

"You come out of it as the Great Communicator and I get a much higher advance on my book."

"Larry, is what we are doing wrong?"

"Of course not. I am your spokesman. What difference does it make if you say it or I say it, as long as you get credit for it?"

"Suppose they find out the words aren't mine?"

"Only you and I know that, sir, and I sure as heck am not going to tell. Look, I won't make up quotes all the time. If you ever come up with anything original I'll use it."

"And you don't think it will hurt us when it comes out?"

"Not on your life. Do you think Abraham Lincoln said everything he was credited with?"

"Can I give you my statement now on how we won the war in Afghanistan?" the President asked.

"Try it out on me and I'll see if I like it."

"You really take over, don't you, Larry?"

"Better me than Gorbachev."

Indiana Warrior

I saw a bumper sticker the other day. It said, VOTE FOR QUAYLE—HE NEVER WENT TO CANADA.

Since I was stuck in a traffic jam and had nothing to do, I asked the driver of the car if he could live with Quayle's war record.

"I certainly can," he answered. "Quayle was in the Indiana National Guard, and that was much tougher than being in Vietnam."

"I didn't know that."

"That's because you don't realize what the National Guard

©1989 St. Mendel

does. It's on call day and night to protect this country against insurrection. Only the best and the brightest are accepted into the Guard."

"Some say that people joined the National Guard as a way of getting out of active service in Indochina."

"The only ones who say that are Democrats trying to steal the election by impugning the motives of Quayle, who just wanted to defend his country in his own state. The reason our boys could fight more effectively in Vietnam was because they knew they had soldiers like Quayle defending their loved ones back home."

"The story making the rounds is that Quayle used his powerful family connections to get into the Guard. Was that a good idea?"

"It may not have been the best idea, but when you're young and full of life you don't always have good ideas.

"The way I hear it is," he continued, "having just finished college, Quayle was about to be drafted into the service. He was told by friends that the National Guard was looking for a few good men. Quayle talked it over with his brother and they struck a deal. He'd go into the National Guard and his brother would join the Marine Corps. That way one or other of them would be guaranteed to fight. Quayle never complained about getting the short end of the stick."

"Assuming that Quayle's friends intervened to get him into the Guard, how is this going to play in French Lick, Indiana?"

"That's the point of it. The voters in Indiana love Dan, and they won't turn their backs on him just because he missed the Tet offensive. What about all the liberal commie pinkos who dodged the draft? Why don't the media talk about them?"

"Because they are not running for vice president," I said. "Not only liberal commie pinkos get upset about someone using his family influence to get into the National Guard."

"Don't worry about Quayle being a negative on the ticket. There are millions of people in the country who didn't want to go to Vietnam, and those are the voters that the Bush-Quayle ticket is going to appeal to."

"How?"

"By being truthful. In a political campaign nothing works better than letting it all hang out. Quayle is going to say that he has nothing to hide—and that should be the end of it."

"For his sake, I hope its true," I added. "If I had been in his position, with a newspaper chain behind me and a great future ahead of me, I'd have done the same thing. Do you know of any particular reason for Quayle's actions?"

"He knew in his heart that someday he would be the vice-presidential candidate of the United States, and he wanted to win one for the Gipper."

No Smoking

The firing squad from Rikers Island marched out onto the parade ground. Six soldiers, led by Captain Loughboro, lined up at attention, facing the wooden post.

Two soldiers, one on each side, marched Tony the Termite to the post and tied his hands behind his back. Captain Loughboro stepped forward with a blindfold and tied it around Tony's eyes. "Would you care for a cigarette?" the captain asked.

"Yes, I would," Tony replied. "I'll take a king-sized mentholated."

The captain drew one out of a pack and placed it in Tony's mouth. He was about to light it when a uniformed inspector from the city's Anti-Smoking Unit ran onto the parade ground and cried, "Halt! You cannot smoke on this property during a firing-squad execution."

"That's ridiculous," the captain exclaimed. "Puffing a last cigarette before being shot is an ancient military tradition."

"Never mind tradition. No one is permitted to blow smoke within ten feet of another person as it's hazardous to everyone's health. Tony isn't doing harm only to himself but to the firing squad as well."

"Suppose I move the squad ten feet back?" the captain suggested.

"That still would be considered secondhand smoke. Don't you have any respect for human life at all?"

The captain turned to Tony. "Would it bother you to give up your last cigarette?"

"It certainly would. This is a free country and having one last puff is my right."

The captain riffled through a book. "He's correct," he said to the inspector. "It says here no one may be shot unless he is offered a last cigarette of his choice."

"But we're only doing this for his health. If Tony sucks on that fag he's going to develop a terrible cough."

"I'll worry about that," Tony protested. "It's too late to quit smoking. I should have done it years ago when it had some meaning. Now let's knock off the sweet talk and give me a light."

The inspector said, "That's the trouble with people who face capital punishment. They think of nobody but themselves. We'll never have clean air if smokers ignore the rights of others. Well, I'm warning you. If the captain lights up your cigarette I'm going to arrest you for violating the law and it will cost you."

Tony asked, "What will I get?"

"Thirty days and a fifty-dollar fine."

"I'll take it. That's better than what they are going to give me now," Tony declared.

The captain barked at the inspector, "I won't hear of it. This man has been sentenced to die by the firing squad and you are interfering in the outcome. Get out of here."

"I'm giving you notice," the inspector admonished, "that you can be locked up for aiding and abetting a smoker, which is a capital crime. I suggest you dispense with the cigarette and get on with the execution."

Tony shouted, "I protest! No one can prove that smoking is hazardous to my health. I will fight to my dying breath to be able to enjoy this last cigarette because I have only one puff to give for my country. I say, 'Give me liberty or give me a Marlboro.' "

The captain snarled at the inspector, "Now you've done it. We're not going to be able to shoot him until he goes to Smoke Enders."

Poor Nancy

Poor Nancy Reagan. She had been trying for seven years to stop drugs from being distributed in the United States. All the while, government agencies working for her husband were smuggling narcotics into this country.

When she read the sworn Senate testimony about it she stormed into the President's office. "I don't believe it," she said to him. "All the time I kept telling the kids to 'just say no' the U.S. was working in cahoots with the drug smugglers in Central America."

The President said, "Don't get so upset. I'm sure there is a mistake. If anyone in this administration was involved in the dope business I would know about it."

"The pilots testified in the Senate that we were," Nancy retorted.

"Well, just hold it—I'll get to the bottom of this. . . . Operator, get me Bill Casey at the CIA . . . HE'S WHAT? . . . Nancy, Bill Casey is dead."

"They don't tell you anything. Are you aware that the contras depended on the drug money to keep the war going?"

"You should not say that unless you have the facts. Nancy, I happen to know that the money for the contras came from arms we sold to Iran."

"Who told you that, Ronnie?"

"George Bush. And if anyone knew what was going on, George did."

"I don't like the idea of the United States being mixed up in narcotics smuggling—it smells sleazy," Nancy said.

"I don't like it either, and if I find out who was behind it I'm going to chew him out."

"Why does the CIA have to exchange guns for cocaine?"

"Because if we don't stop the Sandinistas now they'll be smoking grass on the beaches of San Diego. If the CIA was involved in drug smuggling it was an honest mistake," the President assured her.

"Ronnie, I think you should go on the air and say that no person in your administration knows anything about the arms-for-dope transaction, and you are appalled that anyone in the government would okay it."

"That's a good idea. The Pentagon will bear me out. Operator, get me Secretary of Defense Weinberger on the phone . . . HE'S WHAT? . . . Nancy, Weinberger has resigned."

"Why didn't he tell you?"

"No one tells me anything," the President complained.

"Well, this is a fine kettle of fish. I'm telling everyone to 'just say no' and the cloak and dagger people are loading up their planes with narcotics. I insist that you inform whoever is dealing with the contras that drugs are not the way to fight Communism."

"That's good thinking, Nancy. Send Mike Deaver in and I'll dictate a memo."

"Mike Deaver is no longer in the White House."

"*Caramba!* No one told me that. Well, I know what I'll do. I will turn the whole thing over to the FBI and have them round up the usual suspects. Then I will have the Justice Department try them in a court of law and let a jury decide their guilt or innocence."

"And then what will you do, Ronnie?"

"Then I'll pardon them. That's what presidents are for."

The FBI and the Libraries

As children we all fantasized about working for the FBI. While it seemed like only a dream it's easier than you think.

The FBI recently asked American librarians to keep their eyes open for spies, and report any suspicious activity of library cardholders to local FBI bureaus. The operation is called the Library Awareness Program and the G-men are not kidding around.

According to reports, the FBI wants information on people who come to the libraries to withdraw scientific tomes, linger over maps and photocopy documents dealing with national defense.

The FBI is dead serious because they figure the public library is the main source of information for spies. But the Bureau ran into a major problem with its Library Awareness Program when America's librarians refused to play ball. The overwhelming majority felt it was not their role to act as counter-espionage agents.

The Library Awareness Program cannot work without the cooperation of librarians, and so another solution must be found to provide the G-men with the information they want. This is what is being considered:

There is no law saying library patrons could not volunteer to do the tasks that the librarians refuse to perform. Any American can be deputized to act as a stakeout in a bookstack. Cardholders, unlike librarians, have tremendous amounts of time on their hands and are perfect candidates to keep their eyes on strangers.

If you're interested this is how I suggest you operate. Get a seat near the door. Have a copy of Richard Nixon's book in front of you and bend over and pretend you're reading it. Out of the corner of your eye notice who comes in and what books he is returning. Also note whether his shoes were made behind the iron curtain, or if his hat was made in Cuba.

Once he goes into the stacks, get up and follow him down the aisle. If he heads down the one with a sign reading LASER MANUALS, you may be onto Mr. KGB himself. Pretend you are looking for *Hans Brinker and the Silver Skates*, but keep your eye on him. Remember, this person is not a spy just because he wants to read a book on lasers. If he tears the pages out of the book and stuffs them into his pants, then you should make a note to call the Bureau.

Many espionage organizations are using women to prowl America's libraries and they are more difficult to spot as spies than men. This is how to keep on your toes. If an attractive lady sits next to you in a library and starts playing footsie under the table with your Nike sneakers, be alert. If she follows this up by nuzzling your ear, you know she's in the market for more than an old *National Geographic*. She is probably after everything the library has on microfilm about IBM's latest mainframe computer. She wants it either for the Polish Secret Service or the Apple computer company in California.

The beauty of helping the FBI in their library watch is that a person doesn't have to do it alone. If you're married you can split shifts with your wife. You could keep watch in the morning and she could spy on suspects in the afternoon.

Nobody likes to keep tabs on everyone who comes to a library, but that's where foreign agents are getting their information these days, and since the librarians refuse to be on the lookout for the bad guys, someone has to do it.

One way to check out whether or not a person is a legit library user is to ask to see his library card. According to the FBI there are thousands of spooks walking around with forged cards manufactured in Budapest. To find out if the card is for real, spit on it, and if the ink runs off, you can start searching him for his poison pill.

Winners One and All

When President Reagan heard that the Baltimore Orioles had broken their losing streak of twenty-one games, he immediately called Howard Baker in and said, "Let's get these guys to the White House."

"But sir, it wasn't a good record. It was a bad one. The Orioles lost twenty-one games in a row. No president has ever invited a team to the White House because they *lost* so many games."

"Nevertheless, Howard, I think I should greet and honor them for their fortitude. That's what the Gipper would have done. When a team drops that many games and then wins one, a president should recognize it. Why don't we hold the ceremony on the White House lawn? While I'm vetoing a trade bill, the Orioles can play fetch with Nancy's dog."

"Mr. President, don't you think it's a mistake for you to be photographed with people who have dropped the ball so many times?"

"I don't see anything wrong with it. We're not honoring a team for losing twenty-one games, we're recognizing them for winning one. By inviting the Orioles to the White House, I believe that we are paying tribute to all Americans who strike out most of their lives."

"Since you put it that way, Mr. President, it does make sense. After all, we have had losers in the White House before."

"Who were they, Howard?"

"I can't remember the names, but many of them worked right here in this building."

"Well, no one ever told me about it. Now what should I say to the Orioles?"

"Why don't you say, 'As always, victory has a hundred fathers, but the Orioles are orphans'?"

"Maybe I ought to say something about what losing to Congress has meant to me."

"How about the reason the Orioles have been able to accomplish what they have so far this season is that they're team players?"

"That doesn't sound right. What about this? 'The Orioles represent the best in America because they lost their twenty-one games and never asked for federal money.' "

"I think you've hit upon just the right tone, Mr. President. From there you could speak about the difference between Soviet and American teams."

"What is the diffference?"

"In the Soviet Union you pay for mistakes. In the United States you get paid for them."

"That sounds good. Maybe instead of greeting the team on the White House lawn I should hold a black-tie state dinner in their honor?"

"Mr. President, we're not talking about the World Series winners. Baltimore deserves a reception but I think a black-tie dinner is overdoing it."

"But it would give me an opportunity to include all the losers Nancy and I forgot to invite to the White House during my eight years in office."

"Sir, one of the reasons those people are losers is because they have never been invited to the White House. You don't want to change that at this late date, do you?"

"No, I don't. We better go back to the White House lawn idea. I think I'll declare the day I meet the Orioles a national holiday and give government employees the day off."

"But suppose, sir, the Orioles win a second game? What will you say then?"

"I don't know . . . it's times like these when I miss him."

"Who, sir?"

"Larry Speakes."

Look to the Stars

Behind every great man in Washington there is a great astrologer. The story that Donald Regan tells in his book is that the Reagans used astrology as a means of arriving at decisions in the White House.

Before the know-it-alls make their comments I would like to say that there is absolutely nothing wrong with a president governing a country by the stars. It is a foolproof system and one that has paid great dividends for the country.

I don't know the name of the President's astrologer or even if she had an office in the White House. But what we do know, according to Donald Regan, is that not only Nancy, but the President consulted her.

We shall call the presidential astrologer Zodiac.

A dicey matter has come up in Panama and Noriega won't leave the country. After meeting with the National Security Council, the President calls in Zodiac. "What do you think?"

"I would do nothing until Wednesday, when Pluto conjoins Jupiter."

"This week?"

"No, next year. You can expect big problems from a full moon and a recalcitrant Congress. Your chart says, 'Don't make any new friends when you go to the Republican Convention this summer.' "

"I would prefer that Noriega get out by Thursday, but I hear that he won't do it until Saturn lines up with Venus."

"As an Aquarius, Mr. President, you have a right to be upset about Panama. After all, your chart indicates that Noriega should have fled the country last month."

"Did you come up with any predictions on my meeting with Gorbachev?"

"Well, sir, I would not give up any long-range missiles until the sun enters Gemini. Gorbachev is a Pisces and is dreamy, sensitive, artistic, romantic and a really tough SOB when it comes to making a deal. His astrologer has told him not to come to any decisions this year unless you give up Star Wars."

"Why is he so hell-bent on me giving up Star Wars?"

"Because Gorbachev's astrologer is afraid Star Wars will mess up the entire universe map and make every astrological chart in the world obsolete."

"What signs do you see for Nancy?"

"Her natal chart indicates Nancy should wear red when visiting Lenin's tomb, which will prevent Raisa from blocking her out of the TV cameras. It also says this is not a good time for Nancy to spend a lot of money or invite the Donald Regans over for dinner."

"Anything in the solar system as to what's in store for Colonel Ollie North and Admiral Poindexter?"

"If Neptune stays on its present path you will pardon them."

"How do you know this?"

"I read it in the Evans and Novak column. Poindexter and North's destinies are entwined astrologically with yours, and you are responsible for them."

"Why?"

"Because they did all the things they did when there was a full moon over the White House. If you recall, when I dealt you a Tarot hand two years ago I told you somebody was doing something in the White House that could injure you. You just laughed at me and said, 'Gin.' "

"Zodiac, I don't know what Nancy and I would do without you. You've been in on every decision I've made and you have never been wrong except on my nomination of two Supreme Court justices. I've never doubted you since you told me Saturn indicated Ed Meese would have money problems."

"This country is blessed to have a president and first lady who believe in astrology. Where would we be if we had nothing to depend on but the CIA?"

Deal, Jesse, Deal

What makes Jesse Jackson such a simple man is that he has so many simple ideas. I love the one where he wanted to sit down with the terrorists and negotiate the release of the hostages in the Middle East. Jesse believes all it takes is understanding and goodwill to persuade Middle East kidnappers to give back the people they are holding.

"Hi, I'm Jesse Jackson and I'm here to talk you people into returning to me the Americans you're holding."

"Lie down on the ground with your nose in the dirt."

"Hold it. I am ready to reason with you. Don't you remember the last time I was in these parts you gave me a Navy ensign hostage?"

"That's because he was black and we wanted to embarrass Ronald Reagan."

"I, Jesse Jackson, am somebody. I'm willing to make a deal. What do you people want?"

"A truckload of dynamite and a free parking place in front of the American Embassy in Beirut."

"Be reasonable. How about a boatload of Ritz crackers and two dozen Ralph Lauren suits?"

"Who told you that you could come and see us?"

"I came here because we're brothers. I am a man of God and you people are men of God and you are committing a sin holding the Americans in captivity. I am willing to continue this conversation but first you must take that machine-gun muzzle out of my nostril."

"Jesse Jackson, may a thousand Mayor Koches fall down on your head. You want to make a deal? We desire a 747 airplane."

"Are you going to fly somewhere?"

"No, we want to blow it up. We haven't blown up a 747 since Khomeini was a pup."

"Listen to me. Let me tell you why I need you. I'm running for President of the United States. It would be quite a coup for me if you released the hostages into my custody, because it would show that terrorists deserve a better press than they're getting. Can we negotiate?"

"We will let you have the hostages if we can sink two American aircraft carriers in the Persian Gulf."

"Well, at least you are starting to talk seriously. I'm not in a position to grant you this request, but I will pass it on to the people in Washington."

"We want the entire Kuwaiti royal family delivered to us tied up over the humps of camels."

"I'll also transmit that. The fact that we are discussing terms is a big plus. I don't think it's necessary to take the pin out of that grenade you're holding to my stomach."

"You know we don't like you, Jackson. You sound like a big know-it-all."

"I'm very likable. If I get to be president I'll invite all of you to the White House for a state dinner."

"How much money will you give us for the hostages?"

"I can't pay ransom but I could arrange to wire every terrorist's home with cable TV."

"It's not enough. We need arms and explosive devices and hand-held rockets."

"None of those things are out of the question. You have the

197

right as have-nots to want the same weapons the haves have. Please give me the hostages so I can go back to the United States and tell them that face-to-face diplomacy with well-meaning terrorists really works."

White House Intern

"Mr. Richard Thompson, I see by your records here that you are sixteen years old, and that you are applying for a high school internship at the White House."

"Yes, sir. It has always been my dream to intern for the President of the United States."

"Could you tell me why you're interested in working at the White House?"

"I wish to write a book about my experiences there."

"You what?"

"Yessir. But I don't want to do one of those vanity-type histories. I will tell the truth as I see it. I'm going to call it *The Last Emperor with No Clothes.*

"You sound very ambitious, but slightly disloyal."

"It isn't a question of disloyalty. The public has a right to know what the first lady is really like. If she's running the country, the citizens should be informed. I intend to describe in detail how it feels to work in a place where all decisions are controlled by the zodiac."

"And that's the reason you want to be a White House intern?"

"No, of course not. I hope to find out how the President makes up his mind and why so many of his advisors wind up in front of grand juries. This is not a 'kiss and tell' book, though I am determined to discover why the Reagan kids are always trashing their parents."

"Richard, what you've told me so far is very impressive, but it seems to me that you must have better motives for becoming an intern. Could you give me a few?"

"I could, but they don't sell books. The way I see it, if this book is a hot seller I will earn enough royalties to go to college. Three publishers have promised to give me advances if I can become part of the White House inner loop."

"Is there any particular position in the White House that you have in mind?"

"Yes, I want to be a gofer in the Oval Office. That way I can be in on everything the President does. Don Regan says that Mr. Reagan is very wishy-washy when making the big decisions. I'd like to see this for myself, because to make the book work I must be an eyewitness to history."

"I'm not sure that the administration is looking for a high school intern who wants to be an eyewitness to history."

"Everyone else is writing a book about the Teflon president. Why shouldn't I? Please don't think it will be entirely negative. I plan to say nice things about the Reagans unless, of course, Nancy engineers my dismissal. You have to understand this, sir, I'm a fighter and if the first lady starts to push me around I'll get even."

"I'm looking over our requirements for the summer intern program, but I can't seem to find an empty slot on the White House staff for someone who wants to write a book about us."

"I think it's very important that you have an intern who can author the definitive story on what happened here during the

199

summer. It is essential that we know what the Reagan administration was like at the very moment it started to fall apart. Only a sixteen-year-old intern is capable of doing it."

"Well, Richard, I must say you make a convincing case for an internship. Can we get back to you?"

"Okay, but please hurry it up. The Book-of-the-Month Club needs my story by September.'

What Does Noriega Want?

"Hello, is this Elliott Abrams? This is the President. What have you worked out with Noriega?"

"We have it all wrapped up in a neat package, Mr. President."

"That's what you told me two months ago. Why hasn't he stepped down?"

"He's making a few demands—but none that we can't live with. For example, he says if he has to leave Panama he wants to be Attorney General of the United States."

"That's out of the question and you know it, Elliott. I'm

sticking by Ed Meese. If I replace Ed with Noriega it will look as if Meese did something wrong. You tell him it's no deal."

"I will, but I know what he is going to say. He'll tell me that if he can't be attorney general he wants to be chief of the Drug Enforcement Agency."

"No way, Elliott. The head of the DEA has to be an American citizen, hopefully with an unblemished record."

"I'm aware of that, but the trouble is Noriega thinks he's calling the shots because he knows we'll do practically anything to get him out of Panama. The last time I talked to him he told me that if he can't be director of the DEA he wants Lee Iacocca's job."

"Why does he want to do that?"

"He said he has a bad image in the United States and he thinks he could improve it by doing television commercials for the Chrysler Corporation."

"I might consider that."

"There is more. He not only wants to head up Chrysler but he also wants a free pass to Space Mountain at Disney World."

"That's too much. As President of the United States I can't okay a free pass for Disney World. Congress will say I'm soft on cocaine smugglers. Tell Noriega if he doesn't step down in a week I will resort to stronger methods."

"That's what you said to tell him the last time we made our absolute final offer. Noriega told me to inform you that he is sitting tight unless we give him a Trident submarine."

"What does he want with a Trident submarine?"

"He feels it is perfect transportation for cruising from Colombia to the Florida Keys. Mr. President, I think he's toying with us. I have a hunch he would accept a plain, everyday missile destroyer if we made a hard offer."

"Elliott, the Pentagon is not for sale. If we give Noriega a destroyer how do we know he won't come back the following week and demand twenty Stealth bombers? We must let him know we are a superpower and that we will not be subjected to blackmail by a tinhorn dictator."

"We could always offer him Jimmy Swaggart's evangelical TV program. Noriega can raise more money on the show than he can selling dope."

"Try it out on him. If he turns us down, what do we do then?"

"We have intelligence, Mr. President, that Noriega mentioned to several cronies that he would like to be a guest on 'Wheel of Fortune.' "

"What for?"

"He is very excited about the prizes someone can win if they get lucky. What I suggest is that we telecast a 'Wheel of Fortune' show from Panama and have Vanna White rig it so Noriega will win an electric organ, a camper and a ceramic bulldog. But he has to pick them up in Guatemala."

"All right, Elliott. But that's our last offer. Tell Noriega that if he won't listen to reason I'm going to send Don Regan down there to write a 'kiss and tell' book about him."

Gun Volunteer

When it was announced on television that a very troubled lady in Winnetka used three handguns to shoot several schoolchildren, Esterhazy grabbed his coat and hat and headed for the door.

"What are you doing?" I asked him.

"I'm a volunteer gun lobbyist and I have to get down to the office because the shrapnel is going to hit the fan."

"The Winnetka story has nothing to do with firearms," I told him.

"Don't you believe it. Every nut who wants gun registration is going to be out tonight demanding legislation to stop the sale of handguns in the United States. The shooting in Illinois couldn't have come at a worse time. We just started a big TV advertising campaign telling everyone how great guns are."

"They can't blame the American gun lobby for what a deranged woman did."

"Yes, they can. They'll do anything to disarm this country. Something like this happens and people start asking all sorts of questions about how guns are obtained."

"It seems to me I heard that the lady who did all the shooting had a gun permit. How did she get one if she had a history of mental illness?"

"I don't know, but you can't keep an eye on every firearm sold in the United States. That's why I'm going down to the office. This is the kind of news story that has people calling their congressmen."

"What do you intend to do?"

"We have to get out wires to all our members notifying them that war has been declared against handgun owners, and everyone must be on the alert to stop the bad guys from hurting the good guys who own weapons. We're going to need money and political pressure, and we're also going to have to call in a lot of chits."

"You mean from legislators who took your money?"

"That's right. When they accepted our donations they knew we would call on them when we needed them. I can't tell you how many fund-raising dinners I have attended to make this moment pay off."

"You're a good man, Esterhazy. You believe in your cause, no matter how many people are shot."

"If we don't speak out against handgun control now, when do we?"

"How is the gun lobby going to explain the shooting in Winnetka?"

"We intend to counter the bad publicity by showing celebrities who shoot their sidearms just for pleasure. We plan to hand out press releases that say for every person who shoots someone with a handgun, there are ten who would rather hit a tin can."

"You've certainly got your work cut out for you," I said.

"We haven't lost a battle yet. You really scare the hell out of a shooter when you threaten to take away his pistols. Once we get the word out that the big bad wolf is at the door, every member will send us twenty bucks. Then it's up to the lobbyists to defeat those congressmen who are tilting towards an antihandgun law."

"I'd hate to be a congressman on the wrong side of you guys," I said.

"Of course you would—people don't kill gun control laws, congressmen do."

Twelve O'Clock High

The wonderful thing about air travel today is that it gives people an idea of what it was like flying missions over Europe in World War II.

As I sat crouched over my hand luggage in the waiting area at the airport, writing a farewell note to my wife, I saw Gregory Peck, in the full uniform of an airline counter attendant, march to the front of the room.

"ATTENTION," someone shouted.

"At ease," Peck said. He picked up a pointer and pulled down a map of the airport. "Passengers, I'm here to brief you on the situation. It is serious and the outcome is still in doubt. Pay close attention. You are here." He pointed to Gate C. "Your plane is here."

"Where is that, sir?"

"You can't tell by looking at the map, but as we talk it is being towed to a hangar for failing to pass inspection."

"So what do we fly?"

Peck pointed to the map again. "There is a plane coming in from Minneapolis at twelve o'clock high. We hope it will get here at 0300 hours and be gassed and ready to go at 0400 hours."

"Is that the scheduled takeoff time?"

"No, because this plane does not have a crew. The crew walked off in Detroit."

"Then how do we get out?"

Peck looked out at all of us. "Is there anybody here who can fly a jet?"

No one raised his hand so Peck said, "Then two of you are going to have to learn."

"Sir, can't you dig up another crew to take us out?"

"The only crew available to fly right now can't get here because there is no room in the employee parking lot. I've asked headquarters in Texas to supply backup flying personnel, but Texas is down due to bad weather and there is no one in the office to process the request."

"Then what are you going to do?"

"I'm issuing everyone in this room a chit for a box lunch in the cafeteria. But it does not include beer or diet drinks. The cafeteria is located here next to the luggage merry-go-rounds."

"After we eat lunch can we sleep on the floor until you get a new plane?" someone asked.

"No, you have to stand here by the gate because you never know when your flight might take off."

A lady in front of me started to cry.

Peck said sternly, "Knock off the tears. I want everybody here to buck up and behave like the air passengers you were trained to be. No one promised you that flying would be fun when you signed up. If you're too chicken to carry out one of our missions you can turn in your wings at the ticket counter."

"Sir, we'll follow you anywhere," I said.

"Even if I did have a crew right now," Peck told us, "I couldn't put anyone on board."

"Why not?"

"There is no gate for the plane. Everything is backed up from here to Chicago."

"Then what do we do?"

"I've asked the airline chaplain to say a few words to each one of you. We may not have enough pilots but we have the best sky ministers in the business. All right—that's the morning briefing. I want everybody back here at 0400 hours for the latest weather reports."

"Don't you have any news to cheer us up?"

"Just remember this when you get discouraged: Waiting for a plane that is five hours overdue is a dirty business, but somebody has to do it."

Dukakis Blindness

Something kept happening with my vision during the presidential campaign. Every time I saw a headline with the word "Dukakis" in it, my eyes glazed over.

I was worried enough about the situation to go to my ophthalmologist, Dr. Kip Robinson.

I told him my symptoms and he said, "I'm familiar with your problem. I've had many patients complain about the same thing."

"I'm glad I'm not alone," I replied with relief. "What's the cause of it?"

"It's more than an eye problem. When you read the word 'Dukakis,' a message is sent to the brain asking what you should do about it, and the brain responds by telling you to go to sleep."

"It's hard to believe," I said.

"All right, now read the chart on the wall."

"D-U-K-A-K-I-S."

"How do you feel?"

"Groggy. I can hardly keep my eyes open."

"And yet your eyesight is fine. Let's put some statements up here, and then you tell me if your vision is better or worse when reading them."

" 'I want to make this country as great as it was before,' " I read out loud.

"That's good. Now I'm going to flash another statement: 'I am the governor of a state that has no unemployment.' Is that any better, or is it worse?"

"It's more blurry."

"Okay—the last one: 'I think what a president needs around him are people he can trust, and who are also honest and loyal.' "

"My eyes glazed over completely on that one."

"There is no doubt in my mind that you have what we call the Dukakis Syndrome. The Dukakis Syndrome works like this: You will read every story that has Ed Meese's name in the headline, and pass over every one that has 'Dukakis' in it."

"But I'm a Democrat."

"Democrats are not immune to the Dukakis Syndrome. Some of them are so sensitive to the disease, they will turn him off as soon as he comes on television."

"Can you suggest any medicine?"

"There is none. We're predicting that it's going to get worse as the election draws nearer. The interesting part is that the polls are showing most people afflicted with Dukakis Syndrome are going to vote for him no matter what."

I told Dr. Robinson, "I have as much trouble reading about the INF treaty as I do reading about Dukakis. My eyes automatically close when I see a story about the missile agreement. Is there any connection between Dukakis and the INF pact?"

"It's part of the same virus family. We know that the eye is a very sensitive instrument and will try to avoid sending boring stories to the brain. It senses when something isn't worth reading about. I think that the best thing for you to do is go home to bed and just accept the fact that you cannot concentrate on a Dukakis story. If you continue to worry about it, you'll only get a headache."

"I'm grateful to you, Doctor. If you hadn't told me what was wrong, I would never have been able to get through the election."

"It's nothing to fret about. I have a similar problem. I go into catatonic shock every time I see a story on the front pages about George Shultz and NATO."

Red Golf

A small item of news from the Reagan-Gorbachev Moscow summit was overlooked by the Western press. Armand Hammer announced through Soviet officials that he is going to build a golf course just outside Moscow. For the first time the Russians will be able to play the sport that has made capitalism what it is today. So revolutionary is the idea that Soviet experts refer to Hammer's proposed golf course as The Eighteen Holes That Shook the World.

I hate to think what will happen to the Communist system once golf makes its inroads.

Decisions now made at Politburo headquarters will be resolved on the people's putting greens. High-ranking members of the party will not be judged by their weaknesses as Soviet administrators, but rather by their handicap at the Moscow Country Club.

Brian Nessim, the top Kremlin sports watcher at Columbia University, predicts that golf will change the entire Communist order. "I am surprised that the Soviets would permit it," Nessim told me. "The Russians haven't played golf since the 1917 Revolution."

"I didn't know they had ever played it."

"Oh, yes. The czar even had a driving range in St. Petersburg, and he made the serfs catch the balls with their teeth. Things were very bad and caddies were beaten with seven-irons by the royal family whenever Rasputin hit into the rough.

Finally, the caddies couldn't take it any more and decided to go out on strike. The czar was furious and ordered his mounted Cossacks to run them down on the fairways. When word leaked out about what the czar had done, the greenskeepers mutinied and that was the beginning of the revolution. No one has swung a golf club in the Soviet Union since."

"So bringing back golf is a giant step for glasnost," I said.

"Gorbachev knows what he is doing. He cannot improve the economy of the country if his managers do not play golf. Everyone is aware that all the deals in an advanced industrial society are made on the golf course. In a consumer-oriented economy it is impossible to have top-flight leaders unless they are able to plot five-year plans in a locker room."

"I knew that golf was essential to a high standard of living, but I didn't know it was that important."

"The sport is what made the U.S. number one. Never forget it was America that invented the golf cart, the greatest advance in transportation in the twentieth century. The game, as the Soviets now realize, is more than just a sport. It's a way of life which gives human beings an opportunity to buy and sell. It's obvious that if the Soviets want to catch up with us they are going to have to construct many golf links around their major cities. This is what the Armand Hammer course is all about."

"Better late than never," I said.

"There are problems. For example, who will get membership in the club and what will it all mean? Whereas the Soviet hierarchy now stands atop Lenin's tomb for all the world to see, in the future we will have to watch how they line up to tee off on the first hole. The nearer they stand to the golf pro, the more importantly they will rate in the Politburo."

"Could you see the day when the American and Soviet presidents meet on a Moscow golf course instead of Red Square?"

211

"Why not? When people drive down a Soviet fairway together, they can't help but want to make a better world. That's why Lenin said: 'A person who chokes in golf, chokes in life.' "

"I didn't know Lenin said that."

"Well, maybe it was Marx. We Soviet experts can never keep them straight."

"Do you believe that they will allow wives of world leaders to play on the Moscow course?"

"I doubt it. I don't think you could ever put Nancy Reagan and Raisa Gorbachev in the same sand trap together."

Abstaining, the Key

Congressman Henry Dogged has just published *Abstaining, the Key to Good Voting.*

As soon as the book came off the presses, the congressman's staff went to work selling it.

"Is this Richard Tissiere, of the High Thermostat Manufacturers Association? This is Chris Pohle, Congressman Dogged's ghostwriter. We wanted you to be the first to know that the congressman's latest book is now in the bookstores, and he is anxious to send you an autographed copy—off the record, it is dynamite. The lobbyist for the Crank Case Oil Workers Union told me, 'Dogged makes Solzhenitsyn look like a hack.' Lawyers for the Television Antenna Manufacturers wrote us, 'Only

Congressman Dogged would have the guts to write about how it feels to sit out an important vote,' and Helen VerStandig just called and said, 'I rarely stay up late to read books about abstentions, but I couldn't put this one down.'

"Mr. Tissiere, Lee Iacocca never had such reviews. What the congressman would like to do is set aside a few copies for you and members of your association. Because the publisher didn't print enough, we can only allot a thousand for you now. But we could always send you more from a second printing. . . .

"Before you hang up, the congressman is having an autograph party next week, and he wanted to make sure that you were invited. . . . It's five hundred dollars per person, but all the money goes to finance the congressman's next book, *Recess, the Congressional Answer to Jet Lag.* It would be nice if you could attend. Besides talking to him about literary matters, you would also have an opportunity to discuss your opposition to Japanese thermostat controls."

"Hello, I want to speak to Walter Witherspoon of the Teflon Workers' Union. . . . Walter, have you seen the blurbs on the congressman's latest book? They're boffo. His colleagues in the House compare it to *War and Peace;* the United Antacid League bulletin says, 'Rarely has a story caught the imagination of so many literati in America.' The National Rifle Association says, 'Dogged opens his book with a bang and hits his target with a bull's-eye.'

"Walter, we're having a prayer breakfast to celebrate the publication and we'd like you to take a table. Martha Jenkins is entertaining and it's going to be an inspiring morning. We're keeping it to a thousand dollars a plate so that the little lobbyists can afford it. But get this, Walter—every person who attends will receive a personally inscribed copy of Dogged's book.

"I know you bought a table last week to Mrs. Dogged's forty-seventh birthday party, but this one is different—it's going to be a literary breakfast. How often do you get to eat scrambled eggs with the author of a great work of art? I wouldn't be surprised if William Styron, Saul Bellow and Tom Wolfe are there.

"Walter, you don't necessarily have to talk about books the whole time. If you want to discuss factory closings with the congressman, he'll do that too. But I think you should be aware of how much pride of ownership Dogged has in his book. He had six of us working on it day and night, for ten months, and he thinks it's the best thing he has ever done. . . . Good, then you will take a table, and you'll order twelve hundred books. Thanks a lot, Walter."

"Hello, give me *The Washington Post* book department, please. . . . I wish to report a best-seller."

The Common Touch

To win the election, George Bush had to persuade the electorate that while he was truly a man of the people, Mike Dukakis was a born elitist.

The Vice President got off to a good start by pointing out that Dukakis attended Harvard, which specializes in boutique foreign policy education, while Bush went to Yale, a poverty-stricken, land-grant school in the heart of the New Haven ghetto. Bush told reporters that Yale has no symbolism associated with it, while Harvard represents elitism of the worst kind.

It was obvious to all that Bush was playing down his upper-class background as a means of persuading the electorate he is really for the little guy.

It's one thing for a candidate to decide what his political strategy is going to be, and another to execute it. So every spare moment they had, Bush's campaign managers briefed the Vice President on how best to demonstrate the common touch.

"Okay, sir, let's start where we left off yesterday. You don't go into a Jewish restaurant and ask for quiche."

"Look, Dan, I know that. I should order a tunafish salad on white bread."

"My name isn't Dan, it's Ted. You ask for a tunafish at the Burning Tree Country Club. In a Jewish delicatessen you ask for a pastrami on rye with sauerkraut and a kosher pickle."

215

"I know that, Artie."

"My name isn't Artie, it's Tom. Why did you order a bacon, lettuce and tomato sandwich from the street vendor who was selling hot dogs, yesterday?"

"I was in the mood for a change. I'm getting tired of hot dogs. Doesn't the man in the street eat anything else?"

"No, and you didn't win too many votes when you had lunch with Army recruits at Fort Dix, and asked them if they missed their mom's key lime pie."

"I just wanted them to think I was one of the boys, Al."

"My name isn't Al, it's Irving. If you insist on wearing that blazer with the New York Yacht Club crest on the pocket, Mr. Vice President, nobody is going to be convinced that you are one of the people. And you can't keep opening Teamster prayer breakfasts by saying, 'Give us this day our daily croissant.' "

"I only did it once, Sam."

"My name is not Sam, it's Gerard. The thrust of the campaign, sir, is to ensure that the American people identify with you. They won't do that if you talk to farmers about the need to subsidize polo matches at Palm Beach."

"I was kidding. I know that farmers have more important things on their minds than polo. But, golly, I have to get their attention somehow."

"Our next stop, Mr. Vice President, is Newark."

"I know Newark. It's not far from Princeton, where they have those neat eating clubs."

"Newark may be located near Princeton, but it is far, far away in every other respect."

"Do they get their elitist ideas from a Harvard boutique?"

"Possibly, but that isn't what is disturbing them at the moment. The city is falling apart. Can you imagine what that must be like?"

"You don't have to be poor to know what it is like to live in Newark, Sidney."

"My name isn't Sidney. It's David Logan the Third."
"Gee whiz. Did your father ever row for Yale at Henley?"

Notes from Russia

Leningrad—In the name of glasnost I was invited to the Soviet Union as part of a "humor" writers' exchange. My host was *Krokodil*, the national Soviet satirical magazine. The thinking behind the exchange was that if the leaders of the Super Powers were willing to talk to each other, then Soviet and American humorists could also forget old wounds and the bitter differences of the past.

I accepted the invitation, but the reader must forgive my stream of consciousness, because they are seeing the notes of a man who, having been warned about the water, brushed his teeth with warm Pepsi-Cola for a week.

There is a great deal going on in Russia under perestroika, which was hotly debated during the Communist Party Congress in Moscow. Like so many Americans who have spent seven days there, I am now an expert on Gorbachev's reforms, and what they mean to the world.

While there is a tremendous effort to liberalize the entire infrastructure of the country, old habits die hard in the USSR.

Let me explain what perestroika is all about: The white hats are the liberals, who are demanding complete change in the

217

way the Soviet system works. The black hats are the conservatives, who want to keep the same laid-back life-style that the Russian people enjoyed under Stalin, and all of his successors. (By the way, their conservatives have no affiliation with the conservatives in this country.)

The reason that the majority of the Soviet people are supporting Gorbachev is they are sick and tired of dancing in Red Square every time a new cement plant is built in Minsk. They have declared that from now on they will celebrate only when a new shipment of Reeboks arrives at the GUM department store in Moscow.

Here is another reason why people want change. For years Natasha has tried to buy a box of soap powder. Every day she faces Anna behind the counter. Anna takes great joy in torturing her by telling Natasha that there is no soap powder. Natasha wants to know why there isn't any, and Anna, an old-line Communist, says it is because America has imperialist designs on Nicaragua.

That response would have been enough for Natasha before perestroika, but now she is not buying it. She tells Anna that she doesn't care what America is doing in Nicaragua. She is going to support Gorbachev because he wants the people to have soap powder, and he will ensure that those who don't deliver will be sweeping the streets in Chernobyl.

So that is what perestroika is all about—a battle over whether Natasha will get soap powder, or Anna will be able to send her kicking and screaming out the door.

I met with writers and humorists in Moscow and Leningrad. They are very happy with perestroika and are anxious to get on with writing books, plays and movies about the bad old days. (Most of them kept notes.) We had frank and open discussions about the present literary scene in both countries. I explained to them that the main advantage American writers have over their Soviet counterparts is that we have a Domino's Pizza delivered to us in less than thirty minutes, or Domino's will take three dollars off the price.

The Soviet writers were not impressed by this information, and one turned to me and said, "We had a similar delivery system under the czar."

The subject everyone agreed upon was that Gorbachev went much too far in abolishing vodka as the national drink. The Russians feel that he acted in haste. As one writer put it, "Perestroika is not well enough established to enable the people to face life in this country completely sober."

Trust, Don't Verify

Leningrad—These are more notes of a man who spent only a week in Russia because he would rather trust than verify what the Soviets are doing.

Traveling first class in the Soviet Union is like traveling fourth class in the Soviet Union.

My tour bus drew up alongside a jammed city bus in Leningrad, and I saw a man with his nose pressed against the window talking to himself. I asked my guide what the man was saying. The guide shrugged his shoulders and said, "He is probably saying that he hopes his wife stood in line and got some sugar today so he can make vodka in the bathtub when he gets home. That way he can forget that he doesn't have a bathtub. But knowing his wife, she'll probably buy cucumbers instead, and if you had to eat cucumbers for three hundred forty-five nights in a row, you would be talking to yourself on a bus, too."

There are certain scenes that stick in your mind when you are traveling. The one that remains most vivid to me took place at Peter the Great's Summer Palace outside of Leningrad, which was almost completely destroyed during World War II and then rebuilt by the Russians. I was walking through one of the great halls talking to Jim Berry, the cartoonist, and Jim Boren, the professional bureaucrat, and his wife Alice, when a group of tourists angrily went "Shshshshh." It turned out that they were German and became furious about the noise we were making because it prevented them from hearing their guide relate how the German Army destroyed Peter's palace.

Food still presents a problem for tourists as well as residents in the Soviet Union. There is a suspicion that all menus are decided by a Food Czar in the Kremlin, and that the exact same meal is served to everyone, four hours after the waiter takes the order. There are no chefs left in Russia. There are just dissidents cooking bad meals while waiting to get their exit visas for Brooklyn.

The only tourists I observed who were able to handle the bad food, the heat, the long waits and abuse from hotel employees were little old American ladies in Nike tennis shoes. No matter how many times they were knocked down, they came up off the mat for another round, thus convincing Gorbachev once and for all that America is not a paper tiger.

Why are such large numbers of tourists fighting to get into the Soviet Union? It's part of glasnost. The Evil Empire has opened its doors, and all nationalities are dying to see what

220

they have been missing. It turns out it is everything they thought it would be—and less. Because automobile production is down, the Soviet Union now has more alternate parking places than any country in the non-Free World. And the good news is that if you are a tourist, you don't have to worry about spending any money in Russia because there is nothing to buy.

But there are some disappointments. In the old days, the KGB followed all foreign visitors. If you were important enough, they would compromise you with a Russian bimbo and then take pictures of the two of you with a hidden camera which were later shown in the first-run movie houses in Samarkand.

Now, however, because there are so many tourists in the country, the KGB has thrown in the towel, and the bimbo who picks you up in a bar is just that, and not a sexy agent provocateur of the second-greatest secret service in the world.

Each person in our group was allowed to make one request of Soviet officials. "Please," I begged, "don't send America any more Russian taxi drivers—at least not until the ones you already sent us learn how to get from Kennedy Airport to Manhattan."

It was a short visit, but very pleasant. The one question we were constantly asked was, "Why do Americans like Gorbachev?" Our answer was simple: "Because he doesn't look like a Communist."

My last act before leaving Mother Russia was to present a carton of cigarettes to one of my Soviet hosts.

"Thank you," he said.

"Don't mention it," I replied. "My government has ordered me to bump off one Russian on every trip."

White-Collar Sentence

I am happy to report that in cases of white-collar crime, justice is being served because these criminals are receiving sentences of community service rather than being sent to jail. This occurs so often that there is now a shortage of jobs for white-collar criminals to perform.

I know, because not a day goes by without someone who has plea-bargained his way out of a prison sentence showing up and volunteering to work for me as part of his punishment.

Only last week a gentleman in a Ralph Lauren double-breasted suit and cashmere sweater, holding a mop in one hand and a squeegee in the other, appeared on my doorstep.

"How do you do, sir," he said. "I am the former president of a Texas savings and loan association, and I embezzled the whole stack from my depositors. I was given a choice of twenty years in prison or doing one thousand hours of community service. I chose the latter and I was wondering if I could wash your car."

"That's very kind of you," I told him. "But we had a convicted felon from one of New York's largest brokerage houses wax our car yesterday. He was working off fifteen hundred hours in order to pay his debt to society."

"Perhaps then," the S&L executive said, "I could clean your windows. I believe I am the only white-collar criminal who does windows."

"I'm sure you do good work. But we don't really need any windows washed today."

The man sounded nervous. "I hate to beg, but if I don't put in five community service hours by the end of the day, the judge will send me to jail. How about letting me shovel snow from your walk?"

"But it isn't snowing."

"The court will never know," he said.

"That's perjury, which probably got you where you are to-day. The object of a sentence like this is rehabilitation so that a person will never commit a nonviolent white-collar crime again."

"Absolutely," he agreed. "But how can I do it if no one will let me perform the work? I am also a trash man—the best in the sixth circuit court."

"We could use someone to handle trash. But you're a white-collar criminal. How do we know you won't come into our home and juggle our household account books while we're not watching?"

"Trust me. Ever since I have had to cut lawns, I realized the folly of putting large sums of other people's money into my own account. Nobody who has ever cleaned toilets in com-munity service goes back to a life of crime again."

"You sound contrite," I admitted. "And I think it only fair that we give you a chance to rehabilitate yourself. But if you try to open so much as one Swiss bank account while you work for us, I will see that you never perform an hour of community service again."

"Yes, sir. Thank you—oh, thank you. If you let me take out your trash, I will have only eight hundred ninety-six more hours to complete."

"After you have finished with the trash, my neighbor, Rob-ert Parrish, needs his gutters painted."

"I don't do gutters. But I have a friend putting in seven hundred hours for illegal computer entry, and he's a whiz with a paintbrush. He loves it so much that when his sentence is up, he is thinking of asking the judge if he can stay on marking lines down the middle of the road."

I said, "What I like about you white-collar criminals is that once you're caught, you have a good attitude. You seem eager to carry out your sentence."

"Community service may not be the same as working for Merrill Lynch," he replied, "but it beats the hell out of making license plates in the Big House."

A Lawyer's Field Day

Not long ago, I was nearly run over by a Maserati. The driver was a friend we all call Louie the Lawyer.

He had a huge grin on his face. "We're back in business," he said, wiping the windshield with a $100 bill.

"I didn't think lawyers were ever out of business," I answered.

"This is really big. We're talking about a scandal that could reach to the very top of the teapot on the Pentagon. We're looking down the road at hundreds of indictments of officers, civilians and defense contractors. This is a legal bonanza the likes of which Washington has never seen."

"How did it happen?"

"I guess we just got lucky."

"I'm not talking about you," I told Louie. "I mean how could so many people have committed so many criminal acts under the watchful eye of the vigilant Secretary of Defense?"

"Nobody committed any criminal acts, at least none that can be proved. That's the reason they all need lawyers. Our job is to prove their innocence, and if we can't do that, then we will at least plea-bargain with the government to keep them out of jail. Because it involves a great deal of work, it means we have to burn a lot of oil late into the night. But that's what we get paid for."

"How can you be sure that you will get paid?"

"We have to assume that all the clients who are pleading innocent have put away enough money from their activities to ensure that their lawyers' fees will be covered in case they're caught."

"I bet you there are some who didn't," I said.

"Then they will have to go to jail as common criminals. Lawyers have no use for indicted clients who don't think ahead."

"According to the newspapers, the players in the Pentagon scandal are defense officials, consultants and contractors. Is there anybody you prefer to represent more than the others?"

"The defense contractors always come first in my book. They eat in the best restaurants, and the government rarely has the heart to send them to jail. White-collar tradition dictates that the best way to make them atone for their sins is to have them pay a fine. After contractors, I like to defend consultants because I can always ask the Justice Department to allow them to rat on clients in exchange for a suspended sentence."

"I didn't know that consultants ratted on their own clients."

"It's not in the contract, but they'll do it if they have to. The last group, government employees, have to be examined with caution before I'll take them on as clients. I don't mind defending an assistant secretary of the Navy, or some general in charge of engine contracts for the Air Force, but I'm not going to help out an Army clerk who typed up the bids sent to competing contractors."

"Why not?"

"Because when it's all over, he's the guy they'll throw the book at. It doesn't matter how I plead him, they won't let him off because they want to teach all Pentagon clerks a lesson."

"Well, at least you have enough work to keep busy."

Louie said, "I thought last year was a vintage one for lawyers, but this summer is going to break all records. We've doubled our office space, and because of the number of indictments our lawyers have agreed to make house calls."

"So this is your way of saying how happy all the lawyers in Washington are these days."

"Greed has been good to us."

Up in Arms

Every night on the television you see people shooting at each other with everything from naval guns to rubber bullets. The screen is full of tanks smashing through villages and tear gas wafting on campuses. Whether it is the streets of Beirut or Northern Ireland, the entire world now appears to be an armed camp.

Nobody ever takes the time to ask, "Where is all this stuff coming from?"

The big surprise is not that it is so easy to buy equipment to start an insurrection, but rather that the people in sales don't even know whom they're selling the arms to.

Feaster, an arms merchant prince, said, "I love this crazy business. You never run out of surprises."

"What kind of surprises?" I asked.

"Look at this newspaper. The Israelis are helping the Chinese develop a new and improved Silkworm missile. As soon as it is tested, the Chinese are going to sell it to Saudi Arabia, and the Saudis will probably use it against the Israelis."

"Do the Israelis know this?" I gasped.

"Sure, but that's what makes the arms business so much fun. Take Iran. The country is the enemy of everyone in the world, and at the same time everybody's best arms customer. So what are they doing right now? The Iranians are buying weapons from France to sink ships belonging to the Western alliance, which France supports. Meanwhile, France is selling missiles to Iraq to sink Iranian ships.

"I guess you could lose your mind if you tried to keep track of whose side anyone is on in the armaments business."

"The Iraqis used the missiles they bought from France to hit a U.S. Navy ship despite the fact that the U.S. is helping Iraq in its war with Iran."

"I expect terrorists are big customers of arms dealers."

"The best. And they're getting bigger all the time. For a while they just bought the stray case of machine guns here, and a gross of hand grenades there. But now they're really upgrading their matériel and ordering designer weapons. As a result they have to be treated with respect."

"Do you impose any restrictions on what you sell terrorists?"

"No, but we ask them to try and avoid using the stuff in their own country. There is nothing wrong with selling bazookas to the Japanese Red Brigade to shoot down planes in Rome, while the Italian terrorists blow up an air terminal in Tokyo. It is what is known as terrorist reciprocation."

"Every country seems to be selling arms to the people it considers its enemies."

"That's what makes the business profitable for us. The reason weapons are so plentiful is that when we have orders from both sides, we can provide them so much more cheaply. Take Lebanon for example. There isn't a group in the entire country that won't buy everything we can supply. Every car bomb in Beirut has our name on it."

"And you don't feel guilty that you are playing a small part in fanning the flames of war?"

"No. We're for peace. The other day a man from Lebanon came into the store and wanted dynamite, detonators and a Volkswagen to blow up the headquarters of a medieval church. As I was wrapping the package, I happened to mention that that particular faction had purchased one thousand mortars just the day before. He thanked me and bought a tank to knock out their mortars. If I hadn't brought this up, someone in Beirut might have gotten hurt. So we do a lot of good in this business. Unfortunately, no one ever hears about it, mainly because arms dealers prefer to keep their good deeds to themselves."

One Party for All

When the Founding Fathers met in Philadelphia to form a more perfect union, they didn't know how to do it.

"We have to select a king or an emperor or somebody like that to head up the country," a delegate from Delaware said.

"No," said the speaker from New Jersey, "we should have a president who will answer to the people and can only be in office for four years at a time. He must be a person who worries about the homeless and the poor and a balanced budget. He has to be a friend of business, but most of all he has to be concerned about the colorization of black-and-white motion pictures."

"That's all well and good," the delegate from Rhode Island said, "but how do we select this president or whatever you are going to call him?"

The delegate from New York suggested, "I think we should hold political conventions where the candidates can be anointed by their respective political parties. For example, the

230

Democrats could hold one in Atlanta, Georgia, and the Republicans could have theirs in New Orleans, Louisiana."

"Point of order," the delegate from South Carolina yelled. "Louisiana will not be part of the United States for many years."

"Well, then, that's the Republicans' problem," the delegate from New York said.

The Georgia delegate rose to his feet. "Can we serve peach daiquiris on the floor of the convention?"

"Of course you can," the Pennsylvania delegate replied.

"How can you have a political convention without peach daiquiris?"

The Georgia delegate added, "I promise you Atlanta will provide one cocktail party for each delegate who comes to the convention. And we'll even throw in valet parking for Jesse Jackson."

"If we select the leader of the country this way, will there be a lot of hospitality suites where lobbyists can entertain their elected representatives?" the delegate from Virginia asked.

"We have already put that in the Constitution," the Maryland delegate pointed out. "You can't have an honest, dignified convention without free liquor and lots of fat cats."

"Will the band at the convention be permitted to play 'Dixie'?" the man from Georgia wanted to know.

"They will be permitted to play it two hundred twelve times," the man from Maryland replied.

"Gentlemen," the delegate from Georgia said, "I am authorized by my state to accept the idea of a presidential convention as a method of selecting the leader of our nation, and we promise to throw in three hundred seven more dinner parties than we originally agreed upon."

"What about the Republican convention?" the delegate from New Jersey inquired.

The man from New York replied, "I suggest we buy Louisiana right now so that it will be legal for the Republicans to hold their convention there."

To save the Union, it was so voted.

Then the delegate from Massachusetts said, "It is agreed that forevermore this is the way we will select our presidents."

The delegate from Connecticut concluded, "We now have the presidential selection process in great shape. All we have to do is get approval from the three TV networks."

Fair Is Fair

"Daddy, can we watch baseball on TV?"

"That's a good idea. You'll learn fairness and sportsmanship from it."

"Daddy, why is the manager jumping up and down and waving his arms in front of the home plate?"

"Because he thought his man was safe when the umpire called him out. The manager is very angry, and well he might be."

"Look, Daddy, the manager is butting the umpire in the stomach with his head. Is he allowed to do that?"

"The manager was provoked, and while he's not supposed to butt an umpire, he just can't stand there while the ump

232

calls one of his players out at home plate. Umpires have been getting away with murder lately and somebody needs to say to them, 'Enough is enough. If you can't call the game right, you have to expect to get hurt.' "

"Will the official change his mind after he's taken so much punishment?"

"No. And that makes the manager hopping mad. It doesn't matter what kind of case the he makes, the ump will just stand there and shake his head. That is why for a baseball manager life is so unfair."

"Why have umpires if baseball managers are always getting mad at them?"

"It's an old tradition and no one wants to be the first to break with it. Most fans hate officials and if they had their druthers, they would keep them out of the ball park."

"Why is the umpire pointing towards the tunnel?"

"Because he's kicking the manager out of the game for ramming him in the stomach. Since umpires get to wear shiny black suits they think they can send managers to the showers anytime they feel like it."

"The manager doesn't seem to want to go."

"Of course he doesn't. No one likes to be sent to the locker room in the middle of a game. But do you think the ump cares? Nosirree. An official will throw someone out of the game these days for nothing more than having been called an illegitimate child."

"Why doesn't the umpire allow the manager to explain his side of the story?"

"Well, if the manager told his side of the story, the umpire might have to reverse himself in front of everyone in the park. It would be a public humiliation. Also, umpires hate managers because they make more money.

"Baseball is not the only sport being ruined by officials. Look at hockey. A player can't even hit someone in the stands with a hockey stick without a referee making a federal case out of it. And basketball is no better. All a coach has to do is throw a chair across a basketball court at the opposition's cheerleader, and some stuffed-shirt referee will be all over him for unsportsmanlike conduct.

"Tennis used to be a gentlemen's game until every linesman started picking on John McEnroe for no reason at all. Now they won't even let him open his trap without fining him. That's what's wrong with sports today. No one is free to do what he wants anymore."

"Do you think this baseball game will ever start again?"

"It's hard to tell. I believe the manager is demanding an apology, and that could take a little time."

"The fans look like they are on the manager's side."

"Why shouldn't they be? The umpire is lucky they haven't lynched him yet. Mark my words, the officials are trying to gain control of the game so they can appear in TV commercials. It's no wonder the managers feel the cards are stacked against them. Any umpire can send a manager to the showers, while the only defense the poor, helpless baseball managers have is to kick sand in the umpire's face."

Mike & Jesse

The story of how Michael Dukakis and Jesse Jackson settled their differences finally leaked out. This is what happened, according to sources who were close to the scene.

Members of the Dukakis staff sat down with Jackson at a round table, not because Dukakis put any significance in this shape, but because he found that it was cheaper.

The Dukakis man spoke first. "Jesse, we're ready to deal and make up for any embarrassment we have caused you. What do you want?"

"Nothing. I'm just happy to serve my party as a simple worker in the fields."

"You're a good man, Jesse Jackson."

"On the other hand," Jesse said, "if you expect me to campaign for you I would like a DC-10 for myself and my staff."

"Jesse, no one deserves his own plane more than you do. If we give you a DC-10, will you bury the hatchet?"

"No, there is more," Jesse continued. "I want my own TV show on prime time, and if Dukakis is elected, I get to give the state of the union address to Congress."

"No problem with that."

"I would also like to use the White House tennis court tomorrow."

"Jesse, we can't ask President Reagan to let you use the White House courts."

Jesse said, "I knew you people weren't serious about wanting to make up with me. Okay, I have another demand. When Dukakis meets with Gorbachev, I get to be in the picture."

"Sure, Jesse. It will be just the three of you."

"But I don't want Bentsen in the picture because he took my job. I could have been a contender if it hadn't been for him."

"That's why we're trying to make it up to you. But this pact requires you to be nice not only to Dukakis but also to Bentsen."

"If that's the case, I'm going to up my demands. I'm not making an agreement unless I get a stretch limousine to take me to the Atlanta airport."

"We can't agree to that. Mike Dukakis goes to and from the airport on a city bus, and he would have a fit if he knew he was paying for your limo."

"You owe me a lot because you didn't inform me when Dukakis chose his VP."

"Jesse, we have a proposal to make it up to you. Suppose we offered you the second spot on the ticket?"

"You just selected Bentsen. How are you going to put me on the ticket?"

"We're not talking about our ticket. We're talking about George Bush's ticket. He's still looking for a running mate, and you would make a fine candidate."

"Why would George want me on his ticket?"

"Because you've proved yourself to be a vote-getter and an electrifying speaker. You could tear down the house in New Orleans if George announced you as his running mate. Don't forget—it's Dole, Jack Kemp or you. You're by far the best man."

"I don't want to be Bush's running mate."

"Then what *do* you want?"

Jackson replied, "I'll shut up if you give me Dukakis's snowblower."

Wish You Were Here

At last—the vacation is about to begin. The summer homes have been reopened, the tennis courts swept, the fish are jumping, and the voice of the turtle can be heard in the land.

Zeigfrass entered the kitchen at eight A.M.

"Shall we jog through the woods and sing with the birds?" I asked him.

"We can't," he replied. "I just stopped by to take you to a meeting of 'Save the Bluefish.' "

"I didn't know they were endangered."

"They're not," he said. "But somebody has to save them anyway. People are pulling them out of the sound as if there were no tomorrow."

"When will the meeting be over?"

"About ten o'clock."

"Good, then we'll play some tennis."

"We can't. At ten there's a demonstration in front of the town hall to protest the zoning commission's decision to allow thirty townhouses to be built on the waterfront. We expect you to be there."

"Lunch," I said. "I'm free to go to lunch at the Black Dog Tavern with my children, aren't I?'

Zeigfrass looked at his list. "No. We're having a strategy meeting with our lawyer to see how we can limit the rate of growth in East Chop. He's going to tell us how to tie the developers up in knots."

"I know I shouldn't ask this, but how am I fixed for the afternoon?"

"At two o'clock I've got you down for an anti-apartheid demonstration in front of a South African guy's summer home."

"What a coincidence. That's exactly when I was going to the beach. What happens at three?"

"We're raising money for a boys' club at the Old Whaler's Episcopal Church. Then we go over to the sewage disposal plant and block the entrance gate with our bodies."

"Will I be home for dinner?"

"If you don't get arrested you will. You know there is a potluck dinner at the American Legion for the Order of the Sisters of Massachusetts tonight?"

"No one told me," I said. "Hey look, I only have a couple of weeks here, and while I am sympathetic to all your causes, you've got me doing just what I do at home, only more so."

"You can go sailing or play golf if you want to," Zeigfrass said, "but that isn't what vacations are all about. If you can't be counted when we're trying to save the environment, then why don't you just go snorkeling and forget about the world you inhabit."

"I'm all for the environment, but if I spend my whole time protecting it, when do I get to enjoy it?"

"I never thought I would hear you say that you would rather ride the waves than save an osprey from extinction."

"I didn't say that," I protested.

"You said something almost like it," Zeigfrass retorted. "Look, if you want to have a good time on your vacation, that's your business, but you're the one who will have to answer to your grandchildren forty years from today."

"You're right. Why would I want to have a good time when there is so much work left to do? I'm willing to help out. The ocean will always be there, if not during my time here—then somebody else's."

Zeigfrass handed me a bridge table.

"What am I supposed to do with this?"

"We're going down to Main Street to collect signatures."

"What for?"

"I haven't decided yet."

He's Out to Lunch

So many readers ask, "What do people in Washington do all day long?" Believe it or not, we are no different from super-achievers in other parts of the country.

Most of the time we make telephone calls, leave messages and then wait for someone to return them. We measure our importance by how long it takes for a person to get back to us.

Because of this, many Washingtonians have become experts on the smokescreen messages the secretaries are sending out when we call.

Here's one that is heard frequently. I phone and give my name. I am put on hold, there is a pause of about forty-five seconds, and then the secretary returns and says, "He's not at his desk right now." This makes me wonder. How far is her desk from the boss's desk for the secretary to take forty-five seconds to discover he is not there. Once in a while, when I lose my temper, I say, "Well, if he's not at his desk would you look and see if he is hanging outside the window?"

Many of the people I telephone are "in a meeting." Sometimes I want to know what kind of meeting so I ask, "Is it a Cabinet meeting, an executive meeting, or a bowling team meeting?"

"What difference does it make?"

"I'd like to speak to him, and the only meeting I wouldn't want to interrupt is the one with the bowling team."

The excuse that always bothers me is, "Mr. Dominick is tied up at the moment." An image immediately comes to mind of Dominick tied to a chair with a gag over his mouth, listening to an IBM saleswoman trying to convince him to buy a new personal computer.

Another notorious excuse for not talking to me is, "Mr. Califano is out to lunch." What's wrong with this message is that my call is at nine-thirty in the morning. So I ask the secretary to have him get back to me before dinner as I have a two o'clock dental appointment.

I have a terrible problem with being rejected on the phone. My fears run amok when I call someone and he won't talk to me, although I am certain he's there. In my mind I not only see him shaking his head at his secretary, indicating "no, no," but I also see his face breaking into a wide grin while he is doing it.

As the day goes on I keep imagining a large pile of pink slips on Califano's desk, and the one with my name on it is at the bottom. The worst part is that if I have to wait more than a few hours for the call to be returned, I usually forget what I telephoned about in the first place.

The most painful blow of all is when one's children don't call back.

I leave a message on my daughter's answering machine and days go by, maybe weeks, until she telephones.

"Why didn't you get back to me?" I ask.

"I only listened to my messages this morning."

"Suppose it had been important?"

"Why are you calling if it isn't important?"

In Washington, our livelihoods and our self-respect are hooked up to the phone. It is an instrument that can either bring much happiness or destroy a fragile ego overnight.

The only way to avoid letting the telephone call get you down is to make a game of it. I keep score. If someone calls me back within the hour, I give myself ten points; four hours, six points; eight hours, three points. If a person doesn't return my call within twenty-four hours, I deduct fifteen points. At the end of the day I add it all up. If I have accumulated more points than I have lost, I figure I'm still someone in Washington who has to be reckoned with.

Shrinking
the Campaign Field

Some years ago I did a slide show on Watergate. It started with a photo of Thomas Eagleton. The question posed was, "Do we want a vice president who has been treated for a mental disorder or . . . (slide of Spiro Agnew) one who hasn't?"

The issue arose again when Michael Dukakis was accused by the LaRouche people of having sought psychiatric help for depression. President Reagan, the Great Communicator, said he did not want to comment about an invalid, thus proving once again that it isn't safe for the President to answer questions from the press without his three-by-five cue cards.

Meanwhile, back at Dukakis headquarters, they immediately put the candidate's doctor on live television to deny the charges. According to him, Dukakis had never sought any medical help for any mental problem.

The country breathed a sigh of relief.

That is, everyone but Starkist. "I would trust someone who had psychiatric consultation before I would trust a person who says he never needed it."

"I don't think you're right," I said. "If a person is in therapy, that means he has had personal problems, and presidents should never be perceived as having any."

"But," said Starkist, "if he did have problems and refused

to see a doctor, we could be in a lot more trouble than we are now. We have had many presidents who would have been better off if they had gone to a shrink."

"Such as?"

"Richard Nixon for one. You know he suffered from paranoia while he was in the White House. He thought everyone under twenty-five was out to get him."

"Everybody who lives in the White House has paranoia. You don't need medical help for that," I said.

"According to Henry Kissinger, Nixon talked to the pictures on the wall. Don't you think a doctor could have helped him with that?" Starkist asked.

"Maybe, but had Nixon gone to a psychiatrist he might have destroyed his political career," I pointed out. "The American people will accept anything except a president who seeks out a doctor when he gets depressed."

"It might have helped Lyndon Baines Johnson. He was down a lot when the Vietnam War wasn't going his way," Starkist said.

I replied, "Lyndon would never have gone to a shrink because he wouldn't have been able to display his head on television as he did the scar on his belly."

"That's not the point," Starkist said. "Americans are too quick to breathe a sigh of relief when they hear a candidate has never been to a psychiatrist. What they should realize is just because he has never gone to one doesn't mean he doesn't need one. I believe that rather than making therapy out to be something bad, it should be looked on as profile in courage. Every candidate should be assigned a psychiatrist at the moment he is given his Secret Service detail. That way he can be observed and protected at the same time," Starkist said.

"What a terrible idea. I don't think we should be required to vote for one candidate because he is less depressed than the other. I believe that people are more sanguine this morning knowing Dukakis has never sat in a head doctor's waiting room."

Starkist responded, "Nobody wants a leader who isn't perfect, but will you grant that someone has to be slightly off-the-wall to run for President of the United States?"

I said, "Next you're going to tell me that any president who calls Dukakis an invalid and thinks it's funny should have his head examined."

The Good Republican

At the 1988 Republican Convention there were some winners and some losers. Humbold Hoover, a black Republican delegate, turned out to be one of the biggest winners.

Humbold and I had breakfast in the same coffee shop every morning, so I had a chance to talk to him about his success.

"You stole the show," I told him.

"I just lucked out," he said modestly. "The networks needed a black delegate to interview, and at a Republican convention there aren't that many to choose from."

"Were you the only black in the hall?"

"There may have been others, but I didn't see them. Then again, I was sitting up front."

"How did you manage to get that seat?" I asked.

"Well, when I came in and presented my credentials, they put me in the balcony, but then as soon as I told them I was black, they got all excited and had the sergeant at arms escort me to row A. They also assigned Jeane Kirkpatrick the job of ensuring that I had enough funny hats and noisemakers. I thought I was in heaven."

"So tell me, how did the networks discover you?"

"I was just sitting there waving an American flag at Jack Kemp when Connie Chung came up to me and said, 'What do black people think about Quayle for vice president?' I said that most blacks consider him an asset to the ticket since he is viewed as a tireless supporter of Star Wars, a strong opponent of abortion and a man who believes that prayer should be back in our schools. I would have elaborated on this but Walter Cronkite shoved Connie aside and wanted to know how black people feel about a balanced budget. I told him that we have always been in favor of a balanced budget provided it guarantees people's right to take the Pledge of Allegiance whenever they want to.

"After Cronkite left, George Will shoved a microphone in my mouth and asked me if my black brothers are in favor of higher taxes. I said we could go either way, but what we're really opposed to is manufacturers having to give sixty days' notice before they shut down a plant."

"It was probably the only good interview George had all night," I added.

Hoover continued, "Once the word got out that the Republicans had a black delegate in the hall, it wasn't long before I was surrounded by so many TV cameras that they had to put a red velvet rope around me. Sam Donaldson was forced to stand on a chair to yell his questions."

"What did Sam ask you?"

"He shouted, 'Are black voters going to win one for the Gipper?' I told him that we certainly will in spite of Jesse Jackson and all of the free spenders who keep fumbling the ball."

"Did you ever think that Dan Rather might come down from his booth and speak to you personally?"

"Just after George Bush finished his acceptance speech, there was a moment when Dan started to head my way. I know he was dying to ask me what the black voters thought about Bush's remarks on arms limitations talks, but at the last moment he sent Diane Sawyer to talk to me instead."

"What was Diane's question?"

Hoover said, "She wanted to know if black voters can be counted on to deliver the big cities to the Republicans. I told her that there is no doubt in my mind that once black people get to know the children of both Bush and Quayle, they will desert the Democratic Party in droves."

"What did the Republican leaders do when they heard you say that?"

"The minute Phyllis Schlafly heard me come out for Quayle she brought me a free hot dog."

Small Talk

For a while, all you heard at parties was talk about Dan Quayle. Everyone seemed to have an opinion and I took note of some of them.

"I don't care if you went to the Mekong Delta, the Indiana National Guard or Canada during the Vietnam War—as long as you went somewhere."

"I think Quayle is lucky to have a dad who would use influence to get him into the service of his choice. Most fathers would make their sons do it on their own."

"The National Guard plays an important role in wartime, especially if you have an ugly strike in Indiana."

"The press is making a big deal of Quayle's lousy record in college. But everyone knows that you don't need a Ph.D. to be Vice President of the United States."

"If Clint Eastwood had spent six years in the National Guard in Indiana he never would have had to look for movie material again."

"Quayle may not have had a great senatorial record, but don't forget he is awfully young to vote."

"Sure, Quayle had lousy grades when he was admitted to law school. But there is nothing wrong with that. He's running for vice president—not county judge."

"Bush knew he had the right running mate when he asked Dan Quayle if he had ever burned an American flag, and Quayle said he hadn't."

"Another plus of having Quayle a heartbeat away from the presidency is that if he ever has trouble with Iran he can call up his father and mother and ask them to fix it."

"Dan Quayle is getting a bad rap on his military service. If he had known someday that he was going to be the vice-presidential candidate, he would have paid his own way to Vietnam to participate in the Tet Offensive."

"Dan is strong on Star Wars and weak on veterans' benefits, but that doesn't mean he fooled around with Paula Parkinson."

"The question of influence should not be a political issue. You don't put down people just because they have a bigger Rolodex than you do."

"The trouble with George Bush is that he is taking all the attention of the campaign away from Danny. It's the vice-presidential campaign that deserves the people's attention."

"I don't know what it takes to qualify for Vice President of the United States, but I believe once you nominate that person no one has the right to embarrass him with a lot of personal questions."

"Bush could have chosen anyone he wanted for his running mate. The fact he picked Quayle without checking him out means Bush is his own man."

"Quayle may not make the greatest VP, but at least he'll look great at a state funeral."

"I'm glad the brouhaha on Quayle broke because it brings the entire presidential race down to the lowest level where it belongs."

"The reason I would trust Dan Quayle to put his finger on the button in the Oval Office is that he is probably one of the best golfers in Washington."

Zap, I Gotcha

The networks are terribly worried about losing their audiences these days. Between the writers' strikes, cable television, VCR machines and independent programming, the American people are having an entertainment orgy and driving the television moguls up the wall.

Probably what affects TV more than anything else is the remote-control clicker, which has put all programming decisions into the hands of the viewer.

Before its arrival, most people, particularly men, were too lazy to get out of their chairs or beds to change the channel. Sometimes the set stayed on the same station for weeks. But those days are gone, now that some genius has invented the remote-control device which makes it possible for every man, woman and child in this country to zap any show off the air.

The greatest remote artist I know is Frederick Steinmetz, who has tuned out more commercials and situation comedies than any zapper within the continental United States.

His living room wall is covered with five hundred different TV remote-control models which were handcrafted by a Japanese Sony dealer in Osaka, New Jersey.

Fred showed me the calluses he has developed over the years from clicking programs.

How does he operate?

For starters, he practices on the morning shows.

"I usually begin by zapping Bryant Gumbel and Jane Pauley off the face of the earth."

"Any particular reason?" I asked.

He tried to reassure me. "It's nothing personal—I just don't like Willard Scott wishing hundred-year-old people 'Happy Birthday.' When I tune out the 'Today' show, I try to catch thirty seconds of 'Good Morning America,' and from there it's just an easy click to the 'CBS Morning Show.' "

"Do you watch the 'Morning Show' for very long?"

"That would be a waste," he responded. "I switch it off as soon as the commercials come on. By then my fingers are limbered up, and I can start working on the cable stations. They're really the pits in the morning, although some times I get lucky and hit an old 'I Love Lucy' or 'Barney Miller' segment."

"When you find something like that, do you stay with it?"

"Why would I want to stick with one show when I have twenty-six channels to choose from? The reason I became a zapper in the first place was because no matter what program I had on, I was always sure that the grass was greener on the next channel. Once you start clicking, you have to keep doing it to assure yourself that you are not missing anything. Let me give you an example: It's six-thirty P.M., so I tune into Dan Rather and the evening news. Okay, so he starts talking about Burma. Good night, Dan. Now I click over to Brokaw. He's doing an exclusive interview with Lloyd Bentsen. I say to Brokaw, 'I'm sending you to the ozone.' "

"So that leaves Jennings on ABC as your only hope."

"Are you kidding? I have CNN, C-Span and ESPN for my news."

"ESPN is not news," I corrected him. "It's all sports."

"Right. And if they're showing Oklahoma playing a 1967 football game against Texas, I'm going to zap Jennings even if he makes me Person of the Week. What you have to understand is that we zappers are in charge of programming now, and they can no longer make us watch anything we don't want to."

"You play tough, Steinmetz."

"Somebody has to make the life-and-death decisions in TV programming and I'd rather it be me than Larry Tisch."

Dirty Pool

You never see them, but the key men in the presidential race are the members of the elite Special Scurrilous Presidential Campaign SWAT Teams. They are stashed away in the bunkers of the candidate's headquarters and their job is to disseminate wild and hairy stories about the opposition. I managed to get into a command post to find out how they operate. There was one man in charge of five political yuppies sitting around a table under an electoral map of the United States.

The man on the phone yelled out, "Upstairs wants us to attack what's-his-name for his soft stance on crime. What can we come up with?"

One of the workers suggested, "How about our candidate saying that his opponent is not only soft on crime but he is the Hillside Serial Killer of Cape Cod?"

"It is dirty enough," someone agreed. "But upstairs will never let our guy say that."

"All the better. We'll insert it in a TV commercial, and then our candidate will insist he had nothing to do with the charge and deplores that kind of political tactic in a presidential campaign. It's a twofer. We get to play dirty and he gets to play clean with the same story."

"Good going," the man in charge said. "Now we have to do something to dramatize the opposition's stance on defense."

"I've been working on that one," said Red Suspenders. "We will say the reason what's-his-name is weak on defense is that he has refused to recite the Pledge of Allegiance to the flag for the last twenty years."

"We better trial-balloon it, just in case people don't buy it. Anything happen on us maintaining that what's-his-name burned the American flag during the war in Grenada?"

"We're putting out a story that it was not the candidate but his mother who did it."

"Will they believe it?"

"Of course they will. How could anybody make up something like that?"

"Has anyone dealt with the 'God Bless America' issue?"

"We're going to leak a story that if he is elected president, what's-his-name has promised the ACLU that he will ban the song from all three networks, even if he has to stack the Supreme Court to do it."

"That should play in Orange County. Our man will gladly insert it into his speech without asking us where we got the information."

"We can get more votes by accusing their side of a 'God Bless America' ban than explaining how we're going to balance the budget."

"Speaking of votes, the boss wants us to give him something as good as the stuff we put on what's-his-name's mental health," Striped Tie said.

"Tell him we're working on it. What do you guys think of this? We say that if Shorty is elected, anybody over five-feet-

252

one will lose his right to bear arms. That will scare the hell out of Texas."

"That's a little far-fetched. Who is going to believe it?"

"The people. They won't believe it the first time we say it, and they won't believe the second time we say it—but the third time around they will eat the whole thing."

"How can you be so sure?"

"When I went to college, I studied Advanced Jingoism 104."

The Electrician Cometh!

I was playing tennis when the phone call came from my wife. She sounded excited as she said, "The electrician is coming in an hour."

"He's been saying that for a month. Why should we believe him now?"

"Because he initiated the call. I just know he'll be here. It's a feeling I have."

When I arrived at the house, my wife was dusting the furniture and rearranging the flowers. "You had better shower," she told me, "and wear a shirt and tie. I don't want him to think we can't afford his services."

"But he's only an electrician," I protested.

"He's more than that. He is the key to our entire fuse-box problem. Something has been blowing every electrical appliance in this house, and I'm not going to take it anymore."

I showered and put on my best dress shirt and Italian silk tie, plus the blue blazer which I save for British royalty and American workmen.

My wife was chilling a bottle of wine. "I hope he likes Pouilly-Fuissé."

"He wouldn't be in the wall socket business if he didn't," I reassured her. "I still don't know why we couldn't get another electrician when he didn't show up last month."

"It's impossible to find one because they're a dying breed. Most electricians won't even allow you to leave a message on their telephone answering machines." She powdered her nose and sighed, "I hope he likes us."

"What difference does it make if he likes us or not?" I asked.

"If he doesn't like us, he'll walk out the door and put a curse on our fuse box forever. Now, as soon as he arrives, take him into the living room and make him comfortable. I've put pictures of the children out on all the tables. I want him to realize how important the family is to us just in case he's a Republican. Now, above all, do not discuss politics with him. I don't want to lose an electrician over the prayer-in-school issue."

"What do you discuss with an electrician?" I wanted to know.

"Benjamin Franklin. After all, he was the father of electricity. Then there was Thomas Edison. Electricians think Edison was the cat's meow."

"I could talk to him about the stock market," I suggested. "I understand that anyone who is a licensed electrician automatically becomes one of the Fortune 500."

My wife said, "I'm a nervous wreck. It's such a long time since I met a man who works with pliers."

"Be yourself," I told her. "An electrician puts on his pants one leg at a time, just like a plumber."

"I'd feel so much better if I had cleaned the cellar."

"You're worrying unnecessarily. After he knocks off the bottle of Pouilly-Fuissé, I wouldn't be surprised if he goes straight down the stairs, tears the fuse box off the wall and finds the short in no time."

"I only hope you're right. I suppose we should consider it an honor that he would even stop at our house," she said. "Do you think we should call the Larrimores? They have been waiting for an electrician for four years."

"That would be rubbing it in. Besides, I'm not sure they'd know how to behave in front of a licensed electrician. It wouldn't surprise me if they fell to their knees and made damn fools of themselves."

The Reagan Democrat

Almost everyone is predicting a very close presidential election result with maybe 48 percent for Bush and 48 percent for Dukakis, with the remaining Reagan Democrats deciding the outcome.

With this in mind, both sides are trying to win over the undecided voters.

Freddy Dumstart, who is listed in both the Dukakis and Bush computers as one of the key "don't-know" voters, is therefore receiving tremendous attention from each camp.

Three of Dukakis's people called on Dumstart the other day.

"What do you want with me?" Freddy asked.

"We are appealing to all the Reagan Democrats to come home," one of the Dukakis men said. "We wish you to know how much we love you and want to tell you what you personally mean to the governor and his dear wife, Kitty."

"That's nice to hear, but I still haven't made up my mind about who I'm going to vote for," Dumstart said.

"Can the governor take you to dinner at an extremely good ethnic restaurant and explain his position on agricultural price supports?"

"I have already eaten at a good ethnic restaurant with the Bush people and am not really interested in that particular issue."

"Then maybe you would like to attend a night football game in Texas with Lloyd Bentsen while he tells you what a squirt

Senator Quayle really is. Fred, we want you on our team now."

"You're barking up the wrong tree, gentlemen. I am not going to make up my mind this early in the game."

"Why not?"

"Because as soon as I announce how I intend to vote, no one will take me to dinner anymore. Look at the millions of voters already lined up for Dukakis. You know you have them in your pocket, so you don't even care if they exist or not. All your time and energy is devoted to people like me who are still on the fence."

"Would you consider a tour of Boston Harbor in the governor's pollution-free launch? Surely that would be a wonderful way for you and your family to get to know him."

"I'm not giving in. Many years back I voted the straight Democratic ticket and LBJ wouldn't even accept my calls. Then eight years ago I announced that I was an Independent, and rather than vote along party lines, I would choose the best man for the job. That decision changed my life. The pollsters called me the most sought-after person in the presidential elections."

One of Dukakis's people said, "I think you exaggerate your own importance. We couldn't care less if you vote for our candidate or not. How would you like to be Secretary of the Treasury?"

Freddy answered, "The Bush people offered me head of the CIA."

"They have no intention of delivering on that, Mr. Dumstart. We're not asking you to give us your vote without proof that you would be backing the right man. Governor Dukakis is prepared to show you a slide presentation on the miracles he has performed for the state of Massachusetts."

"I'd rather hear the dirt he has on Bush. George was over

at the house last night and you can't believe what he told me about Dukakis's behavior when the Japanese bombed Pearl Harbor on April Fool's Day. I'm one of those voters who always prefers the candidate who takes the low road."

"Look, it's your vote and you can do anything you want with it."

"Then why are you here?"

"To prevent you from making a fool of yourself. The country needs leadership as it has never needed it before. When you pull that lever all America will face either four years of pain or four years of low-interest rates from sea to shining sea."

"I'll give you my answer on election day."

"It may be too late. We're holding a seat on the Supreme Court for you, but if you don't decide right away we'll have to give it to another fence-sitter from Hoboken, New Jersey."

Cross My Heart

I recently visited an arms factory where George Bush was expected later in the day.

"Does this plant make firearms?" I asked Baskerville, one of Bush's advance men.

"No," he said. "They produce arms that you can place across your chest when you're reciting the Pledge of Allegiance to the flag. It's the largest right-arm factory in the world, and business is booming since the candidate made the flag the main issue of his campaign."

"Are they meant for people who don't have right arms?" I asked.

"No, these are for citizens who have their own arms. The manufactured arm makes it possible to recite the pledge and applaud Bush at the same time."

"It's a miracle," I exclaimed.

"Before Reagan, Americans didn't care if they had an arm to pledge with or not. But the Republicans changed all that, and the demand for a right arm to put over one's heart has swept the nation. They're not very expensive. They sell for $9.95 each."

"Does Bush own any of these?"

"Of course. If you say the Pledge of Allegiance as often as he does, you have to keep a trunkload for emergencies. They're going to give him a Teflon-coated one at today's ceremonies.

It's supposed to be very special because not only can he place it across his chest to salute the flag, but it can also be held up in a V-for-victory sign when he's taking a bow."

"What does George do with his real right arm?"

"During his speech he uses it to point out Dukakis's mistakes and to question the governor's patriotism. Anytime you see Bush sticking his finger into the air, you can assume that the rest of the arm belongs to him."

"And when he has his arm across his chest?"

"Almost certainly it's a plastic one made in this factory."

"How did you discover such an operation?"

"The owner called us. He sent a sample to the Vice President as soon as he heard that George had a bad case of tennis elbow caused by placing his hand on his heart while reciting the pledge. The VP was really impressed and told me to check it out. What made it exciting to us was that Michael Dukakis had never been here. It seemed the perfect spot for a follow-up to George's visit to the flag factory in New Jersey."

"That was good thinking," I told him, "you'll probably be on all three networks tonight."

"We hope so, but that isn't why George is coming over."

"Why is he coming?"

"It's his way of showing that he cares about this country, and that he admires any company that makes it easier for Americans to recite the pledge. Many people complain about how hard it is to put their arms across their chest. With these arms they have no excuse."

I said, "Since I'm here, I think I'll get one. How long are they good for?"

"Twenty days if you keep them in a dry place."

"Can I use the arm to wave to George after he makes a speech?"

"Yes. We waved them at the convention in New Orleans

when Dan Quayle was nominated and they worked like a dream."

"What time does today's ceremony begin?"

"Any minute now. We can start as soon as they've measured the VP for a flag to wrap himself in when he leads us all in reciting the oath."

Getting an Appointment

A group of us were having lunch the other day when Beeman came hurrying in. He was flushed with what seemed like victory.

"I think I've got it," he exclaimed.

"What is that?"

"I just made an appointment with my daughter. I haven't been able to see her for two months, but she informed me that she can fit me in at six o'clock on Thursday."

"That's neat," I said. "How did you do it?"

"It wasn't easy. I kept leaving messages at her dorm saying I would be grateful to simply meet with her and talk over how things are going.

"The first time she turned me down because she was going to Vermont to look at the leaves. The second time she actually made a date with me, but then canceled it as she had been invited to wash her boyfriend's car. And three weeks ago, she called to say that she couldn't see me on her birthday because she wanted to enter a twenty-six-mile marathon where you could meet a lot of neat guys."

"How can you be sure that she will show up for the appointment she's made now?" I wanted to know.

"She sounded serious. But it's not firmed up yet. There is some talk about her floating down the Delaware River in a rubber tube, or going to Ohio for a touch football game with the League of Women Voters—but I'm optimistic that she'll keep the date with me."

"You're a lucky man, Beeman," one of the group said. "I haven't been able to arrange a meeting with my son for two years. He's one busy fellow."

"They all are," Beeman answered. "And you can't fault them for refusing to put us on their calendars. You know what's really funny? I wanted to talk to George Shultz the other day, and it was arranged in an hour. I called Lee Iacocca and he said he'll see me as soon as I arrive. It's been like that all month. The only one I am unable to make contact with is my own flesh and blood."

"What are you planning to talk about when you do see her?" I inquired.

"I am going to ask her if she loves me. And if she says she does, I'll start to wonder why she doesn't answer the calls I leave on her answering machine. I'll try to find out if I'm the father she really wanted."

"I wouldn't do that," one of the men said. "You'll only make her feel guilty."

Beeman remarked, "If I could make her feel guilty I would consider our meeting a big success."

"Have you decided what to wear?" I asked.

"What difference does it make?"

"Seeing your daughter isn't an everyday occurrence, and you should at least be dressed for it."

"I'm not applying for a job," Beeman yelled.

"Don't get so excited. There are five of us at this table and, if you added it all up, we haven't seen our children for a total of ninety years."

Beeman said, "I'm sorry, guys, I don't want you to think I've got it made. Just because my daughter gave me this appointment doesn't mean she'll give me another one. If she gets a better offer she will cancel this date just like that."

"If she did, would you take away her school allowance?"

"Of course not. What kind of father takes away his daughter's allowance just because she doesn't return his calls?"

And the Winner Is . . .

My wife and I were eating dinner in the kitchen, watching Peter Jennings on the ABC news. I didn't hear his exact words, but Peter indicated that on the basis of a nationwide poll, ABC had given the election to George Bush.

"Is that it?" my wife asked. "Is it over?"

"Dukakis is a dead fish," I replied.

"But election day isn't until November eighth. How could they announce the results in October?"

"One guy with a clipboard spoke to ten thousand people, and based on those results Bush has all rights to the White House tennis court."

She seemed shaken. "If the ABC poll is correct why should anyone bother to vote?"

"You don't have to if you don't want to," I told her. "But balloting in this country is a tradition. We don't do it for ourselves, we do it for the children."

"You're not taking this seriously. That poll just took my ballot away from me. Why should I go out and pull the lever if I can't make a difference?"

"Look, it had to come to this sooner or later," I told her. "Remember the election nights when they used to concede states to the presidential candidates by eight P.M.? Now the technique is so refined that they can give you the results in October. It wouldn't surprise me if the next time around they declare the winner on the Fourth of July. I am glad it's over. Bush was starting to turn into a nice guy."

264

"Are they going to give up campaigning?" she asked me.

"I imagine so. There's no sense spending all that time and money when the results are poll-ordained."

"There is something fishy about this whole thing. Both sides are urging their troops on, the dirty commercials have just been released, and the hecklers are stretched out in the streets. How can anyone declare that the election is over?"

"You can't fight computers. They not only know who lost but why he lost. Once you crunch the numbers there is nothing left to do but put your hand on the Chief Justice's Bible and solemnly swear."

"You sound happy that they've announced who our next president is going to be."

"I'm not happy about it—I'm just realistic. If we can be informed a month in advance who won, the time will come when we don't have to have an election at all. We'll go out onto the sidewalk, tap someone on the shoulder and the next day we'll have a new gipper in the Oval Office."

"I thought we were going to have an election-night party," she said.

"We were," I replied, "but I didn't know they would announce the winner tonight. That's the only part about jumping the gun I don't like. The pollsters didn't give us enough time to stock up on cold cuts."

"Well, what shall we do on November eighth if there is no suspense?"

"Maybe the candidates will have another debate just to kill time. Besides, there is a lot more to election night than choosing a president. You get to see the families of the winners and losers. The political experts tell us what the losers did wrong, and maybe Dan Quayle will finally reveal what his grades were in school."

My wife said, "The people I feel most sorry for are those who live in California. In the East we now know who our next president is, but they have to wait three more hours before somebody out West is permitted to give them the word."

Don't Panic, It's an Embargo

Dear Gun Lover:

The government has imposed a ban on the importation of semiautomatic weapons from abroad, including the AK-47, the Uzi, and other "hunting and target weapons" which are absolutely essential for sport.

But don't get too depressed. It's only a temporary measure to give the administration an opportunity to "study the problem." President Bush wants a cooling-off period until the NRA finds a legal way to get the Chinese weapons into the country, as guaranteed by the Founding Fathers, who never lived in a drug-infested neighborhood.

The good news is there's no ban on the manufacture and sale of domestic weapons. You can buy all the semiautomatic weapons you need as long as they are made by Americans.

There is now a run on domestic machine guns, but once the stampede is over, you'll be able to buy as many rapid shooters as you want.

The reason gun lovers should remain calm is that the President, a lifelong member of the National Rifle Association, doesn't see any difference between a hunting rifle and a weapon that can knock over a bus. George Bush is not a wimp when it comes to guns. His embargo on foreign semiautomatics is just a temporary way of appeasing the country's police forces who become hysterical every time they see an armed dope gang walking down the street.

While the machine-gun ban is on, we gun lovers need to remain cool and keep our powder dry. They may stop us from importing our guns from China, Italy and East Germany for a few months, but most of us can easily manage with what we have in the ol' linen closet. We just have to wait until common sense comes back into the gun game, and it will as soon as the NRA begins scaring the politicians on the Hill again.

If you want to know what really threatens the safety of the American people it's Chilean grapes. Nothing can rip apart the fabric of our society as much as two grapes with cyanide in them. The truth of the matter is it isn't safe to go to the grocery store anymore.

The National Grape Association has one of the strongest lobbies of any group in Washington. Their slogan is, "Cyanide grapes don't kill people—people kill people."

On the Ted Koppel show the NGA keeps asking, "Why should law-abiding grape eaters be punished because of a few bad apples in Chile? The criminals will find ways of getting their cyanide grapes no matter how many embargoes are placed on them."

The NGA says that the panic about the poisoned grapes could lead to people having to register each grape before they

NATIONAL
BACCHANALIAN
GUN LOVERS UNITED

©1989 S.H. Mendelson

eat it. Most citizens who use grapes for sports or target practice would not even be allowed to stomp on them for wine.

That's the kind of hogwash the NGA is putting out. But people like Charlton Heston, another lifelong member of the NRA, does not believe that everybody should be permitted to buy grapes without restrictions. "There are a lot of kooks out there and you have to have laws to keep them from spitting seeds at innocent Americans," he told an Egyptian pharaoh in Cairo.

For reasons none of us will understand, the government banned grapes and guns on the same day. It's like mixing apples and oranges. You shouldn't confuse them because guns can't hurt you but grapes can kill you. It is a known fact that ten times as many accidents are caused in homes with grapes than in those with guns.

If you want to reduce the hysteria of the antigun propaganda in this country, then I urge all of you to write to George Bush and tell him that we are never going to have a safe and sane gun policy if he keeps letting Barbara Bush push him around.

More Questions

I am sad that there will be no more presidential debates. The reason for this is that there are so many questions left unanswered. The panel members for the three debates did what they could to draw the candidates out, but I believe that they should have been tougher. Here are the questions I wish they had posed to the contenders:

"Sir, if you were a gypsy moth, what kind of gypsy moth would you be?"

"Name the last three Dead Sea Scrolls you have read in the original, and why you would recommend them to every American child."

"If your wife were knocked down on a dark street, brutally kicked, and her purse snatched away from her, would you still pardon Ollie North?"

"Do you believe a man on welfare, who refuses to look for a job, is entitled to a zip code?"

"Would you recommend three good restaurants in the Boston area to a convict who is going on a weekend furlough?"

"If you were a guacamole dip, what kind of guacamole dip would you be?"

"Do you believe that card-carrying members of the ACLU should lose their driving privileges on federally funded interstate highways?"

"If someone took all the garbage in Boston Harbor and dumped it off the beaches of New Jersey, would the people of New Jersey consider it a cheap shot?"

"Please give me four dates on which the Japanese might have bombed Pearl Harbor."

"If Senator Bentsen is elected, will those lobbyists who could not afford ten thousand dollars for breakfast in his office, be entitled to meet with him for five thousand dollars in the Senate cafeteria?"

"If you were a Scotch-tape dispenser, what kind of Scotch-tape dispenser would you be?"

"Would you advocate the death penalty for any pregnant woman who does not believe in the right-to-life movement?"

"Governor, when you play baseball with a kid for the TV cameras, do you ever put pine tar on your glove?"

"Mr. Vice President, do you think Mike Tyson and Robin Givens represent the family values that you hold so dear?"

"Senator Bentsen, if Dan Quayle is no Jack Kennedy, does that make Mrs. Quayle no Jackie Onassis?"

"Senator Quayle, if we refuse to embargo American wheat and sell it to the Russians, won't they become healthy and want to kill us?"

"Governor, the polls indicate that the only way you can win the election now is to tell us how you made Massachusetts one of the great states in the Union. Are you prepared to break your vow of secrecy and tell us how you did it?"

"Senator Quayle, would you agree to enroll in the Electoral College if your father made a large donation to the school?"

"Please tell us the names of all your heroes, and whether any of them has done TV commercials for Wheaties?"

"Do you think a gun is the best answer to poor grades in school?"

"If you were President of the United States, and someone asked you to recite the Pledge of Allegiance to the flag, knowing what you know now, would you do it?"

"If you were a Manhattan telephone directory, what kind of telephone directory would you be?"

"If you were Vice President of the United States, and the President just had a meal on Northwest Airlines, what is the first thing you would do to restore confidence in the country?"

The Boomers

George Bush said he picked Dan Quayle as his running mate because Quayle represents a younger generation of voters. The people who make up this generation have been described as baby boomers—the ones who were conceived after World War II.

The question I've been noodling with is, are baby boomers ready to fulfill the great dreams George Bush has for them?

James Grove, the president of the Baby Boomer Defense League, believes that the boomers, now hitting their forties, are thrilled to be finally recognized as a voting bloc.

"If I asked you why is it a good idea for a baby boomer to be a heartbeat away from the presidency, what would your response be?"

Grove replied, "The baby boomers took a long time growing up—but George Bush believes they are now ready to run the country."

"Who exactly are the baby boomers?" I wanted to know.

"They are a generation of children who never had to make their beds. The males didn't pick up their pants and the females didn't hang up their skirts."

"Why not?"

"Their parents wouldn't let them. The mothers and fathers of baby boomers were very frightened of their young because they became hysterical when criticized," Grove told me.

"It's hard to imagine that boomers were so powerful within their own families."

"Look at Dan Quayle, who Bush says is representative of his generation. Quayle's father had to help him do everything. Quayle couldn't even get through law school without his father carrying his lunch pail for him. Bush wants Quayle to be his liaison with the boomers because Dan knows what it is like to have it all."

"Are baby boomers yuppies?" I asked Grove.

"While yuppies are baby boomers, baby boomers are not necessarily yuppies."

"Do baby boomers have a dream?"

"It's the same dream everyone in America has. We want to have our own golf carts."

"And Quayle can do this?"

"He's forty-one years old. Only one baby boomer can appreciate what another baby boomer yearns for. Bush was no fool when he selected Quayle as his running mate. Dan is his own man. He looks exactly like they do."

"Do you think baby boomers will vote as one?"

"Definitely. Boomers see a lot of each other in supermarkets and at football games. All they really have to talk about is what a great president Dan Quayle will make if George Bush falls off his horse in the Rose Garden."

"It's hard to believe that we would send a baby boomer up against Mikhail Gorbachev."

Grove assured me, "Quayle is well qualified. He has been marshal of the Indianapolis 500 for three years in a row."

"Do baby boomers believe in Mom's apple pie?"

"If you are talking about Japanese Mom's apple pie, they do. They have never known what an American Mom's apple pie tasted like."

"The big question remains, however, will the boomers come out to vote on election day?"

"It doesn't matter. In order to prove their love just one more time, their parents will come out and vote for them."

Dress Blues

I guess that the only election question left is, will Barbara Bush or Kitty Dukakis borrow clothes from American fashion designers when one of them becomes first lady of the land?

It probably wouldn't have come up if *Time* magazine had not revealed that our best couturiers were throwing millions of dollars' worth of outfits over the White House fence for Nancy Reagan to wear. Mrs. Reagan's press secretary explained why, after promising not to do it anymore, Mrs. Reagan continued to borrow from the designers. The press secretary said, "She set her own little rule, and she broke her own little rule."

You could argue that by wearing borrowed clothes, Mrs. Reagan was helping the domestic fashion industry. Or critics might suggest that in taking $20,000 gowns, Mrs. Reagan was putting the White House under obligation to the designers who dress our upper classes. On the other hand, you could defend Nancy's actions because there is too much to lose if we allow our first ladies to be dressed by Sears-Roebuck.

Finally you could do what most people do when they read the Nancy Reagan yarn and exclaim, "This is terrible. I am so shocked. I don't know if I have the strength to turn to the inside page and read the rest of the story."

But, as Oscar de la Renta once said, "Those who do not remember the past are doomed to repeat it."

Which raises the subject of how many dresses Kitty or Barbara intend to borrow while in the White House.

I called the Bush headquarters to speak to someone high up in the campaign. They gave me the person in charge of the motor pool.

At first she seemed wary about answering questions concerning Mrs. Bush's clothes.

"Will Mrs. Bush continue the Nancy Reagan policy of calling up Adolfo and saying, 'I don't have anything to wear for a tea today with the wife of the Prime Minister of the Solomon Islands'?"

"At this point in time, Mrs. Bush will continue using her own wardrobe because she intends to be with Mr. Bush when he goes out to fight crime in the streets."

"Suppose Galanos, or Valentino, comes up to Mrs. Bush and says, 'If you wear my gowns, the country will prosper and your husband will balance the budget.' Would that persuade her to borrow some dresses?"

"No, because Mrs. Bush does not make such a big thing out of clothing. By the same token, Mrs. Bush admires Mrs.

Reagan's taste in clothes, even though we have to assume that there are many skeletons in Nancy's closet."

"Does this mean that Mrs. Bush will say 'no' to Halston?"

"I didn't say that. If she becomes first lady, she will wear what she thinks is appropriate for the occasion—no more and no less."

"If Mrs. Bush moves into the White House on inauguration day and finds all the clothes that Mrs. Reagan wore still in the closet, what will she do?"

"She'll give them to Vice President Dan Quayle, who will be in charge of crisis management."

I decided to try and get through to Kitty Dukakis.

The Dukakis people turned me over to a high-level messenger in the Washington office. He told me that Kitty has no intention of wearing any designer outfits in the White House. "Mrs. Dukakis feels that wearing couturier garments would detract from her husband's efforts to give the country catastrophic health insurance coverage."

"Is Mrs. Dukakis a clotheshorse to start with?"

"No. As Michael Dukakis told Kitty the other night, 'You are no Nancy Reagan.' "

He added that Kitty intends to stick with Filene's basement, which Mike is going to make the summer White House.

"What does Mrs. Dukakis think Nancy should do with the clothes she borrowed?"

"Give them to the Imelda Marcos Fashion School of Design."

He Won One for George

After a presidential election is over, political debts must be paid. The men and women who did the most for their candidates have to be rewarded.

And so it will be after November 8.

If George Bush wins, there is no doubt that the person who'll get all the credit is Willie Horton, the murderer-rapist who was given a weekend furlough from a Massachusetts prison and then committed rape and beat up a couple.

A Bush staffer said, "We owe Willie everything. He was probably the most important issue in the entire election, and the candidate doesn't forget the people who were there when Mr. Bush needed them."

"How did you find Willie?"

"The campaign was looking for a murderer-rapist to illustrate how soft Dukakis is on crime. Willie's name popped up in the computers and we rushed it over to the boss. At first, George, who is by nature a kinder, gentler person, didn't want anything to do with it. He told us, 'This will make Dukakis look bad because Willie's furlough took place on his watch.' But Bush's handlers said, 'You owe it to the country to reveal what a sleazy governor Dukakis really is.' "

"That should have sold George," I said.

"When Bush traveled out on the stump with the Willie Horton issue the crowds went wild—and just in time. Up until then, the candidate had put his audiences to sleep with his plan for the environment, and every time George discussed the deficit, it was Valium time. The minute he listed the world leaders he has met, everyone stretched out on the floor and snored. But as soon as George mentioned rape and murder and Willie Horton, he got nothing but standing ovations. All he had to say was 'death penalty' and the crowds went into paroxysms of joy."

"Were his supporters cheering murder and rape as an idea?"

"No, they were cheering the fact that the governor had let Willie Horton out of the pokey, which showed what kind of a president Mike Dukakis would make. At first we thought that Willie would be a good issue for a couple of weeks—but it turned out that Bush got to like it. The people couldn't get enough of the speech. It was like asking Irving Berlin to sing 'God Bless America.'

"Supporters drove hundreds of miles just to hear George tell them how dumb it was to have let Horton out of prison. We circulated pictures of Willie on the covers of programs at GOP fund-raisers, and people doubled their contributions. It made this a one-issue election."

"Have you ever thought of having Mr. Bush meet and thank Willie for all he's done?"

"It's a great photo opportunity but we decided not to do it until after the election. Don't forget, Willie endorsed Dukakis for president from his cell."

"Was that your idea?" I asked the staffer.

"No, Willie's. He thought of it all by himself. I think he's hoping to be awarded the Medal of Freedom if Bush gets into the White House."

"It's going to be hard for the Bush administration to find a job for Willie now that he is back in the pen."

"Something will come up—maybe an ambassadorship to a small country that doesn't mind a diplomat with a criminal record."

"Perhaps you could name a government building after him?"

"Bush was thinking of 'The Willie Horton Post Office' across from the governor's mansion in Boston, just to stick it to Dukakis for the sleazy campaign he ran."

"I'm sure Willie would like that. You know, it's quite possible that if Willie had known he was going to be the most important person in the 1988 presidential race, he might have gone straight and never committed a crime at all."

"That wouldn't have done him any good. If he had kept clean, no one in the Bush campaign would have even mentioned his name."

My Son, My Son

Every political campaign manager saves a thunderbolt for the last week before election day. George Bush's people are no exception.

I've known Rovere for ages. He is one of the best political handlers in the business, and except for getting the date of Pearl Harbor wrong, he has never missed kicking the ball through the goalposts.

We were sitting in the bar and he said, "I suppose you're wondering if we're going to pull a rabbit out of the hat."

I replied, "I don't believe a newspaperman should inquire into a politician's business."

"We intend to take care of the Quayle problem once and for all," Rovere announced.

"I'm ready if you are," I told him.

Rovere looked around the room and then whispered, "Bush is going to adopt Dan Quayle as his son."

"Before the election?" I asked.

"The news will wipe Dukakis off the networks. He won't be able to get a sound bite on a cable station in Butte, Montana."

"I understand the publicity value, but why else would Bush want to adopt Quayle?"

"To silence the critics once and for all. They will no longer be asking why Bush chose Quayle as his vice president. The answer will be obvious. It's because Quayle is his son."

"There has never been a father-son relationship like that in the White House. Was it hard selling it to Bush?"

"Not very. We explained to him that by adopting Quayle, the voters will see the warm, compassionate side of Bush that he has been hiding since the campaign started. Also, this allows George to deal directly with the 'President Quayle' issue. When people see them together as father and son, it will make the country feel less nervous that Quayle is a heartbeat away from the White House."

"Does Quayle want to be adopted?"

"He doesn't mind, provided the Bush people don't assign handlers to him to tell him how he should behave as a son."

"This has the makings of a news story. When are you going to go public?"

"In a day or two. We want to get Barbara Walters to film the actual adoption ceremony with Ronnie and Nancy holding the Bible. When the press asks him why, Bush will say he decided to go ahead with it because Quayle is the most qualified son a president could have."

"It's good," I said, "and it's good because it's true. I have nothing but admiration for the way you people have handled this campaign. And having Bush adopt the vice-presidential candidate as his son is the final stroke of genius. When did you decide about this?"

Rovere ordered another drink. "The trick in politics is to do the unexpected. When Quayle's military record was exposed, everyone expected Bush to drop him. We decided to have him adopt Dan instead, because no one could complain about a father not wanting his son to go to war."

"What puzzles me is that with the polls showing Bush so far ahead, why would George want another son?"

"Because although he has several of his own, there is nobody quite like Dan Quayle."

"J. Danforth Quayle Bush has a nice ring to it," I told Rovere.

He said, "The adoption won't affect the true believers, but

when the undecideds see George carrying Quayle on his shoulders, they'll be so moved that they will give Bush a landslide."

Fans

You see them on television holding their fingers in the air and sticking their tongues out, and you wonder where they come from. They're the fans that the cameras pan to between football plays. They are the people who make everything about TV sports worthwhile.

How do sports fans qualify for a moment of fame at the football game? I asked Bill Pearson, whom you probably saw in the final quarter of the Redskins-Bears game. Aw, come on, don't say you've forgotten him. He was the fellow in the Redskins knit hat, who waved his arms up and down and yelled, "Hi, Mom" into the camera. Everyone was talking about it the next day.

I accidentally ran into Bill on the corner of 16th and K streets in Washington, D.C., where he was mobbed by autograph seekers.

"You were fantastic," I told him. "I thought that the fans were going to go crazy when you jumped onto your seat to declare that the Redskins were number one."

Bill blushed modestly. "Everyone was great. I couldn't have

done a good job on TV without the little people behind me—
the directors, the cameramen and the scriptwriters, not to
mention the network vice presidents who had the faith to put
me on the screen knowing I had a sore throat. I'd also like to
thank my grandmother Quayle, who told me many years ago,
when I revealed to her my dream of appearing on TV, 'You
can do anything you want, if you just put your mind to it.' "

"You were lucky to have had such a wise grandmother," I
told him. "But in the long run you were the one who did it.
What gave you the idea to declare that the Redskins were
number one?"

"I'd been thinking about doing it for some time. In the game
before the one with the Bears I had noticed that the number-
three camera was panning closer and closer towards me. So it
dawned on me last week that I better be prepared just in case.
I had several options, including waving my Redskins banner
or even my hot dog. But I decided to fool them with the old
we-are-number-one play. As soon as the red light went on I
was ready."

"You certainly were. I never saw a football fan who was
more believable on television."

"In order for the cameraman to get the full shot, I had to
push down Arnie Blauvelt, who was in the row in front. He
isn't talking to me."

"People are still buzzing about that unforgettable moment
when you looked straight into the camera and yelled, 'Hi,
Mom, I'll be home for dinner.' That was inspired and I don't
think the viewers expected it."

"My mom's been good to me and she deserved the recogni-
tion," Bill said.

"Not only did she deserve it, but it was so real that everyone
had the feeling that she was putting the roast beef in the oven.
Did she know that you would be on?"

"There were no guarantees, but I did tell her to be sure and watch the last quarter. There had been a lot of talk that the director was looking for new faces because the home audiences were turning their sets off. I guess when I appeared it was a bigger moment for my mother than it was for me. What's nice about it is that she called up everyone in advance, so the whole neighborhood saw me."

"How great."

"The only thing wrong is that she told them I was going to be on every week," Bill said.

"Since you've been there, what would be your advice for another fan who might wind up on the TV screen?"

"Be yourself. No matter what you do, give it your best shot whether it's yelling, making ugly faces or sticking your tongue out at the camera. Above all, don't let them see you sweat— and mind your manners. TV audiences can't stand someone who makes a fool of himself. If they decide they don't like you, they'll all get up and go to the bathroom at the very instant your big moment comes."

Factory Closed

The election was over and all the campaign staffers had been laid off. I stood by the gate as they poured out of sleaze headquarters holding their pink slips.

"What are you going to do now?" I asked a dazed worker.

"I don't know," he replied. "I've been offered a job making cheap shots for the private sector."

"You manufactured cheap shots for the presidential campaign?"

"I was the best. I took plastic ACLU cards and turned them into Saturday-night specials."

"It was a winner," I said. "Were you the one who polished up half truths to produce the specter of crime in the streets?"

"I ran the whole assembly line. They gave me a hundred-dollar bonus for inventing a faster way of making unsubstantiated charges. I also designed the 'L' word which scared the hell out of the South. No one ever did understand what the big 'L' really was, but it became a more important symbol than burning the American flag."

"I'm surprised that they fired you. Won't the candidate need cheap shots when he gets into office?"

"Apparently not, but in my opinion he is going to miss the sleaze factor, especially when he doesn't get what he wants from Congress."

A second man came up. "Did you make cheap shots also?" I asked him.

"No, I was in charge of taking the low road. For example, we leaked the story that an opponent had suffered from mental illness. Then we had our headquarters say they had nothing to do with releasing it, which gave the story a further shove. We followed that up by announcing we could neither confirm nor deny the story, and so were unable to comment on it."

"Is that the furthest you sank?"

"No. I think we really hit bottom when we sent the press a photo showing the girlfriend of their candidate secretly doing Jane Fonda exercises."

"Did you have permission?"

"You don't need permission to take the low road."

"Whatever they paid you wasn't nearly enough."

"It was a living. But now I'm out on the street. Nobody cares about a mudslinger once the fighting is over."

"I wouldn't be too sure. There are a lot of talk shows like Morton Downey's that could use somebody as lowdown as you."

"I never thought of television."

By now hundreds of people were pouring out of the factory.

One lady complained, "We've risked our health manufacturing negative charges and then they dump us out in the cold."

"There is just so much sleaze you can produce in an election campaign," I reminded her.

"I didn't make sleaze. I wove scurrilous lies."

"You did? Such as?"

"I fabricated the one which said that, if elected, our opponent would shoot any gray whale which had escaped from the Arctic Circle."

"I heard that one but I didn't believe it," I said.

"I was also in charge of distorting the opposition's stand on defense. When it came off the production line it looked like a Polish sausage."

"You shouldn't have lost your job," I remarked.

"I guess it's part of the game. You lie, cheat and steal for the candidate, but then when he wins he doesn't know you and goes around telling everyone he is really a kinder, gentler person."

Marriage Blending

One of the busiest periods for marriage counselors is directly after a presidential election. Nerves are raw and the wounds are deep.

That's the way it was when the Clydesteins walked into Dr. Orange Gimlet's office.

"What seems to be the trouble?" asked Dr. Gimlet.

"I'm finished with this marriage," Mrs. Clydestein told him. "I decided I can't stand the heat and I want to get out of the kitchen."

"What did he do wrong?"

"Well, for starters, every time we've gone somewhere during the last three months he's called me by my 'L' name."

Mr. Clydestein said, "I only called her the 'L' name during

the Republican Convention when she jumped up and down on our bed and shouted, 'Where was George?' "

Dr. Gimlet reassured them. "So far you sound like a very normal couple. I haven't heard anything to warrant a split-up."

"He's a brute," Mrs. Clydestein said. "I asked him what if a store clerk took my credit card and forgot to return it? Should that salesman get the death penalty? Mr. Conservative responded that there was no other choice. I don't want to spend the rest of my life with someone who is so lacking in compassion for his fellow man."

"And I don't want to live with a bleeding heart," Mr. Clydestein added. "She claims that the only reason Willie Horton got into so much trouble was because Dan Quayle refused to play golf with him on weekends."

Dr. Gimlet remarked, "There seems to be a slight ideological breakdown between the two of you. Can you pinpoint the moment when you started drifting apart?"

Mr. Clydestein answered, "I had my first suspicions when she refused to recite the Pledge of Allegiance before the Monday-night football games."

"Some women are like that," Dr. Gimlet pointed out. "It doesn't necessarily make them disloyal wives."

"I cannot remember a day when she offered to salute the flag voluntarily," Clydestein told Gimlet.

"How could I?" Mrs. Clydestein asked her husband. "You slept in it all the time. Whenever I put my hand over your chest you said, 'Get your arm off Old Glory. It's my flag and I paid for it.' "

By now Mrs. Clydestein was in tears. "He never understood my stand on the environment. Every time he disagreed with me, he told me that if I didn't like it, to go water-skiing in Boston Harbor."

Dr. Gimlet said, "This is starting to sound serious. There could be a negative element here much deeper than mere politics."

"There is," Mrs. Clydestein agreed. "It's a question of competence. Things really fell apart for us when I mentioned to my husband that I didn't want to be married to a man who gets turned on by dirty commercials."

Mr. Clydestein said, "All she has against Bush is his shrillness. If she listened to what his handlers had to say, instead of reading George's lips, she would know what Bush will do for this country."

Dr. Gimlet told them, "All right, I've heard your passionate pleas, and I must say that each of you has a strong argument. But the election is over, and whether you like it or not, you both have to live with the same president for the next four years. This means that you must forget all the cheap shots and think about the kinder, gentler world that George Bush promised every American. Are you prepared to do this?"

Mr. Clydestein replied, "I'm willing to try if she will just stop yelling when she goes to bed, 'Don't forget to turn out the thousand points of light, dummy.' "

Wall Street—
Two Weeks Later

One of the ironies of the postelection season is that many of George Bush's strongest supporters are beginning to doubt his policies. This is odd since he doesn't have any yet.

Wall Street stands out as a case in point. Before the election almost everyone was rooting for Bush and his brilliant sidekick, Dan Quayle. Now it's another story.

I talked to Thomas Fernando, a hotshot broker who specializes in reading George Bush's lips.

When the market kept skiing downhill I put the question to Thomas, "Why have America's investors lost faith in George?"

"They haven't lost faith. They just think he's a disaster," he told me. "Wall Street doesn't believe that Bush has what it takes to lick the deficit. When attempting to solve budget problems, he looks like a man up the Boston Harbor without a paddle. Since we have no idea what his intentions are, we're recommending that our customers sell instead of buy."

"What does George say?" I asked.

"Every time I read his lips he keeps talking about what a great family he has. This doesn't make for a bullish stock market. We want his lips to tell us what he plans to do about the yen."

"But he hasn't even slept in the Oval Office yet," I protested.

"I'm sure he has a plan. No politician would dare ask the American people to elect him president if he couldn't cut the deficit."

"Don't bet on it. Some people want that office so badly they would even advocate a flexible budget."

"I know deficits are not to be sneezed at. At the same time, we had this debt for eight years and it never fazed Ronald Reagan."

"That was Ronald Reagan. He never had to admit to anything. But George Bush is a different kettle of fish. Wall Street expects signals from Bush that can be read by the average investor."

"If Wall Street has no faith in Bush, why did they vote for him?"

"Because he promised that Willie Horton would never get a weekend furlough again."

"What did Willie Horton have to do with the deficit?"

"Not much, but it impressed Wall Street that George Bush was interested in the little picture as well as the big one. What we didn't know was that he is dead set against asking for new taxes and cutting back on defense spending—which are the only two ways you can reduce the deficit."

"Bush made no secret that he was against taxes and defense cuts," I reminded him.

"Maybe he spoke about it, but it never got on the evening news. In any case, what we're dealing with on Wall Street right now is a lack of confidence in Bush and Quayle which is knocking the hell out of soybeans."

"I can see the financial market's problem," I admitted, "but I don't see a solution. Bush and Quayle were chosen by the people because they had complete faith that the nation's debt could be reduced. It's unfair for Wall Street to start complaining less than one month after the fat lady sang. By driving down the Dow Jones you are not getting George off to a good start."

Fernando became angry and said, "Just because we're perfect doesn't mean we know everything."

"When will the market stop sliding?"

"When George and Dan take off their suit jackets and say, 'Gee whiz, guys, we have a problem here. Let's tackle this job with a will and a smile.' "

"Is that the only sign Wall Street needs?"

"Bush must also level with this country and tell us that all he can offer for the next four years is blood, sweat and voodoo economics."

A Sigh of Relief

There was a great sigh of relief in Washington, D.C., when a vindictive ethics bill was vetoed by a benign President Reagan. The veto preserves the opportunity for retired administration appointees and former members of Congress to make a buck the same way they have done in the past.

A White House insider told me, "If signed, this bill would have destroyed the democratic American way of life. What good does it do for a man to serve his country when he can't sell his connections to the highest bidder once his term is over?"

"Does that mean you are against ethics in Washington?" I asked him.

"I am *for* ethics. Everyone in Washington supports ethics, but at the same time, too much can choke you. One of the reasons many people join the government is for the golden parachute they get at the end of the rainbow. Some former congressmen and executive appointees have few skills other than the sale of their influence to the highest bidder. An ethics bill would destroy the profit incentive for many who are now leaving the Reagan administration."

"You see no conflict of interest in peddling your connections to the private sector?"

"Of course not. It is essential that lobbyists maintain access to the right people in our government. And it is also important that clients deal with legitimate influence-peddlers rather than phonies who pretend they know somebody but don't."

"Now that the bill has been vetoed, is it your intention to solicit new accounts from the business world?"

"I wouldn't say that. But if I can give people an informative and worthwhile tour of the Pentagon for a small fee, I feel that I am doing my share for the defense of my country. With an ethics bill, it would be every man for himself. Without such a law, those who know the ropes will receive the greatest rewards."

"Some people feel that you shouldn't grease the wheels for the same officials who knocked on your door when you were in the government. What do you have to say to that?"

"No bill in Congress can stop anyone from doing wrong. Look at the members of the Reagan administration who have been convicted. Do you really believe an ethics bill would have prevented any of their misdeeds? The congressional law that Reagan vetoed was no more than a dagger aimed at the heart of every insider. If you start passing laws restricting lobbying techniques you will deter good men from joining the government. There are many people out there who will not sign up if they can't sell out when they leave."

"Doesn't that add to the sleaze factor?"

"Why are you introducing the sleaze factor, when all we're talking about is honest influence-peddling? Washington has always operated by the old-school tie. When you're on the inside your actions are affected by those on the outside, and vice versa. It is important that everyone knows who the influence peddlers are. Ethics regulations will only drive them underground and then we will never find out who is being paid off and who isn't."

"You make a convincing argument for the Reagan veto."

"I have to. I'm joining O. Joy, Malloy, and Nufsinger, as soon as I leave government."

"What will you do for them?"

"I have been hired to get a photo opportunity with the President and Ferdinand and Imelda Marcos in the Oval Office."

"Can you do that?"

"Just because I'm leaving the White House doesn't mean they are going to shut the revolving door in my face."

Where's the Money?

As any self-respecting outgoing president would do, Ronald Reagan spent his last weeks in office blaming others for everything that went wrong with the country's finances during his administration.

In discussing the enormous debt he left behind, Mr. Reagan said that those responsible were an "Iron Triangle," consisting of Congress, the press and the Washington special-interest groups. Had liberal congressmen been more responsible, and a responsible media been more vigilant, and vigilant lobbyists butted out, we would not have billions of dollars of red ink all over our hands.

White House aides joined in the criticism. Doberman Pincher, who coined the phrase "Iron Triangle," told me that the President decided to go public about the people who wrecked his dream of a balanced budget because he still had some Teflon left from his first term.

"It's time we pinned the deficit on the donkey's back," he declared. "You, the press, are as responsible for the trillion-dollar debt as anyone."

This got me mad, and I said, "I am only responsible for three hundred fifty billion dollars of it. The rest of the blame goes to the liberal Congress and the special-interest groups. By the way, does the President intend to accept any responsibility for the deficit?"

"Why should he?" Doberman asked. "He had nothing to do with how the money was spent while he was in office."

"I thought perhaps he might admit to his Defense Department wasting a few dollars here and there on weapons that don't work."

"The President doesn't know of any such weapons. Don't think that you can use defense expenditures as a way of making him part of the Iron Triangle."

"Why did the President include the press as one point of the triangle?"

"Because had the press done its job and reported on the spending bills passed by the liberal Congress, we would not owe any money."

"We tried to report on waste in government," I told Doberman, "but every time we attempted to talk to someone, you had the whistle-blower locked up on a prison ship in the middle of the Potomac River."

"Whistle-blowers can't be trusted. They are always trying to embarrass the President."

I said, "There is still some question as to why Ronald Reagan would talk about a trillion-dollar deficit so late in his term."

Doberman answered, "The President didn't know about the debt until he cleaned out some papers in his desk. He was horrified by what he read. So he immediately called me in and asked what he could do so that history would not hold him responsible. I suggested he create an 'Iron Triangle' and blame everyone else in Washington for the mess. We included the press and the lobbyists who kept pushing a liberal Congress for bills that broke the bank."

"What about the lobbyists who helped the President get congressional funding for Star Wars and the Stealth bomber?"

"Those people were not acting as lobbyists, but rather as patriots. If there was any waste and fraud in his administration, the President didn't know about it."

"How can you be so sure?"

"Because Mr. Reagan didn't know about a lot of things and the deficit was one of them. If the press had done its job, the President would have read about it or seen it on the Ted Koppel show and then taken action. As it happened, Mr. Reagan was living in a fool's paradise."

"Is there anything we citizens can do about the Reagan deficit?"

"For starters, you can stop calling it the Reagan deficit. It is now the Bush deficit and don't you forget it."

Christmas Choices

It's the age-old yuletide problem which has no solution. When a couple has four parents, maybe five or six, depending on how many divorces there are in the family, how do they decide where to go on Christmas Day?

Dr. Victor Template, who specializes in Christmas mental diseases, told me, "Fear plays an awfully important role in this decision. If the couple is more afraid of the wife's mother, they would be smart to go with that side of the family. On the other hand, if the husband's mother is the strong figure then you opt to go to her house."

"Suppose both mothers are very strong?"

"Then you try to get the two of them to come to your house. I can't guarantee this will work because mothers do not feel they are contributing anything to the holiday if they don't cook the dinner. When they are guests on Christmas Day they usually sulk a lot."

"Is it better to have two sulking mothers rather than a happy one, and another who is really ticked off?"

"It depends on how close the ticked-off mother lives to you. You have to remember that Christmas is the time when everyone gets insulted. There is nothing that wounds the mother of a nuclear family as much as having the role of cook taken away from her. We're not talking about cooking as much as holding on to power. The last vestiges of power for a mother are in the roasted turkey and pecan pie. There is no hurt greater than her daughter going to the in-laws on Christmas Day—just as there is no greater injury a son can inflict on his mother than to inform her the family is going to his wife's parents in Minnesota for the holidays."

"How about splitting up the couple—the husband going to his parents' and the wife going to her folks' home on Christmas Day?"

"That's no good because the husband's mother or the wife's mother will spend all her time telling the children what terrible spouses they married because they won't spend Christmas with each other."

"Suppose the couple visits one mother on Christmas Eve and the other on Christmas Day?"

"This is fine unless one of the mothers lives in Florida and the other resides in Michigan."

"We're sort of running out of combinations," I said.

Dr. Template replied, "The most sensible solution is to have both parents come to the couple's house. But sometimes this can't be done because the mothers are entertaining their other loved ones for dinner. No one can fault young marrieds if they insist on staying home to prepare their own Christmas meal. But at the same time they're not going to get any kudos for it from their parents. We're talking about an insult that will last forever."

"Fathers don't seem to take much offense over all this."

"Most fathers don't care where they eat dinner as long as there is enough gravy and mashed potatoes. The power struggle we witness at Christmas is almost always between the women. It was Nietzsche who wrote, 'She who has her hand on the chestnut stuffing controls the world.' "

"How do these women control the world?"

"Through tough love. It was Confucius who said, 'The journey of a thousand miles begins with one call from your mother making sure the entire family is coming to her house for Christmas dinner.' "

"No one should ever have to decide between a mother and a mother-in-law," I said.

"Who ever said that Christmas was easy?"

The Term Paper

I receive a lot of interesting calls at my office. A recent favorite was from a mother who lives in Bethesda, Maryland.

"I wonder if you'd mind answering some questions on the U.S.-Soviet missile treaty?" she asked.

"I would be happy to," I told her. "Why do you need to know about it?"

"My son is home from college and he has to write a term paper on disarmament."

"I see. Why doesn't your son call me himself?"

"He's very busy. He needs to get his car tuned, and the only time he can see his girlfriend is when he comes home."

"Don't you think there is something wrong with a son asking his mother to do his term paper for him?"

"I don't mind," she replied. "There is so little he needs from me these days. Was it Reagan's idea or Gorbachev's to reduce the missiles in Europe?"

"Look, ma'am, I don't mind answering your questions, but if you do the work, your son isn't going to get anything out of it."

"Oh, yes he will. If the paper is any good they'll give him an A."

"That's not what I mean. Mothers shouldn't be writing term papers for their children."

"Why not? We pay their tuition."

"The term paper itself isn't important—gathering the research for it is what helps make the scholar."

300

"Well, I'm sure my son would research the material if he could spare the time. He was never lazy when he lived at home."

"Whose idea was it for you to do this paper?"

"Both of us. He kept complaining that his entire vacation would be ruined because he had to look up facts about ICBMs. Since I didn't have any other commitments, I volunteered to help him. After all, he is flesh and blood."

"But if you just give him all the information, he won't understand any more about disarmament than he does now."

"If he gets stuck he can call me. I always like to hear his voice."

I didn't know what to tell her. "Somehow I feel party to a crime," I said.

"Mrs. Lipkin always helped her son Milton with his papers, and now he works for the State Department. Will you please tell me everything that took place in Geneva before they reached an agreement?"

"That'll take a long time."

"I'm not going anywhere. My son is using my car."

"Apparently there is no child abuse in your family."

"None whatsoever. We're very close."

"I'm sure you are. But I would still prefer to discuss disarmament with your son."

"What's the matter? Are you afraid that a woman can't understand it?"

"It's not that. What concerns me is if something I tell you about the missile treaty is wrong, your son would never forgive you."

"He has in the past," she told me. "Once I did a paper for him on Tolstoy. Are you going to help me or not?"

"Why are you so impatient?"

"The paper is due in four days, and my husband needs at least a day to type it for him on his computer."

Goodbye to the Old

What big changes occur in Washington when there is a new president?

If there are any at all, they are taking place amongst the lawyers and lobbyists who make their living persuading our elected officials that what's good for their clients is good for the country.

I dropped in to see the lawyer-lobbyist Norton Nesbitt the day after the inauguration. He was removing all the photographs of Reagan appointees and replacing them with autographed pictures of Bush people.

"Redecorating the office?" I asked.

"Just changing the decor a little," he replied. "One gets tired of looking at the same faces all the time."

"You're not throwing an autographed picture of Ed Meese in the trash can, are you?"

"What kind of a friend do you think I am? I'm taking it home and putting it in the bathroom. Ed was good to me. He always took my calls."

"I can understand taking Ed Meese off the wall, but how can you discard a picture of you and Cap Weinberger, particularly when he signed it 'To Ted, with Admiration'?"

"I need that space for a golf photo of me and Secretary of State Jim Baker."

"May I see it?"

"I don't have it yet, but I'll get one at the next Republican fund-raiser."

"I notice that there is a big gap where you used to have an autographed photo of Ronald Reagan."

"Yeah, I decided to take Ronnie down and put him in the storeroom so that no one will steal him."

"Who are you planning to put in his spot?"

"I'm waiting for a picture of the big guy."

"You mean President Bush?"

Nesbitt said, "I could kill myself. I had thousands of opportunities to have my picture taken with him when he was vice president. I remember one time I was at the New Jersey State Fair for the crowning of Miss Bergen County, and George wanted to get a photo with me. I turned him down and went off to get myself a beer."

"You really blew it."

"How was I supposed to know he was going to be president? Who ever heard of having your picture taken with a vice president of the United States?"

"I just hope for your sake that Bush doesn't remember that you walked away from him."

"I doubt it. People were doing it to him all the time. I have someone in the White House working on an autographed picture of the Prez right now. They owe me for all the money I raised for the party in Michigan."

"Nesbitt, people will consider you a good lobbyist whether you have a photo of yourself with the President or not."

"That may be true of those who know me, but what about the potential clients who don't? They will judge me only on the basis of whose picture I have hanging on the wall. This is a dog-eat-dog business and the reason that they hire you is because they think you have access to the top dogs."

"I guess once they're out of power there is no reason to keep in touch with the Reagan people anymore."

"Some folks may feel that way, but I don't. Those I dealt with during the Reagan years are still my friends, regardless of what they are doing now."

Nesbitt's secretary came up to him and said, "George Shultz is on the phone."

"Well, for God's sake don't tell him I'm here." He turned to me and said, "The man thinks I have nothing to do but chat with him on the phone."

Slow Down, Japan

According to Mr. David Sanger of *The New York Times*, the Japanese are having a very difficult time persuading their workers to put in a five-day week. For years everyone was content to work six days, so trying to adjust to five has not been easy.

This campaign for a reduction in hours is meant to encourage more leisure time, as well as allow the worker to spend a lot more yen in the homeland. Japanese institutions, from the banks to the unions, are trying to force a radical change of life-style, and there has been great resistance to the proposal. According to Sanger, 30 percent of the Japanese people are in favor of a five-day work week, and 70 percent are against it.

Using leisure time to its utmost is one area where Americans excel over the Japanese. In fact, we spend twice as much time being laid-back (figuratively speaking) as our trading partners across the seas.

Therefore, the Japanese government is hiring American firms to convince the workers in Japan that a forty-hour week is better than a forty-eight-hour one, no matter what their bosses tell them.

One U.S. consulting firm, called TGIFIJ (Thank God It's Friday in Japan) is run by Lawrence Bathgate II, and his company has landed a major contract with the Japanese.

Lawrence told me, "This is the toughest job I've ever had. Every time I try to get the Japanese to relax, they jump up and start welding another bumper onto a car while singing the Toyota Fight song."

"How do you know where to start?" I asked.

"I've been sending over students from the U.S. to teach them a thing or two. If anyone knows how to take life easy, it's the American youngster."

"What approach do the students take?"

"As soon as they set foot on Japanese soil, they go to the beach. Our goal is to persuade the people of Japan that they can get as much pleasure from suntanning as they can from screwing the back onto a Sony Walkman. American kids are great at showing others how not to lift a finger."

"How do you convince the Japanese that a five-day week is better than a six-day one?"

"We have advised the government that they cannot do it unless they build more golf courses. People can't be expected to take the weekend off if they have no golf courses to play on."

"I hope that they have responded positively."

"Yes, they're building golf courses as fast as they can. The trouble is that while they're waiting to tee off, the workers keep heading for the factories because they want to build just one more microwave oven."

"Is there anything you can do about that?" I asked Bathgate.

"My people are attempting to teach the virtues of leisure. We try to impress upon the Japanese that it is more productive to go to a department store than it is to produce a hand-held typewriter which also doubles as a fax machine. Our message is that the only road to true bliss for Japanese workers is the acquisition of as many material goods as their houses will hold. We also tell them that there is more happiness to be found on the ski slopes of Mount Fuji than in all the skyscrapers in Osaka."

"Are they buying the message?"

"Not too well. The male workers are very worried that if they cut down from a six-day week to a five-day one, it will mean spending two days at home with their families. They are afraid that their wives would then make them do chores around the house. That very fear is what drove them to work six days a week in the first place."

"I can see it's not easy to make people relax in a country where the work ethic is so powerful."

"You don't have to remind me. The officials who hired my firm have ordered us to work six days a week until we come up with a solution to the problem."

A Mom and Pop S&L

Those of you who have been wondering if the Bush administration has a sense of humor should be delighted to find out that it does. Secretary of the Treasury Nicholas Brady suggested that savings and loan depositors be taxed with a levy of twenty-five or thirty cents per hundred dollars. When Brady sent up the trial balloon everyone in America laughed all the way to the bank.

How on earth did the S&Ls get into such a mess? Here is a typical case of what happened.

Mom and Pop Parker ran a delicatessen in Hillside Park. When business got slow, the Parkers decided to sell all of the cold cuts and potato salad and open an S&L instead. It was called The First Bonnie and Clyde Savings and Loan.

Pop Parker had no sooner opened the door when he received a call from his brother-in-law, Walter. "I need thirty seeded rolls, two pounds of corned beef, a dozen pickles and a boatload of sauerkraut."

"Wait, Walter. I'm no longer in the delicatessen business. I'm in savings and loans."

"Why didn't you say so? I'll have a ten-thousand-dollar note, one hundred thousand dollars for a mortgage, and a line of credit from here to Oklahoma."

"Walter, your credit stinks. Why should I give you any money?"

"Because you're married to my sister and your family comes first."

307

Pop Parker had no choice but to extend all sorts of services to Walter.

Mom was behind the teller cage when her bridge partner, Mildred, walked in. Mildred said that she would like to take out a $50,000 loan to redo her bedroom.

"What kind of collateral do you have?" Mom wanted to know.

"Listen to Mrs. J. P. Morgan. When people go into banking they immediately forget their friends. You never asked me what collateral I had when I was holding the ace, king, queen and jack of hearts. If I had collateral, I would have gone to the Chase National where at least the pens don't smell of pickles."

"I'm making an exception for you," Mom said, "but don't go blabbing all over the neighborhood that The First Bonnie and Clyde S and L is a patsy when it comes to making loans."

Pop was wrapping the deposits in wax paper when Freddy Moonblatt walked in. Freddy and Pop were Masons and also played on the same softball team.

"Have you heard about the string of condos I'm building in Watershed?" Freddy asked.

"No, I haven't," Pop answered. "When did you go into building condos?"

"I just decided to when I saw who owned this S and L. I want to call it Parker Palace, after you and your lovely wife. I need twenty-five million dollars in small bills."

"That could wipe us out," Pop protested.

"You don't make money in this business by putting it in wax paper. I'll pay twenty-five-percent interest on the loan."

"That's a lot."

"I'd rather owe it to you than to strangers."

The upshot of this was that Mom and Pop Parker took care of their family, friends and acquaintances, and wound up in the red to the tune of forty million dollars.

The Parkers weren't as disturbed as one might think. As Pop told the press when they were going under, "If we still had the delicatessen business, nobody would have bailed us out at all."

The Revolving Door

The revolving door turns and where it stops nobody knows. Ever since President Reagan moved out and President Bush came in, the game of musical chairs continues. Reagan appointees are now working the other side of the street representing private clients seeking assistance.

The most popular profession for ex-administration appointees seems to be public relations. "Public relations" has a nice ring to it and, like "consultant," you can make it mean anything you want it to.

It's interesting to note that these people, who are now charged with buttering up the media, were not too friendly to us when they were doing Reagan's bidding. Some are having a hard time persuading my colleagues and myself that they were really good guys when they worked for the government.

One such person is Sanford Probe, who came into the office to sell me a story on tax breaks for the hot-cross-bun industry.

"Why should I talk to you, Sanford?" I asked. "When you were in the White House you never returned my calls."

Sanford replied, "It wasn't my fault. How did I know that I'd be representing the hot-cross-buns industry when I left the government?"

"That's not a good enough excuse. Remember when I saw you at the Salute to Nofziger ball? You wouldn't even say hello to me. You walked by as if I wasn't there."

"I had no choice. I was with Don Regan and he would have become suspicious if I had spoken to you. He might have thought I was returning your calls."

"All you guys in the revolving door are the same. You treat us like dirt when you're on the inside and lick our boots when you're on the outside."

"You're making that up. Remember the time when I called and told you that the contras had just won thirty million dollars in the New Jersey lottery?"

"It was a phony story. The contras won the money from Ollie North, who sold U.S. arms to Tehran."

"So I was slightly inaccurate. Does that make me an unreliable source?"

"I didn't say that you were unreliable. I just felt that you were suffering from a bad case of disinformation. You thought you would be running things forever. Well, it doesn't work that way in America. You dump on people for two terms, and then it's their chance to dump on you."

"Look, I've learned a lot since I have been working in the private sector. I now understand that everyone has a job to do whether they're in the Oval Office or stuck in a traffic jam on the Beltway. If I don't get a story on a tax break for hot cross buns into the newspaper, I could lose the account."

"Why should the hot-cross-bun industry get a tax break?"

"Because the Japanese are flooding the country with hot cross buns, and are killing our markets." '

"How are they doing that?" I asked.

"They're bringing them into America in the glove compartments of their automobiles."

"That doesn't sound like much of a story."

"You don't think so? I'm new at this game. I know I could have gotten away with it in the White House."

"You can get away with anything in the White House, but when you reenter the real world, your veracity is at stake. Remember this, Sanford. Nobody in the private sector ever lies."

"I wish someone had warned me about that when I took this job."

A Good Salary

The big Soviet secret is out. The press has revealed that Mikhail Gorbachev makes $30,000 a year—not a princely sum by Donald Trump standards, but certainly in the same ball park as a United States congressman.

Many people are wondering how Mikhail and Raisa live on his pay. One person who has the answer is Lem Newsom, a State Department expert on Soviet salaries.

"The reason the Gorbachevs can get by on thirty thousand a year," he told me, "is that they don't spend anything. And

they don't spend anything because there is nothing to buy in Moscow."

"It's hard to believe," I said.

"Let's say that Raisa wants codfish for dinner, which is selling for twenty rubles a kilo. She goes to the store at eight in the morning and stands in line with the other shoppers. At six that evening the fish merchant yells 'No more codfish!' and slams the door. Raisa goes home and tells Mikhail she just saved another twenty rubles out of the household budget."

Lem continued, "The beauty of the Soviet economy is that everything you could possibly spend money on doesn't exist. Therefore, at the end of the year most of a Soviet citizen's salary is intact."

"Lenin wanted it that way," I agreed.

"In the State Department we have observed that while his salary is low by American standards, Gorbachev has many friends in the Soviet Union, just as Ronald Reagan does in California. So, if the Gorbachevs need shoes, the head of the shoe cooperative in Murmansk will provide them. And if they need mulch, it will be delivered gratis within the hour by the mulch commissar of Smolensk himself."

"But what about Raisa's clothes?" I asked.

"While there have been groups critical of Raisa for borrowing expensive clothes from Soviet couturiers, her defenders insist that she has started a demand for Russian creations that no other Communist first lady ever did before. Even Mrs. Khrushchev didn't do as much for fashion as Mrs. Gorbachev has."

"What with the perks and the borrowing, I'd be surprised if any chief of a Super Power couldn't make ends meet on thirty thousand dollars," I added.

Lem said, "I haven't told you the big surprise yet. The one thing that keeps the Gorbachevs alive and well is their American Express card. How they got the card is a story in itself."

"They agreed to pose for an ad?" I suggested.

"No. The CIA went to American Express and said it wanted the company to issue a card to the supreme leader of the Soviet Union. American Express replied that it had had very bad luck with Soviet credit. Brezhnev stuck them for three airline tickets to Tashkent, and once they had to send a bill collector to Moscow to find Kosygin when he stiffed them for twenty dinners in Bulgaria. The collector disappeared and was never heard from again."

Newsom continued, "The CIA was adamant that the Gorbachevs receive a credit card and told American Express that the agency would guarantee the unpaid accounts. American Express put the CIA's name into the computer and it turned out that its credit wasn't any better than the Kremlin's.

"Only after intervention from the White House was a card issued to the Gorbachevs. Mikhail was surprised to receive it, but Raisa told him not to ask any questions. So Gorbachev decided to use the American Express card as a test of sincere relations between the U.S. and the USSR.

"He told Raisa, 'If we can charge and they don't ask us to pay, that means the Americans really want glasnost. If they keep demanding the money, we'll know that when they say they want arms reduction, they are just faking it.'

"Well, the rest is history. All Gorbachev's American Express bills are paid for by the CIA. The arrangement has worked out so well there is talk that if an agreement is reached on long-range missiles, Mikhail and Raisa will be issued a Gold American Express card—the highest honor that any country in the Free World can bestow on a foreign leader."

Pet-Owner Abuse

One of America's best-kept secrets is pet-owner abuse—meaning the battering of owners by their pets. Nobody talks about it, but more and more people are showing up in hospital emergency rooms black and blue all over, and sometimes even with broken arms and fractured ribs. Inevitably, their injuries have been caused by "man's best friend," as these pets are called in the TV commercials.

There are no statistics available on how many battered pet-owners there are in this country because these crimes are rarely reported.

I recently made a hospital visit to a pet owner named Mary R. to hear her story. She was willing to speak for my column on the condition that we didn't show her face and that we disguised her voice.

"How long have you been battered by your pet?" I asked her.

She bit her lip. "For seven years. When he was a Doberman puppy, he was so lovable, but as he grew older he kept sneaking up from behind and knocking me down."

"Why do you think he did it?"

"He comes from a long line of dogs who beat up their owners. It could very easily be genetic."

"How did you break your ribs?" I wanted to know.

Mary R. wiped away a tear. "I was walking Buster on a leash when he saw a squirrel and bolted for it. My mistake

315

was to hold on. He dragged me for almost twenty feet and my ribs cracked when I hit a rock garden dedicated to the Daughters of the American Revolution."

"It sounds like a typical battered pet-owner case."

"What made it even worse was that after he stopped chasing the squirrel, he came back to where I lay bleeding and pretended to passersby that nothing had happened."

"Why did you let him back in the house?"

She answered, "He's not like that all the time. Some days he can be as sweet as Häagen-Dazs ice cream, and I guess I put up with the battering just to have those moments."

"Have you told anyone else that your Doberman beats up on you?"

"I'm afraid to. Buster has a terrible temper and I don't know what he would do if he overheard me complaining about him on the phone."

"Does he knock you down in front of your children?"

"All the time. Once I was trying to adjust the TV set in the living room and he pushed me right through the screen."

"How else does he abuse you?" I asked Mary R.

This time she cried as she spoke. "He licks my face when I am trying to put on makeup."

"Perhaps if he won't go, you should leave him," I suggested.

"Where could I hide?"

I felt it was time to have a serious talk with Mary R. "Pet-owner abuse is practiced all over this country. It has existed for a long time, but people never talked about it. For centuries pets tripped up their owners and bit their ankles—yet no one dared call the police. Then a few owners started to speak out, and now there are support groups to help those in need. Buster is a sick dog, and you have to stop making excuses for him. Otherwise you will wind up in the broken-bone department of this hospital every other week."

Mary R. said, "I don't know whether it's worse to be pounded by a pet or to live alone."

"I can't answer that," I confessed. "We know that Buster will never change and so you must. Does your pet mistreat your husband as well?"

"No, he left home two months ago after telling me to choose between him or the dog."

"And you chose the dog?"

"I had to. He's my best friend."

Good Luck, Frequent Flyer

"Good morning, ladies and gentlemen. This is your Eastern Airlines pilot, Captain Frank Lorenzo, welcoming you aboard our flight from Miami to Anchorage, Alaska, for three dollars.

"We will be cruising at an altitude of thirty-five thousand feet, but because of expected turbulence from striking Eastern employees, we may have to land in Ft. Lauderdale.

"Please fasten your seat belts while we taxi onto the runway. Since our disloyal pilots are refusing to cross the greedy mechanics' picket line, our copilot on this flight is Sam Harris, who handles lost luggage complaints for Continental Airlines. Will the flight attendants take their seats?

"We are now at fifteen thousand feet and I am going to turn off the no-smoking sign. If you look out the window on the left side of the aircraft, you will see hundreds of pickets waving signs at decent Americans who have no use for unions. If you look out of the right side, you will see thousands of people waving papers. Those are my lawyers making sure that nobody stops anyone from flying.

"People don't appreciate what is needed to run an airline. It takes money, which you have to borrow at very high rates. It also requires knowledge of the merger business and how to sell off the assets of one airline to pay for another. Union members can't understand that. Their only concern is feeding their families. The employees don't give a hoot about what happens to entrepreneurs like me. This country will never get back on its feet until it has respect for those of us who watch the bottom line.

"I am about to turn on the 'no-striking' sign to warn the stewards and stewardesses it is against FAA regulations to carry placards up and down the aisles while we are in flight. Ladies and gentlemen, the cabin crew will now begin selling beverages. We would appreciate it if everybody bought thirty dollars' worth of liquor to help keep Eastern flying for the rest of the year.

"Now hear this. This is Captain Lorenzo speaking again. We hope that you are enjoying the flight. As you probably heard before leaving Miami, Eastern will no longer supply meals to passengers. You can blame this on our thirty-five thousand striking employees who could care less if our passengers starve to death. If you don't like it any more than I do, write to the Bush administration. Almost everyone there is a good friend of mine.

"At present we are flying over Niagara Falls and have a treat for you. We are going to show *Labor Unions and How They Destroyed America*. This is a tough, hard-hitting film which depicts the decline of the labor movement, and how one man decided to break the stranglehold that the working class had on his airline. There will be a six-dollar charge for headphones. . . .

"This is Captain Lorenzo. We hope that you enjoyed the movie. If you would like a videotape to take home with you, the cost will be ninety-nine dollars.

"Many of you have asked, What are the issues in this strike now affecting all of us? They are as much about power as they are about money. I want power and my employees want money. When I started running airlines I discovered that it is impossible to have power if you give money to the workers. I know how to operate a damn good airline but I can't do it if the employees have their hands out all the time saying 'gimme, gimme, gimme.' There has to be some way of carrying on a business without paying people.

"Ladies and gentlemen, apparently my strikebreaking tactics are not working so I am going to demand the resignation of three of the cabin stewardesses, and request that they turn in their uniforms immediately. Eastern will never forget their loyalty.

"This is Captain Lorenzo speaking to you once more. At this moment we are flying over Montana and seem to be out of fuel. I am asking all the passengers to fasten their seat belts so that I can declare bankruptcy, and let the courts worry about whether we are going to make it to Alaska or not."

What Does It Mean?

Senator John Tower is gone, but the word "womanizer" lives on. The senator was falsely accused of being one. Even Sam Donaldson doesn't know what a womanizer is.

My Webster's dictionary doesn't seem to know either. It defines womanizing as "To pursue freewheeling relationships with women."

I decided to ask some friends what they think a womanizer is.

Ella Brennan told me, "A womanizer is a man a woman can't stand."

"Supposing she likes him?"

"Then he's a teddy bear."

Lisa Johnson said, "A womanizer is someone who has no respect for anybody. For example, if a guy in my office takes me out on a date, and then the next night has a date with my roommate, he is a lowlife rat."

"And if he called you two nights in a row what would he be?"

"Mr. Right."

Bob Hefty spoke up. "The whole business of courting is full of jokers. I enjoy dating girls, but so far my mother hasn't liked any of them. Does that make me a womanizer?"

I replied, "People believe that if a man has to go from woman to woman, he is fatally flawed."

Bob protested, "But if a man's not married, there is nothing

320

wrong with going out with a lot of women. Everyone has to go somewhere to eat."

I asked Sarah Temple if she thought womanizers are evil people or just poor little sheep who have lost their way.

"I deal with it on a case-by-case basis. Some guys who start out as womanizers can easily be tamed. In a way, it's more fun because it's a challenge to win a man over for yourself. Then there are men who are incorrigible and will never change. They should not even be confirmed as members of Bush's Cabinet."

John O'Donnell was sputtering mad. "The whole mating game is based on female pursuit. Everything from Opium perfume to Victoria's Secret is used to trap us. After spending so much money on themselves, women get mad if the bait doesn't work. So they start bad-mouthing males around the water cooler. What do they call a woman who dates more than one guy?"

"An environmentalist?" I suggested.

I then asked Arthur Buckingham, the lobbyist, "Do certain professions have more womanizers than others?"

"Of course they do. Defense consultants are in a very high-stress business and womanizing is the only way they can wind down."

Roz Ripple thought womanizers should be hanged.

"They serve no useful purpose, and they're always spoiling your fun on a Saturday night."

"It sounds as if you're bitter because there are no messages on your answering machine," I said.

"I can get all the womanizer dates I want. But I wouldn't waste my time with a man who is interested in going to a movie with me one night, and validating his parking ticket with someone else the next."

Steve Trilling interjected, "You can't label a person a womanizer just because he wants to take you out. Underneath his Ralph Lauren sport jacket, he might be as honorable as Ollie North."

Bob Hefty couldn't have agreed more. "What everyone forgets is that men who take out more than one woman need love too."

"It's Off to Work We Go"

I woke up one morning and thought I'd eat an orange.

"Are you sure you want to do that?" my wife asked.

"Why not?"

"They could be from Chile. Somebody from Chile wants to kill us."

"You're right. I think I'll have an apple instead."

She threw herself down on her knees. "Please don't eat an apple. What will happen to all of us if you eat an apple?"

"How selfish of me," I said. "I have no right to consume an apple when so many people depend on me. Any late bulletins on shredded wheat?"

"None so far, but that doesn't mean the milk doesn't have

pesticides in it. I just read an article which said that cows are ingesting all kinds of poisons in their foods. You'd be a fool to take a chance."

"Then I'll have a slice of bread and a cup of coffee."

My wife told me, "Marie Hawke says coffee causes cancer in rats."

"Has she ever seen a rat with cancer?"

"No, but Geraldo Rivera has, and he showed the rat on TV the other night."

"So much for breakfast. I guess I'll be off to work."

"You're not going to drive on the Beltway?" she gasped.

"What's wrong with that?"

"There is ten times as much hazardous waste being transported on the highway now as there was two years ago. One trailer spill and you'll be in cruise control with the angels."

"That's not a very comforting thought. But we can't be intimidated by hazardous-waste trucks. They would like nothing more than for us to stay home so that they can have the highways to themselves."

I put on my driving gloves.

"Suppose you get shot," she cried, blocking the door with her body.

"I'm not going to get shot," I assured her. "Nobody wants to shoot me."

"It's happening to people in Washington every day. Don't you ever watch Dan Rather on television?"

"The odds are still in my favor. I'm going to stay out of the neighborhoods where the shootings take place."

"So let's say you make it to the office. What about the asbestos in your ceiling?" she asked. "Doesn't that make you think twice about going to work?"

"I'm in a new building. It's been inspected."

"What are your plans for the lunch hour?"

"I'm not sure yet, why?"

"Whatever you do, don't take a flight to Europe. The PLO is threatening to hijack a plane."

"I'm glad you warned me. I probably would have flown to Shannon for corned beef and cabbage. Anything else I should be on the lookout for?"

"The air is supposed to be foul today. I wouldn't go jogging if I were you, and don't stare at your computer screen too long or you'll go blind."

"Was that on the 'Today' show?"

"No, '60 Minutes.' "

"I got it. So what *aren't* we going to have for dinner tonight?"

"We're not eating any fish until they stop spawning in acid rain."

"Enough chitchat. Give me my construction worker's helmet and a kiss and I'll be off."

She hugged me as June Allyson always does in her pictures and whispered, "Have a nice day."

A New Skipper

A New Skipper

A federal judge recently ruled that the United States could not
keep the America's Cup. The judge stated that by using a cat-
amaran, the San Diego Yacht Club had raced unfairly against
New Zealand, and many world-class American yachtsmen, including myself, went into mourning. It seemed unfair to lose
the trophy just because we had discovered a new way to dunk
the chaps down under. What to do?

An emergency meeting of the Vineyard Haven Yacht Club
was called. In the past, the VHYC had left it to the New York
Yacht Club or the San Diego Yacht Club to do the racing—
but now it looked as if it was time for others to save the day
for the United States.

Stern proposed, "I think that we should hire the captain of
the Exxon oil tanker in Alaska as skipper."

Brown seconded his proposal. "I'll drink to that."

Clurman rose to object. "How do you know we can get him?
He's the hottest sailor on the West Coast."

Stern answered, "We will appeal to him on navigational
grounds. We'll tell him that he's not just going out there to
win the cup back from the New Zealanders. He's also going to
show them what Americans can do with a tall sail and a compass to steer her by. Captain Hazelwood is the only man for
the job. Gentlemen, I suggest that we begin our trials."

"We can't because we don't have a hull," Guggenheim
pointed out.

325

"It doesn't matter," Stern replied, "he'll never know."

Van Ripper was not so sure. "Doesn't the man have a drinking problem?"

"Everybody who goes to sea has a drinking problem. That's why they have an automatic pilot," Wallace assured us.

I told the group, "My only concern is that he'll hit a reef."

Stern sounded surprised. "How can he hit a reef? The channel is ten miles wide. I'd trust my life to an Exxon skipper on the open sea."

"Do we have any other choices?" Styron wanted to know.

"No one in the same class as Hazelwood," Durr answered. "He's a household name."

"I'll drink to that!" Eaton yelled. "How do we get him?"

Stern spoke up. "He's hiding out now because everyone is trying to sign him up. I think we have the inside track if we appeal to his patriotism and send a case of champagne."

Guggenheim sounded worried. "I just hope that none of the other yacht clubs get to him first."

Stern continued, "It's essential that we move fast. We have to convince him that our boat is the one to win back the America's Cup. Once he realizes how seaworthy it is, he's bound to sign up."

"Wait," I said, "he's only captained oil tankers. Maybe he won't want to take command of a racing yacht."

"There's no difference between an oil tanker and a yacht. They both depend on the wind," Styron explained.

Stern was anxious to finish our meeting. "If there are no objections, we agree to hire Captain Hazelwood to skipper the next race, and to bring back the America's Cup to the shores of this great land."

"Wait a minute! I heard that he has no driver's license," Van Ripper shouted.

Stern replied, "Then we'll ask his third mate to take his place."

Peppercorn U.

It wasn't a serious problem before, but it has now become a crisis. No restaurant worth its salt will let you put pepper on your own food. The reason for this is that waiters in the United States cannot be licensed to serve a meal unless they are able to operate a nine-foot pepper grinder.

In order to handle the demand for qualified grinders, pepper schools are springing up all across the land. Their function is to teach students the art of using a pepper mill in a public place. This includes spraying everything from salads to smoked salmon. A great deal of the curriculum is also devoted to safety.

Pierre au Poivre, the Isaac Stern of pepper grinders, told me, "You need nerves of steel to be in this business.

"Most accidents in restaurants are caused when an incompetent person using a pepper mill misses the salad and hits the diner in the nose or on the head. In the wrong hands a pepper mill is considered a lethal weapon, and we need all the guidelines we can get to prevent serious injury.

"Probably the most important point to remember when holding a pepper grinder is to keep it at a forty-five-degree angle. If you raise it any higher, you could shoot the pepper into someone's eyes. If you hold it any lower, the pepper will fall onto the customer's shoes. Next comes 'twisting the mill.' The twist of the wrist is what distinguishes the great grinders from mediocre ones."

"Is that all there is to it?" I asked.

"You must also practice. I devote five hours a day to my art.

327

My wife makes thirty-four pounds of Caesar salad every morning for me to train on. But it has all been worth it."

Pierre said that there are many waiters aspiring to be pepper grinders who just don't have it.

"Why is that?" I wanted to know.

"Because they close their eyes when they are putting the pepper on the salad. We call it 'fear of sprinkling.' "

"I know this is a silly question, but what are the advantages of having a waiter do your pepper grinding for you?"

"It's a once-in-a-lifetime gastronomic experience. We live in a very frenetic world, and most people do not have the time to put pepper on their food. If you're dining at a restaurant which provides such a service, you know that you're in a classy joint, even if the food tastes like bicycle tires."

Pierre feels that timing is everything in pepper grinding.

"My favorite maneuver is to hide behind a palm tree. I wait until someone starts to tell a story, and just when he gets to the punch line, I jump out with my mill at the ready and yell, 'PEPPER?' "

"It takes a real pro to ruin someone's joke."

"I also like to grind pepper just as a man is proposing marriage to a woman or when a couple is breaking up. It makes me feel that what I'm doing has some value."

He continued, "Recently, however, I have observed that people are starting to grind their own pepper. They have no class and are the same ones who insist on putting gas in their own tanks. Nevertheless, restaurants are no longer ignoring them, and are setting aside a special section for do-it-yourself pepper grinding, and another one where waiters provide the service.

"The biggest criticism heard about self-grinders is that they are inexperienced and badly trained. Many hold the grinders upside down and wind up shooting peppercorn dust at everyone in the room."

I asked Pierre if he owns his own pepper grinder.

"Every great waiter does," he replied. "Mine was crafted by Antonio Stradivari, the celebrated pepper-mill maker from Cremona."

"Why is it so valuable?"

"Because of the pure sound it makes when the pepper hits the lettuce."

A Goes into B

Of all the phrases my wife has uttered over the years, the one that she is most in love with is, "Why don't you read the instructions?" It doesn't matter if it concerns a piece of wooden furniture from K-mart, or an expensive popcorn-maker from South Korea, she thinks I will have an easier time of it if I refer to the instruction booklet (written half in Korean) before I proceed.

This makes no sense. Instructions are for idiots who don't have the magic touch. They are written by nerds to explain to dummies how to operate a piece of machinery which will probably never work anyway.

The other day I brought home a toy Steinway piano. At least the picture on the box said it was a piano. But inside the carton it turned out to be a thousand pieces of wood, some wire and three screws.

Just as I finished unpacking it, my wife went into her usual routine, "Why don't you read the instructions?"

"Because," I said, "it would only be a sign of weakness. This is not a complex nuclear reactor. It is a very simple design that a child could put together."

"But you're not a child," she protested. "That piano has more parts than all the toys in Taiwan."

"Forgive me for sounding so piggish, but women do not understand the excitement that men experience when putting something together without the instructions. Remember the swing set I erected for the kids several years ago? Do you think the children would have gotten any pleasure out of it if I had followed the instructions?"

"You didn't construct that swing. After it crashed, you hired a contractor to put it together."

"I don't remember details that far back. There is a knack to assembling anything. You have to lay all the parts out neatly in front of you, and then screw the little pieces onto the big pieces."

"Is that what the instructions say?"

"No, but that's what logic dictates. When the project is completed, the trick is not to have any screws left over. Instructions don't tell you that. That's where one's engineering education comes in."

"I have no idea where you're headed with this."

"Like most married women your trouble is that you would rather trust a scrap of paper written by a Tibetan student than your own husband."

"All I'm going by is years of experience. The attic is filled with unfinished masterpieces that you tried to assemble without success."

"Every one of them was either short a piece of plastic or included the wrong fasteners or bolts."

"Why do you keep doing it?"

"Haven't you ever heard of the thrill of victory and the agony of defeat? Look at all the money we're saving. If I bought this piano assembled, it would cost ninety-nine dollars. I paid only fifty-nine dollars, because where toys are concerned, I'm my own man. When I finish fitting the black keys between the white keys, even you will not be able to tell the difference."

"Why is it tilting over to one side?"

"Because they included the wrong supports for the legs. One is shorter than the other. But not to worry, I can deal with it."

"How?" she asked.

"Read my hands."

Saints and Sinners

The first time I saw Jimmy Swaggart was on TV in my kitchen at eight o'clock on a Sunday morning. I was making porridge when this voice boomed out, "You are a sinner and you are damned to burn in hell until you beg forgiveness and cleanse your soul!"—or words to that effect.

I was so amazed at how much Swaggart knew about me that I sent him a check for fifty dollars.

The next Sunday I got up and turned on the set. In truth, I

was hoping he would announce the names of those who had sent him fifty dollars. But Swaggart had other fish to fry. He took off after people who bought or sold pornography and said the wrath of God would fall on us and we would be eaten by worms and slugs—or words to that effect. Then he started crying and I sent him a check for $100.

I stopped watching "Saturday Night Live" so I would be fresh when I turned on Swaggart in the morning. I couldn't believe it, but I wanted him to punish me.

The Reverend was unmerciful. He railed at me for my obsessive avarice. He said his God is better than my God. He marched up and down the stage and then stopped and pointed his finger directly at me, promising a plague of locusts in my washing machine—or words to that effect. He gave me no choice so I sent him $500.

Did I feel better after I sent off the money? Of course I did. I had been engaging in immoral behavior ever since I attended the University of Southern California, but Swaggart was the first preacher to call attention to it. I now had someone to beg forgiveness from.

The winter went along as winters do. Swaggart called me a thief, a liar, a scurvy nonbeliever and words to that effect. I, in turn, wept as I sent him checks so he would forgive me.

Then the Jim and Tammy Bakker story broke and I thought to myself, "Surely Jimmy Swaggart will forgive one of his own. But what makes Jimmy a great preacher is he doesn't discriminate. If you slip, you go right down into the cellar with those who have offended the Lord. Swaggart was not going to punch anyone's ticket who had committed adultery on church time. Nobody was as tough on Jimmy and Tammy as Swaggart.

I was so impressed with his stance I sent $500 to him and a supplementary $250 for bashing Jimmy Bakker.

Then it happened. I was watching the Olympics when the

announcer said Jimmy Swaggart was being investigated by his church for having been caught with a prostitute in a pornographic situation that was too weird to be described on television.

I dropped to my knees and cried, "Say it isn't so, Jimmy."

But Jimmy came on TV a little later and said it was so, as buckets of tears flowed down his cheeks. My first idea was that it was a frame-up. Then I thought to myself, if it isn't a frame-up Swaggart is going to need money. I sent him a check for $200.

What really bothered me was that all those months while Swaggart was accusing me of being a sinner, it turned out *he* was the meanest transgressor on the tube. Did this make him better or worse than I?

"The real sin," a fundamentalist taxi driver told me, "is not the atrocity Swaggart confessed to, but the outrage he committed against evangelical broadcasting. People who watch ministers on television want them squeaky clean. I can see the Lord forgiving Swaggart for his sexual misconduct, but I would not bet on the electronic preachers out there who depend on their checks every Monday morning."

I Pledge Allegiance

Just when you think that everyone in this country is at peace with everyone else, the Supreme Court makes a decision which tears us apart. Last Sunday in our backyard, Manchester suggested we all go down and set fire to the Court to protest its ruling that it is no longer a crime to burn the American flag.

I said it was too hot, and Manchester called me a closet flag-burner.

I told him, "I've never burned a flag, and I never intend to. If I did, I would burn Libya's. By the same token, I have no reason to trash the Supreme Court on a lovely Sunday afternoon."

Manchester was livid and yelled that if the Supreme Court didn't stop people from burning the flag, then American citizens should take the law into their own hands.

"How many flag-burners do you know personally?" I asked.

He replied that just because he didn't know any did not mean that they weren't out there.

"Have you ever seen anyone burn an American flag?" I wanted to know.

"No," he admitted, "but now that it's legal, every pervert in the country will buy one just to burn it."

I disagreed with him. "When it was illegal, burning an American flag was the strongest political statement a protester could make. Now, after the Court decision, it isn't considered a radical gesture at all. Do you think that the media has any interest in covering an act that is the law of the land? I believe

334

that the Justices ruled the way they did to cut down on flag-burning rather than encourage it."

"A flag-burner deserves to be executed," Manchester said, pouring too much barbecue sauce on the hamburgers.

"Fear of death never stopped a flag arsonist," I told him. "In the past, the thought of capital punishment convinced him that he would become a martyr. Besides, he knew that by desecrating the flag he could wind up on the Morton Downey, Jr., Show. To be successful, you have to commit the act in public. No one ever got famous for fifteen minutes by burning the flag in his bathroom. Since it is now legal, and the burner will not be arrested for doing it, the protest is meaningless."

Manchester remained unconvinced. "Wait until the congressional elections in November. Any person who doesn't vote for a constitutional amendment will wind up in the gutter. We will put our politicians' patriotism to the test. We'll spread the word about which candidates love their country and which ones don't."

"I worry about that," I confessed. "There will be a lot of mud thrown in the next election over the flag issue."

"Good," Manchester said.

"Let me ask this question. How many flags do you think were burned in the United States last year?"

"Thousands?" Manchester suggested.

"You're wrong. There were fourteen, and of those, six flags were flying from houses that burned to the ground. So there is not a vast pool of flag-burners out there. Most of the American-flag-burners right now are in Iran, Nicaragua and Panama, and they don't care what the Supreme Court of the United States says."

Manchester, who had ruined the hamburgers by this time, declared, "If the Supreme Court Justices don't like it in this country, they should go back where they came from."

335

And Now for
the Good News . . .

According to *Time* magazine, White House Chief of Staff John Sununu has complained that news coverage of the Exxon oil spill was slanted. Instead of concentrating on the 240,000 barrels of crude that escaped the tanker, the real story was how Exxon and the government saved another one million barrels from escaping into the sea. Sununu is quoted in *Time* as saying, "Three-quarters of it was contained within the ship. There's been very little reporting on that."

It so happens that Sununu is right. I wrote that story soon after the *Exxon Valdez* hit the rocks but nobody would print it.

So here it is again:

There was a miracle in Prince William Sound yesterday when one of the largest oil tankers in the world went aground and ruptured on the rocks near the port of Valdez. Only 240 thousand barrels of crude oil escaped from its tanks before valiant Exxon damage-control people managed to pump oil into another tanker.

An oil spill expert said that barely eight hundred miles of shoreline would be affected by the spill, as opposed to

336

the entire West Coast of the United States, if everyone had not been so on the ball.

He told reporters, "You have here an example of how the combination of seamanship and teamwork was able to turn what could have been a major disaster into a piddling incident. All credit goes to the captain of the *Exxon Valdez*. Even though he had been in his cabin, he decided to go out on deck after the accident and save his ship. A grateful nation owes him a debt for salvaging one million barrels of much-needed fuel."

When asked if anyone was to blame for the spill, the expert replied, "Only if the press insists on writing stories about the oil lost to the sea instead of what is now safely inside the tankers. If the media wants to be fair it should focus on how many birds and otters are still alive because one million barrels of oil were *not* spilled. As long as the TV cameras keep filming oil-soaked geese, the true story of the heroic *Valdez* will never be told."

One TV reporter said, "What about the oil on the beaches? Is it all right to concentrate on that?"

"Why don't you show pictures of the black gold that was pumped off the *Exxon Valdez?* You don't help people feel any better by always illustrating the downside of what happens when a tanker runs aground. Everybody makes mistakes, but there is absolutely no reason to draw attention to them with pictures of workers wiping off rocks with damp towels."

According to the expert, no one is sure how long it will take for the oil-spill carnage to be cleaned up. However, everyone is pleased with the smoothness of the operation, especially when compared with how long it would have taken if all the oil on board had leaked.

The expert continued, "It's true that it looks bad from

the air, but that's just because oil and water don't mix. All of us would have preferred not to have had an accident, but if there is one, and only twenty-five percent of your cargo is lost, anyone can live with that."

He was then asked, "Knowing what you know now, is there anything we can do to make this a kinder, gentler Alaska?"

"It's no good dwelling on incidents such as oil spills. You have to look at a grounded tanker as you do a glass of water, and ask yourself if it's half full or half empty. That's what oil spills are all about."

Find Me a Juror

Colonel North's trial is over, and now it is Admiral Poindexter's turn to face a jury. But what jury? The jurors in the North trial were supposedly chosen because they knew nothing about Irangate, had never watched television, and weren't too sure who the President of the United States was.

After a sweep through every neighborhood in Washington, the federal marshals managed to find barely enough jurors for Ollie's trial.

Once again there is a need for twelve jurors with the same qualifications, and nobody knows where to look.

Last Friday a federal marshal went to see the judge. "Sir, we're having a serious Poindexter jury problem. We can't find anybody who is so ill informed on Irangate that they would be suitable for jury duty. Every person we have talked to has either read a newspaper, discussed the contras in a bar, or watched Geraldo Rivera get his nose broken in Cuba. We even combed the streets of Georgetown without success, and the residents there don't usually know anything about anything."

The judge was angry. "In a town this large there must be more ignorant people. Don't tell me that there are no candidates on Capitol Hill."

"There are some congressmen who know nothing about Irangate, but it is not possible to ticket them as jurors because they have immunity. Do you want us to start interviewing the homeless?"

"A person on a jury has to have a domicile," the judge said. "Besides, after the trial, what guarantee do I have that the homeless will leave the jury box? Are you sure there's no one out there who thinks that Poindexter is nothing more than an IBM computer program?"

"I know it sounds crazy, but everyone I talked to has an opinion on the contras. I thought I had a juror until the guy told me, 'I didn't follow the case, but I think that Brendan Sullivan's Nuremberg defense was brilliant, and the prosecutor's use of Hitler's name was an utter disaster for the government. Losing on three out of twelve counts is not bad for Ollie who, allegedly, shredded the Constitution.' "

The judge responded, "He doesn't sound like someone who is lacking views on the situation."

"That's how I felt, sir, particularly when he told me that, as an impartial observer, he has his own thoughts about where the money from the sale of the Hawk missiles disappeared to."

"Marshal, I can't have a trial if I don't have a jury. Come up with some ideas."

"I heard that the Brazilian Navy is due here next week. They probably don't know much about Irangate."

"They would be good," the judge admitted, "but they're not U.S. citizens."

"How about grabbing some taxi drivers from National Airport? Most of them are from Third World countries and they don't know North from South."

"They should be D.C. residents and law-abiding people who love their country but don't read about it too often in the papers."

"How about the Washington Redskins?" the marshal asked. "As far as we can work out, they only read the sports pages."

The judge said, "That's only eleven and we need twelve."

The marshal suggested, "We could get the guy from the White House."

"You want George Bush to be a juror?"

"Why not? He's the only one who has come out and sworn that he never heard of Irangate, and he wouldn't know a quid pro quo if he saw one."

Bail Out Everybody

News Item—Government officials predict that the American taxpayer will have to pay for the vast oil clean-up in Alaska.

As soon as I opened the door I recognized the man from the federal government. He had come to the house before to ask me to bail out the S&Ls.

I told him, "I already gave at the office."

He said, "I'm not asking you to bail out the S and Ls this time, I want you to contribute to the clean-up in Alaska."

"Why me?"

"You're a taxpayer, and we would like every taxpayer to behave responsibly and help Exxon with this problem."

"But I had nothing to do with the tanker going aground," I protested.

"Each one of us is guilty. It's not our role to point the finger at others when it comes to an oil spill. We have to leave that to wiser and more experienced people."

"Such as the captain who was snoozing in his bunk while the third mate steered the ship."

"Someday we'll get to the bottom of all this. For the moment, the only way to make restitution is for John Q. Public to dig deep into his pockets and say, 'There but for the grace of God go I.'"

"I have never been to Alaska in my life. I'm tried of bailing out everything from nuclear power plants to railroads. Someone has to say 'enough is enough.'"

341

"You don't have the right attitude. The position you should take is, 'Okay, we blew it. What can *I* do to save Exxon management and the stockholders whose savings are at stake?' "

"I am not going to say that. Every time you come to the house looking for bailout money you make an appeal to my patriotism."

"There is nothing wrong with a little flag-waving for an American company which makes a teensy, weensy mistake. Just hand over ten thousand dollars as your share for cleaning up Alaska. I promise not to bother you again until I figure out how much you owe me to prevent Third World countries from going bankrupt."

"I don't care about Third World countries going bankrupt."

"It's not them we are worried about. It's the American banks which loaned them the money. If you don't come through on this they could all be broke. Are you willing to take responsibility for the Irving Trust Company running aground?"

"Of course not," I replied. "But if I keep rescuing all these companies, I'm not going to have anything left for myself."

"Surely you jest. You have at least four more bailouts in you. Look, nobody likes oil spills, but they are inevitable when the situation on board a tanker is not as sobering as it should be. Your money will be used to clean up the environment in Alaska once and for all. It will also enable us to study tanker captains who are under the weather and how they behave when they are at sea. Once we have the answer to this question, the only one left for you to bail out is the defense company which makes the B-1 bomber."

Bulldozer

I live in a beautiful, but not very forgiving, neighborhood.

When Adnan Khashoggi was arrested and detained in Switzerland for extradition to the United States, the residents of Wesley Heights were in an uproar. The reason is that just up the street from us at American University there is a large building named The Adnan Khashoggi Sports and Convocation Center. It was donated by the zillionaire arms dealer who is wanted by the U.S. for racketeering, fraud and obstruction of justice, and the people in my area are afraid that real estate values will fall if his name stays on this building.

Feelings are so strong that as I was coming home the other night I saw Jim Lawson backing his bulldozer out of the garage.

"Where are you going?" I asked.

"I'm driving up to American U. to knock down that Khashoggi monument before Wesley Heights becomes the laughingstock of the Western world," Lawson told me.

"You're jumping to conclusions. It's true that the man has been arrested, but people don't knock down a brand-new building just because the person who paid for it is accused of a crime. If we destroyed every edifice donated to a university by a white-collar criminal, the college campuses of America would look like the Arctic Circle. American U. accepted Khashoggi's money in good faith, and you can't expect the

343

school to turn its back on him just because he has allegedly been playing 'spin the bottle' with Mr. and Mrs. Ferdinand Marcos."

"Even though the guy was in on every arms deal in the world?" Lawson yelled. "How does a school know where to draw the line when it comes to deciding which money is clean and which is dirty?"

"The line is so fine that only presidents of universities can see it. Their problem is not the fact that they accept the money, it's having to explain to faculty and students why they put the scoundrel's name on the building."

"Well, I am going to pulverize the Khashoggi Center anyway. If he turns out to be innocent, I'll apologize to him. Why would American U. take money from a notorious arms dealer in the first place?"

"The kids had to have a place to play basketball. Long after Khashoggi does time, and I'm not saying he will, the cheers of students will be resounding from the rafters of the AU Sports Center. We should not concern ourselves with Khashoggi's guilt or innocence, but rather be happy about the olympic-sized pool he left behind."

"Can we at least tape over his name on the building while the jury is still out?"

"No. It would suggest that AU is making a judgment on the case, which the university never does when it concerns one of its white-collar givers."

"Until Khashoggi is judged by twelve of his peers, is there any action we can take?"

"We must strike while he's reeling, and ask him to provide the funds for another building on campus to match the first one. People in trouble with the law are always anxious to perform good deeds to make amends for their bad ones. I know of one white-collar criminal who beat a million-dollar embezzlement rap because the sentencing judge found out that the man had given his Jaguar to a women's volleyball team."

"If you won't let me bulldoze the building, will you allow me to rename it the Michael Milken School of Business?" Lawson pleaded.

"It's too risky. The way things are right now, today's financial heroes could easily wind up as tomorrow's license-plate makers."

Changing the System

"The worst thing that a totalitarian government can do is to give its people a *little* democracy," said Wabash of the Political Dynamics Institute. "It's like making them a little pregnant."

I was in his office and we were following uprisings all over the world on his shortwave radio. He pointed to Soviet Georgia on a map. "Every time Gorbachev loosens up and offers his people a bunch of grapes, they want the whole vineyard. All of the Republics are demanding either autonomy or complete freedom from the mother country. It proves that if you are a dictator and allow just a small amount of light into your country, nobody is going to say 'thank you.' "

"Why would anybody want to live in a democracy when you can't get tickets to *Phantom of the Opera?*" I asked.

345

Wabash answered, "The dilemma is, how to reform the old system when people want a new one? I'm not red-baiting when I say that Communism doesn't work. Gorbachev is offering Marxism with freedom, and it is a contradiction in terms."

I agreed. "I think that the Russians should back off and take a serious look at what they are demonstrating for. We are a society of pizzas and Big Macs. We depend on Japan for our TV sets, and South Korea and Malaysia for our clothes. *The New York Times* crossword puzzle is much more difficult today than it was ten years ago."

Wabash said, "We are not only seeing an internal revolution but an external one as well. All the Soviet bloc countries are demanding their freedom. Every country behind the iron curtain is poised for true democratic reform, including elections and multiple-party voting."

"They must be stopped," I declared. "If they all adopt the capitalist system, there won't be an empty parking place in the whole, wide world."

"The political storm clouds are not only blowing over Eastern Europe but over China as well," Wabash explained. "We are watching Chinese students demanding the same democratic privileges that we have."

"Don't they know if that happens, they will have to read the *National Enquirer* every week, and watch Morton Downey, Jr., and Geraldo Rivera on television?"

"It doesn't matter. They want our way of life, even if it means that students in China will be wearing Ralph Lauren clothes to demonstrations. You can't stop the people once they have taken to the streets."

"Do the Estonian people have any idea what it's like to be ruled by Mayor Barry?" I asked.

"They don't care. They are willing to take Barry over some crooked Soviet bureaucrat who is telling them how to live. The

346

world is a different place now from what it was twelve months ago. No one is demonstrating for Communism or Fascism. They're all yelling for their right to phone in to a radio talk-show host, and make a fortune in the lottery."

"Someone has to tell them before it's too late that democracy has many holes in it. It's a messy system because no one agrees with anybody else. A totalitarian government speaks with a single voice—a democracy talks with a million. Besides, under Communism, you don't have savings and loan banks failing every day."

Wabash said, "I'm afraid that you can't put the genie back in the bottle. Whatever the Russian people wind up with, it isn't going to look anything like Lenin's dream."

"Maybe when the Soviets find out what it costs to stay in an American hospital, they'll reject any ideas they ever had of being like us," I suggested.

Wabash shook his head. "They're buying our system, warts and all. Even the KGB is trying to get prayers back into the schools."

Thumbsucker

The Thumbsucker Report has just been released. Written by Dr. Alfred Thumbsucker, the report deals with the problems that parents have communicating with their children, and the inability of those children to communicate with anyone.

"Most parents," he told me, "admit that they didn't have much luck with child-rearing, but they all have the same defense: 'Look what we had to work with.' "

"In your report, what do you consider to be the main barrier between children and their parents?"

"Rock music," he replied. "When teenagers turned to the Grateful Dead for all their needs, parents lost control over them. It is not generally known, but as soon as a child is born in the United States, the doctor inserts tiny Walkman speakers into the ears. The Walkman is activated when the doctor spanks the baby, and it remains on at full volume right through college."

"You're going to make the front pages with that one."

"As the child grows up, he or she spends every waking moment listening to music, and tuning out on everything else. Parents were always under the impression that when a young person shook his head, he was answering either yes or no to a question. They had no idea that the kid was only keeping time to the Rolling Stones."

"Didn't it ever occur to a parent that something other than thinking was going on in their offspring's head?" I asked.

"No, it didn't. Parents were happy to see their children snap

348

their fingers because it meant that they were still alive. Some teenagers found that the audio level of the Walkman was not strong enough for their rock music habit, so they put large radios on their shoulders to enhance the sound. They also installed loudspeakers in their bedrooms so that nothing else could be heard in the house.

"With so much electronics at their command, it's no wonder that kids have been unable to converse in any spoken tongue. This is the reason that parents never get a response when they shout, 'Why don't you do what I tell you?' The child has no idea what his father or mother is saying."

"How can young people get by without communicating?"

"Most of them have discovered early in life that no matter what they did, they would always be housed and fed. Knowing this, there was no reason for them to try and figure out what was going on in the world."

"At least they know what they want," I said.

"The generations of rock music fans, all of whom are still wired with Walkmans, are now becoming the labor force in this country. They are doctors, lawyers and oil tanker captains, but they all keep time to Bruce Springsteen."

"Did you interview a lot of people for your report?" I asked him.

"I talked to many parents, but they were more confused than helpful. The children were something else again. Every time I asked a question, they rolled their eyes and clapped their hands. I would have been worried had I not known that each and every one of them had a Walkman implant."

"Then your findings are based more on your own knowledge rather than on what anyone said to you?"

"That is correct. But it does have substance. I have never met a child who listened more to his parents than he did to Michael Jackson."

A Phony Docudrama

Not one, but two juries brought in a verdict on Ollie North. One was composed of twelve men and women in Judge Gesell's courtroom. The other consisted of millions of people sequestered in their living rooms, who judged Colonel North based on what they saw and heard in a tough TV docudrama called "Guts and Glory."

I don't know how Gesell's jury reached its decision—but this is how I reached mine. Like most Americans, I assumed that everything depicted in the docudrama was factual. I was all set to buy the whole package, until the second episode when I saw a scene that I couldn't believe. Ollie parked his car on Pennsylvania Avenue in front of the White House—locked it, walked into the Executive Office Building and left the car there all day.

"No way," I yelled at my wife. "I don't care how much national security was involved, Ollie could never have had permission to park in front of 1600 Pennsylvania Avenue."

"Docudrama people don't make things up. Maybe Bill Casey told him to leave his car there," my wife suggested.

"Not Bill Casey," I told her. "He was no fool. If Ollie had left his automobile in that location in real life, they'd have towed it away, and then everyone in the D.C. impoundment lot would have known about the arms swap in Iran."

My wife, who has read up on every aspect of Irangate, said, "Suppose that Casey told Ollie it was okay for him to park in front of the White House, but if the cops caught him, he'd be the fall guy and be forced to take the hit."

"It's possible," I admitted. "However, in order for Ollie to use the parking spot, a lot more people must have been in on it. For example, if North got a ticket, wouldn't General Secord have paid it?"

"Not necessarily. If Ollie was caught, he could say that he knew leaving his car in a No Parking space was wrong, but he didn't know it was illegal."

I added, "There is another scenario. Instead of Ollie showing up in traffic court, he could have given the parking ticket to Fawn Hall and told her to shred it. Fawn admitted that she'd do anything for him."

"I don't like the way Fawn keeps touching Ollie all the time in the miniseries," my wife said.

"Neither do I," I agreed. "On the other hand, you can't have someone like Fawn in the movie and have her do *nothing*."

"If we accept the basic premise of the docudrama, who else besides Casey, Poindexter, McFarlane and Fawn knew that Ollie illegally parked his car in front of the White House?"

"George Bush," I told her.

"How did he know?"

"Bush's main task as vice president was to keep track of everything that happened on Pennsylvania Avenue."

"Did President Reagan know?" she asked.

"I'm sure he did, but he had to say that he would never approve of any illegal parking unless the driver was delivering dresses to Nancy in the White House."

"I only hope that the producers of 'Guts and Glory' can prove everything we just saw. Otherwise people will get the impression that he had no respect for the law," she said.

"Ollie saw it differently. He was a Marine, and a Marine believes that he can park anywhere he pleases."

My wife wanted to know, "If Ollie was so important, why didn't they give him a decent parking spot inside the White House grounds?"

"They couldn't," I explained, "because Ollie was involved in a covert operation."